EXPERIMENTAL TEST PILOT

EXPERIMENTAL TEST PILOT
MILITARY AIRCRAFT RESEARCH FLYING

CHRIS TAYLOR

AIR WORLD

EXPERIMENTAL TEST PILOT
Military Aircraft Research Flying

First published in Great Britain in 2023 by
Pen & Sword Air World
An imprint of Pen & Sword Books Ltd
Yorkshire – Philadelphia

Copyright © Chris Taylor, 2023

ISBN 978 1 39904 885 9

The right of Chris Taylor to be identified as Author of this work has been asserted by him in accordance with the Copyright, Designs and Patents Act 1988.

A CIP catalogue record for this book is available from the British Library.

All rights reserved. No part of this book may be reproduced or transmitted in any form or by any means, electronic or mechanical including photocopying, recording or by any information storage and retrieval system, without permission from the Publisher in writing.

Typeset by SJmagic DESIGN SERVICES, India.
Printed and bound in the UK by CPI Group (UK) Ltd.

Pen & Sword Books Limited incorporates the imprints of Atlas, Archaeology, Aviation, Discovery, Family History, Fiction, History, Maritime, Military, Military Classics, Politics, Select, Transport, True Crime, Air World, Frontline Publishing, Leo Cooper, Remember When, Seaforth Publishing, The Praetorian Press, Wharncliffe Local History, Wharncliffe Transport, Wharncliffe True Crime and White Owl.

For a complete list of Pen & Sword titles please contact

PEN & SWORD BOOKS LIMITED
George House, Units 12 & 13, Beevor Street, Off Pontefract Road, Barnsley, South Yorkshire, S71 1HN, England
E-mail: enquiries@pen-and-sword.co.uk
Website: www.pen-and-sword.co.uk
Or
PEN AND SWORD BOOKS
1950 Lawrence Rd, Havertown, PA 19083, USA
E-mail: Uspen-and-sword@casematepublishers.com
Website: www.penandswordbooks.com

Contents

Foreword ... vi
Introduction ... viii
Chapter 1 Wanting to be a Test Pilot ... 1
Chapter 2 ETPS Interview – Test Pilot Selection ... 16
Chapter 3 ETPS, Class of 1994 – First Term ... 22
Chapter 4 ETPS, Class of 1994 – Summer Term ... 38
Chapter 5 ETPS, Class of 1994 – Autumn Term ... 60
Chapter 6 Wessex ... 85
Chapter 7 Sea King ... 110
Chapter 8 Lynx ... 122
Chapter 9 Simulators and Aeroplanes ... 142
Chapter 10 Royal Navy Appointing – Fighting to stay an Experimental Test Pilot ... 152
Chapter 11 Back to School – A Hell of a First Year ... 164
Chapter 12 ETPS Principal Tutor Rotary Wing ... 188
Chapter 13 Licences ... 211
Chapter 14 Principal Tutor Systems and Short Courses – The Last Straw ... 228
Postscript ... 250
Conclusion ... 253
Glossary ... 256
Index ... 271

Foreword

*'An intelligent person armed with a checklist is
no substitute for experience.'*
Joy Gumz

When you think of a Test Pilot, what sort of words pop into your mind? Skilful? Brave? Crazy? Good looking? All good choices, especially the last one. As someone who's been in the profession a long time, I'd probably choose things like: Flying Ability, Powers of Observation, Analysis, Communication and Integrity. That last one is important. I vividly remember a project manager once passionately advising a colleague 'never take a test pilot to a meeting – when the talking gets tough, they have a horrible habit of blurting out the truth'. Yes, integrity is right up there, and it can make you very unpopular, especially with managers, manufacturers and even the people who are going to use the aircraft. As a test pilot you're often the person pointing out problems. Problems which are going to hold things up and cost people more money; but that's the job. There's a fundamental responsibility to make sure that the aircraft is safe. Safe for those who will fly in it and safe for those whose heads it will fly over. You can't compromise on that, but it can be a hard line to stick to.

It's difficult to teach some of the non-technical skills at a test pilot school. So, as a wise person once said: 'There's no substitute for experience.' But how on earth do you gain that kind of experience in a profession like test flying without coming seriously unstuck along the way? It's a great question, and it's one that I thought about a lot during my time as the Chief Test Pilot at MOD Boscombe Down, the UK's military flight test hub, because although all my test pilots were experienced *pilots*, they were almost all newly qualified *test pilots*. They were yet to experience the realities of working alongside suppliers and customers, where one day they might be the lone voice pointing out a problem.

This book, *Experimental Test Pilot,* is the prequel to Chris Taylor's first book, *Test Pilot,* and it paints a fascinating picture of Chris' earlier career, the ten years in which he learnt his trade and gained his all-important experience, prior to joining the CAA. This is the story of Chris learning the basics at ETPS and then telling us stories of developing the skills which turned him into the total professional that we all enjoyed reading about in his first book. He tells us about his entry to the world of test flying via the world-famous Empire Test Pilots' School, his work as an Experimental Test Pilot at Boscombe Down, his time as a test pilot instructor at ETPS and then his pivotal role in helping ETPS evolve from pure military unit to commercially astute business.

I was lucky enough to serve at Boscombe Down several times during this period and I worked with Chris very closely, especially during my three years as 'The Boss' at ETPS. I loved working with him. He was one of those people who just makes things happen and who always does it with a smile on his face. Yes, he was an excellent test pilot and a talented instructor. But those non-technical skills really shone through. His personality, enthusiasm and sense of humour were infectious, and it was these qualities which made him the perfect person to lead our charge into the commercial world as ETPS transformed itself.

By the end of this book, you'll understand exactly how Chris became such an experienced test pilot and brilliant communicator. Just the sort of guy the CAA would one day ask to go out and deal with the big, wide, sometimes scary, world of General Aviation and to make sure that things were as safe as they could be. And, just the sort of person to write brilliantly readable, fascinating accounts of his incredible life in aviation.

I hope you enjoy reading *Experimental Test Pilot* **as much as I did.**

Dave Best
Air Commodore David Best, OBE

Introduction

This is not my first book. Some of you may already have read, or at least seen, my first, entitled *Test Pilot – An Extraordinary Career Testing Civil Aircraft*. That first book attempts to capture just some of my experiences and anecdotes from the most recent phase of test flying. This book is the prequel. My aim is to cover the ground of my earlier flight test career, which effectively revolves around the decade I spent working at the United Kingdom's military flight test centre, MoD Boscombe Down. For my previous book, the catalyst was mainly to document some of my funnier stories to enable my grandchildren to have some understanding of what I was up to when I went off to work each day or jetted away to far off countries to test a whole variety of aircraft. Having written it I realise that this volume covers ground that will be of more interest to my two children who were aged from 3 to 16 during the decade in question. Again, it may explain the time when I was away or the time when I was swotting hard for examinations on nice sunny days when perhaps I should have been out with them kicking a football around.

My previous book was written as a collection of anecdotes. This book has a more traditional structure with a beginning, a middle and an end. It expands upon my childhood aspirations to be a pilot, which morphed into a passion to be a test pilot, shortly after gaining my private pilot's licence (PPL). I have remembered my time preparing for selection to the Empire Test Pilots' School (ETPS) and the incredibly busy and exhausting twelve months trying to learn the art and science of flight test. I have tried to capture a glimpse into the research and development world, which was the responsibility of Experimental Flying Squadron (EFS) and the work of the boffins of the Defence Research Agency (DRA) based at the former Royal Aircraft Establishment (RAE) airfields, Bedford and Farnborough. I have discussed the challenges of gaining my civilian licences and qualifications and my ultimate return to ETPS to act as an instructor (tutor). I conclude by discussing the final three years of my time at Boscombe Down which were, in some respects, immensely rewarding but ultimately became so frustrating that I felt I had no choice but to move on.

As I reflect on this period I realise the common thread that runs throughout the book is of someone who has worked his hardest to make the most of the 'cards he was dealt'. I am not someone who has 'landed on my feet' at every turn. School became a struggle as I dealt with my mother's increasingly poor health – and I very nearly failed to obtain a degree as my mum took a turn for the worse and passed away in my final year at university. Becoming a Royal Navy pilot took resolve, hard work and determination and progressing to being a Test Pilot even more so. As you read the book you will perhaps pick up on some of the many challenges I faced, which I have chosen not to dwell upon. Ultimately, this decade provided the stepping stone that took me from being a competent operational 'naval aviator', to being able to step into a job with the UK Civil Aviation Authority, test flying every type of aircraft imaginable; a job I could not have dreamed of being competent to undertake only a few years earlier.

Now, as I watch my grandchildren growing up, I am fascinated that even at an early age certain personality and character traits are becoming evident. At my granddaughter's second birthday party she was already playing with a battery powered screwdriver and fixing her new tractor – an engineer in the making for sure. Whereas I think my elder grandson's enthusiasm for dressing as Marvel Super Heroes or enacting huge battles with Lego characters will bode well for a career or hobby in the media industry. In my case I wanted to be a pilot from as young an age as I can remember but must owe that, partially at least, to my dad. Edward Taylor, as a 19-year-old clerk, joined the RAF mainly in the hope that the uniform would help him pull the girls; not that he needed any help in that department if his collection of sepia photos of glamorous sirens was anything to go by. He'd wanted to fly, but the RAF was desperate for medically fit clerks to join the squadrons as they deployed overseas. My dad joined 222 Squadron operating Spitfires (Vbs) and in 1943 transferred to 65 Squadron flying Mustangs (IIIs then IVs). He spent lots of time in Scotland and the South of England but then found himself in France shortly after D-Day as 65 Squadron flew ground attack missions from dirt strips just behind the lines. Some of his funnier, and scarier, stories were generated in this period, including driving a jeep-load of pilots into Brussels to get hammered only, on the way home, to notice blokes in grey uniforms standing on street corners. The Germans (who clearly hadn't been on the memo my dad had read about the city's liberation) were so amazed to see a bunch of drunks, being driven at such speed, they had no time to unsling their rifles. In contrast was the occasion where he had been driven into a French town with some mates; reading between the lines, my dad had evidently managed to charm a local lass, and was late getting back to the pick-up point where he arrived to see the Bedford truck disappearing in a cloud of blue exhaust smoke. Said truck ran over a mine a few miles up the road and *there were no survivors*. His mates were nearly all pilots and he had the unenviable task of drafting the letters to mothers and wives following such incidents, and sorties when they failed to return. Summer holidays in France, Belgium and Holland included tours of numerous cemeteries. My dad almost certainly suffered from what we would now describe as PTSD. He spent several weeks in an RAF Hospital at one stage and had a nervous breakdown running up to his planned wedding years after the war.

As a youngster our beach holidays were taken in Anglesey, just along from RAF Valley. Shiny silver Lightning fighters, bright yellow (then red) Gnat trainers and Whirlwind Search and Rescue helicopters would all overfly us while we were building our sandcastles. Kites made way for Kiel Kraft balsa-wood, elastic-band-powered aircraft and hard-earned pocket money was spent every Saturday morning at the local newsagent who sold Airfix bagged models of Spitfires and Hurricanes which could be built in a day and hung from bedroom ceilings the same evening. Dad loved it that I wanted to be a pilot – and I did from as soon as I could build Lego or Meccano planes. I dreamt of flying Spitfires and read all of W.E. Johns' books about my all-time hero, James Bigglesworth – aka Biggles. There was nothing he couldn't fly or do with an aeroplane. However, in my teens I became more aware of the activities of the Fleet Air Arm (FAA) and at the age of 16 spent two weeks drinking, at the expense of the tax payer, in the Wardroom bar at Royal Naval Air Station Culdrose, where every day the Royal Navy flew me in a different type of aircraft. Not content with that 'sales pitch', they awarded me a Flying Scholarship, as a member of my school cadet force, which allowed me to be awarded a Private Pilot's Licence (PPL) – before I had chance to take my driving test.

Despite suffering a stroke that left him wobbly on his feet and unable to speak, Dad continued to enthusiastically encourage me and must have been the proudest and drunkest 60-something bloke at my 'Wings

65 Squadron RAF 19 June 1944 at Ford, Sussex. Edward is the Corporal without a hat standing on the Mustang's wing. *(Author's Collection)*

Day'. Thankfully, he got to see me become a successful operational pilot, husband and dad before he passed away a few years later.

I should, perhaps, before you dive into the chapters, just give you the briefest idea of the context. After qualifying as a pilot I flew the Wasp and then Lynx helicopters in the Fleet Air Arm, and as such was known affectionately as a 'Pronger', or more fully: 'Third Pronger', based on the idea that a fork has three prongs, with one prong being those that flew to hunt out submarines, the second to support and transport the Royal Marines and thirdly – well us – those that flew off smallish ships that carried a single helicopter with a single crew. As a Lynx pilot I became an instructor and continued to teach and fly at numerous air displays. I ended up running the Lynx training simulator at Portland. In my next book I will write about my time in the RN and the challenges I faced along the way, particularly when operating the Westland Wasp HAS Mk1. This book picks up my story from wanting to become a test pilot and documents my decade at MoD Boscombe Down, flying military aircraft for research and development before returning to ETPS to train the next generation of test pilots. I hope you find the story of my hard work, unswerving singlemindedness and more interesting aviation scrapes illuminating, and perhaps an encouragement not to give up on your dreams or aspirations when the 'going gets tough'.

Health Warning

This book does not aspire to be a history book. It should not be treated as an authentic record of any activity that might, or might not, have taken place at Boscombe Down from 1993–2004. It is my honest recollection of the aviation events that I experienced throughout that decade, but has relied only on my personal flying log book and conversations with colleagues to jog my memory. I have avoided too many names. In my experience the reader will either know who the stories relate to or will not care! Too many names can be counter-productive and frankly there is a risk I will ascribe events to the wrong person.

Photographs

One of the challenges I have faced is sourcing illustrations/photographs. During the period described in the book, personal cameras were not allowed 'on site', so I have no personal photos of any of the aircraft I flew. Some photos have been sourced from MoD/QinetiQ, some from trials officers I flew with, some from my family photo albums, but by far the majority have been sourced from aviation enthusiasts who have patiently waited on a hill top in Wales, or on the flight line at an air show, to capture some unclassified images. I am very grateful to all those that have assisted me in collecting the photos, many of which are breathtaking.

Language

This is, without apology, a more technical book than my previous one and is riddled with technical language and jargon. Additionally I have used, where appropriate, expletives in the text which I confess I am prone to do when bad things happen to me unexpectedly. One of my more readily used mild swear words is 'Blige'. Until I drafted this book I had not realised that the word originates from, and is used almost entirely in, Bristol. Both my wife and her sister lived in Bristol in their younger years and so it is likely I have picked it up along the way. It readily translates to Blimey or similar for other regions of the UK. Apart from my expletives, I would hope that I have captured other technical or jargon terminology within the glossary which is to be found after the conclusion.

Chapter 1

Wanting to be a Test Pilot

Bam!

The screens went red. I had crashed. I tried again.

Bam!

I crashed.

In fact, after three attempts I was improving but still had not managed to land this beast safely following a double engine failure.

I suppose the opening question might be: why on earth did I want to become a test pilot in the first place? As mentioned in the introduction, I had a passion to become a pilot for as long as I can remember. Certainly as a wee boy my hobbies all revolved around aircraft. I was never a plane spotter but I was fascinated by all aspects of flying and attempted to build numerous Airfix models that were easier to glue together than they were to paint. I also loved to construct aeroplanes out of balsa wood and tissue paper that were meant to fly. Nowadays you can buy a fully fabricated, nearly complete, flying aeroplane made from polystyrene foam. Back then, I had to spend hours each evening placing slender bits of balsa onto a paper plan pinned to board. Wood could be bent and glued overnight to build up a rigid enough structure that could cope with being covered in lightweight tissue paper. Painting dope onto the tissue not only added colour but stiffened and shrank the material to become skin tight. Sadly, weeks and weeks were spent making accurate and attractive scale models that rarely survived their first flight. So maybe this sowed the seeds of wanting to improve the designs; to make the aircraft more stable and easier to fly – the very job of a test pilot. Certainly I remember, with some clarity, the 1976 Thames Television documentary by Ken Ashton featuring ETPS and called originally *Test Pilot*.

The show aired after I had already gained a PPL, courtesy of a Royal Navy Flying Scholarship, and my intent to become a professional pilot had already been well and truly embedded in my psyche. But the *Test Pilot* programme sowed an additional seed. So much so, that my deliberations over choosing a degree course led me to consider what degree should a test pilot have? Given that aircraft were becoming increasingly more complex, with the addition of flight control systems, I elected to apply to study Electrical and Electronic engineering. I also realised that the 'chop rate' for aspiring military pilots was very high, and at least as an electrical engineer there would be a very good chance of employment. You will note that I had already acquired a pessimistic streak which was to pervade all aspects of my life in the following years.

With hindsight, which is a wonderful thing, I wish I'd studied something more useful and *fun*. I had expected to be building my own TV by the end of the first term. The reality was I ended up working long, long days and evenings, hanging on by my finger nails, as more and more complicated mathematics was hosed in my direction. I barely made it to my final year having pass/fail examinations every two terms which I never passed on the first attempt, so ended up with exams or resits every term – nightmare. Thankfully, in my final year I didn't have exams until after Easter and my mate Dave and I, teamed up for a project that was actually quite enjoyable. We thought it would be easy to produce a voice activated typewriter. Nowadays, my iPhone achieves very competent voice recognition. Back in the seventies the computing power required would have filled numerous buildings. So after a period of research we opted to concentrate on a simple method of discerning certain sounds in speech that would be a stepping stone to fully fledged voice recognition.

The challenge of our project was amplified by my mother finally losing her fight with bowel cancer. After several years of operations, and periods of remission, she very sadly died in the February of my final year. I owe my mate, Dave, a huge debt of gratitude. He shouldered the burden of our project single-handed for some time and, realising I would need some really hardcore, concentrated revision time to catch up with stuff I'd missed, booked me a room on campus to ensure I had minimal distractions for the few weeks I had left. I worked my socks off and halfway through my final examination (on Telecoms) fell fast asleep at my desk. The invigilator had to wake me because apparently my snoring was disturbing the other candidates who were still busy writing down stuff I'd long since forgotten.

Surprisingly, the results posted on a notice board some days later indicated I had scraped a pass ...

Phew! I had survived another!

My guess is, that the challenges of my teenage years, and this disrupted time at college, actually stood me in good stead later for the focus and dedication I would require to become an experimental test pilot.

I had joined the Royal Navy after my first year at university and spent my leave periods doing stints at BRNC Dartmouth and on various ships. I even got to spend two summers flying RN de Havilland Chipmunk T10 aircraft down to Périgueux, France. Following graduation I was straight off to sea learning how to be a Navigating or Operations Officer before commencing flying training in 1982. I became a relatively proficient Wasp and Lynx pilot and instructed on the Lynx for a few years but, given my short attention span, had begun to become rather bored of 'just flying the Lynx'. In 1986 a second documentary about ETPS had aired. This one, filmed by the BBC, was screened at about the time I had been starting to think again about the possibility of becoming a test pilot. The programme featured many characters that would, in time, become colleagues, but as I watched, as an ab initio Lynx pilot, I was blown away by the intensity of the course, in particular the ground academic studies which seemed to revolve around more and more dreaded maths. So despite my earlier aspirations, I parked them. Instead I began to toy with the idea of getting out of helicopters into aeroplanes. The RN was trying to fill Sea Harrier cockpits with mixed success. The supply of ex-Phantom and Buccaneer pilots had dried up and selecting pilots straight from Bulldogs hadn't always produced satisfactory outcomes. So the RN designed the SMAC 309 Course which with hindsight (again) I wish I'd had a go at. It comprised of learning to fly the Hawker Hunter at RNAS Yeovilton under the watchful, and very judgemental, eye of a bunch of former FAA pilots working for FRADU (Fleet Requirements and Direction Unit). I did my research and for a number of reasons 'chickened out' – not least because Sea Harrier pilots were routinely expected to embark for six months at a time and my wife, Ally (Alyson) was already expecting our first child.

So, instead of becoming a Sea Harrier pilot I thought an alternative might be to join the RAF. At the time they had an officer employed specifically to poach pilots from other services and the Commonwealth. A number of my colleagues on the Lynx training squadron (702 NAS) embarked on a change of uniform. By then I was a Lieutenant Commander which should have meant transferring as a Squadron Leader, but the RAF was rather weird about that and wanted me to become a Flight Lieutenant initially, albeit on my current pay and pension.

The selection process was also strange. I was asked to attend RAF Biggin Hill for interview. At the time the RAF still retained part of their former wartime base and used it specifically for conducting interviews and aptitude tests. I rocked up as required on the afternoon of the scheduled day and my first surprise came when I was invited back at 0600 the following morning to conduct initial aptitude tests. I protested. I made it clear that I was already a fully qualified service pilot (QSP) with 'wings' and in receipt of flying pay. The 'jobsworth' corporal could only go by the papers on his clipboard, so sure enough I was up at 0500 and undertaking an O level/GCE style maths paper an hour later. Not surprisingly I didn't do brilliantly in this paper – mainly due to being still half asleep, but also because I hadn't had to do this kind of maths for over fifteen years. I managed to pass though, and did much better at all the other piloty kind of papers. In fact, once I'd got past the corporal with the clipboard, all the 'grown-ups' were very friendly and took me aside to give me a personal debrief on my results. Given that I was already a successful military pilot they were keen to see how their test methods stacked up against reality. Having survived that ordeal I was presented with another fascinating challenge. Just before lunch I was approached by some RAF chap who took me aside and asked me to change out of uniform. 'What?'

'I'm sorry sir, I'm going to have to ask you to change out of uniform.'

'Why?'

'Well, you are a Lieutenant Commander and you are about to be interviewed by a Flight Lieutenant – if you are wearing uniform he will have to call you "sir" in your interview so he has asked that you change into civvies.'

'Sorry, I'm not living on site and it will take me over two hours to go and change. So I'm going to go and have a drink in the Officers' Mess. Let me know when it's time to meet the Flight Lieutenant!'

This caught my interrogator quite by surprise as they were mostly used to dealing with meek and earnest sixth formers. Suitably calmed by copious amounts of beer I finally met said Flight Lieutenant who called me sir and I ordered him to address me as Chris … problem solved.

I passed my interview process with flying colours and the RAF offered me a commission which I accepted. I was off to RAF Cranwell to learn how to march and salute in a funny fashion followed immediately by thirty-plus hours roaring around Yorkshire in a Jet Provost – I could learn to march funny for that. I was then heading to the Central Flying School (CFS) to convert my Qualified Helicopter Instructor (QHI) qualification into a Qualified Flying Instructor (QFI) qual. Turns out the RAF were desperately short of experienced instructors and within a few short months I could become a senior instructor on the Shorts Tucano before moving up to the BAe Hawk T1. This was enough for me. I was going to become a fast jet instructor, and then, all being well, I would head to the front line in a single seat Jaguar or Harrier. Cool!

I got to within a week or so of changing my navy blue uniform for a light blue one. *But* … just as it was at university, I was now facing an equally challenging medical issue. My wife had previously been diagnosed with a brain tumour which had needed immediate surgery. Apparently, as brain tumours go, it could have been worse. I'd found out when I was embarked in a ship off the coast of Portugal. I'd dashed back to the UK via Gibraltar and twenty-four hours later was at Ally's bedside. A twelve-hour operation failed to remove all of the tumour and we were advised a further similar operation would be required within months. We started to muddle on and make the best of the 'cards we had been dealt'. I was playing at being a single parent for our toddler son when it became evident we were expecting our second child; without us knowing, Ally had been newly pregnant at the time of her diagnosis. Despite her being zapped by all sorts of scans and drugs, our darling daughter, Emily, arrived in the nick of time for Ally to undertake further surgery. While she was recovering in hospital we chatted to her consultant and I explained my planned career change that was now imminent. He almost laughed. In fairness, I knew that the straws being pulled were going to leave me holding a short one. In spite of massive amounts of time, energy and angst invested successfully in this potential career modification, it turns out that looking after two young children and a wife firing on less than two cylinders, even with the help of family and friends, was not compatible with the turbulence the next year of training would bring.

Bugger!

I have to say, at that stage, the Royal Navy were just the best of employers. They had given me some compassionate leave to try and sort things out, and, despite my impending betrayal, phoned me every other day asking me to stay. Ultimately I responded to such a kind invitation by requesting a specific job. I asked to be appointed Officer Commanding of the Lynx Simulator at RNAS Portland. This would achieve a number of things:

> It was a Commanding Officer type job, so I would get to be in charge of something. I could manage my instructional sorties to fit in with dropping children off at carers and nursery. I would continue to fly as an instructor – and would now fly on all three Lynx Squadrons. And most importantly – it would give me the opportunity to study for the dreaded academic papers that formed part of the interview process to become a test pilot.

So, weeks later I started working at the simulator and started my planned preparation for ETPS selection. This involved visits to Boscombe Down and RAE Bedford to chat to current TPs about their jobs and to do some research regarding the interview process. This included a meeting with the then senior RN TP – Mike. He was a Commander and had already been a working test pilot and commanded the Rotary Wing Test Squadron, or D Squadron as it was previously known. I'm pretty sure his opinion counted for a lot in the process and I was relieved to apparently receive his endorsement for my application. Following an extensive tour of the school and chatting a good deal with Andy, the Principal Tutor, I gathered there were at least two written papers. One solely concerning maths and the other mostly about 'principles of flight'. They would be followed by two face to face interviews, one with the academic tutors and the next with the flying staff. Finally I would face a very formal interview by the senior military TPs wearing my 'best bib and tucker'. Apart from the academic papers, I would be expected to have an intimate knowledge of my own aircraft type and role, then know lots about other helicopters and aeroplanes. I'd be quizzed on my general knowledge of other aviation matters including space flight and all sorts of whacky futuristic concepts.

So to business. I started to work out how to address all of the above. As a stepping stone and catalyst, to knowing more about my own aircraft, I initiated another self-inflicted challenge in addition to caring for young children and my recovering wife. I was a QHI teaching on the Lynx. The instructional system in the armed forces was, and still is, managed by the

CFS. As a newly qualified instructor we were awarded B2 status. After six months or so we could upgrade to B1, and then after another year we could be assessed to become A2 instructors which was effectively a senior/experienced instructor. The A1 grade was reserved for exceptional instructors – at the time there had never been an A1 category instructor on Lynx helicopters. So why not me? Knowing the Lynx inside and out would be a requirement for both ETPS and CFS, and we simulator instructors probably knew more about the aircraft than most. So that covered getting to grips with the basics. What else could I do? Next on my agenda was to talk to the Westland Helicopters' TP responsible for the type. Ted very kindly invited me up to Yeovil to spend a day with him talking about the aircraft. Ted is one of the most helpful characters around and, having been a tutor at ETPS, was able to impart all sorts of knowledge and information. I ended up knowing the background to all the aircraft's limitations and understanding comprehensively the quirky flight control system that was fitted. And I got to learn from Ted how to make homemade pasta.

The next challenge was to broaden my aviation experience. A number of things came together. The RN was in the process of a programme to update the Lynx by the fitting of a sensor turret and better radar. This new aircraft was designated the Lynx HMA.8. As the boss of the simulator, I had been campaigning for some time that we would need to purchase a new high fidelity 'sim' to train a whole new generation of pilots and observers. I was tasked with researching the requirement and putting together detailed specifications that eventually would form a core part of an invitation to tender. I needed to know more about such training aids. I spent a week at Cranfield University on a dedicated course of training and started to visit other UK-based training devices.

The next piece of this jigsaw was when Ally's best friend from university, Pat, invited us out to Houston, Texas. Her husband Doug was a 'sedimentologist' – whatever that is. He was on an exchange posting with BP. The RN had already been very generous with compassionate leave, but now I hatched a cunning plan. If I was willing to self-fund my travel to the USA, could I be given a leave of absence to spend some time fact finding about training simulators? That would also allow me to visit other aviation facilities and broaden my knowledge. My boss, Ian, a well-respected hero of the Falklands campaign, heard my pitch with interest and enthusiasm. The following day we booked to spend a whole month in the States. So what to do with the two or three weeks I would have. Well, I started researching places to visit and after several transatlantic phone calls had organised some rather interesting venues.

With my plans for America firming up I turned my attention to my A1 recat. At the time there were no A1 Lynx instructors in the Royal Navy, so I would be assessed by a team of three A2s from RN Flying Standards. These guys were known as 'trappers' and would conduct routine inspections of all the Naval Air Squadrons on a regular basis. They were also responsible for flying with as many Fleet Air Arm aircrew as they could, to ensure our standards were maintained and that we followed normal procedures where appropriate. I learnt that I was to fly with Mike, the Lynx trapper who had an office in my building, and Ian from Yeovilton. I was also going to be grilled for a day by Mike, Ian and Dave who was the commanding officer of RN Standards Flight (Rotary Wing) at the time. I guess this was their way of ensuring I reached the required 'Exceptional' standard without any one of them being accused of bias. Both of the instructional flights I flew were incredibly stretching. I had, thankfully, beforehand had two or three work-up flights with the other experienced A2s at RNAS Portland. It was on one of these work-up flights with a mate where we nearly ended up crashing into a field; following a simulated double engine failure we were both waiting for 'the other' to tell us to abort the planned forced landing – I chickened out inches above the ground. The assessed sorties with the trappers were, without doubt, designed to test me to the utmost. The first sortie was built around a scenario of being a student's first conversion flight. I had to brief him comprehensively on the aircraft including all the controls. As soon as we were airborne I was informed I had an engine fire. I had to deal with this slickly without any assistance from my 'ab initio student', and had to give him my most calming BA-pilot-patter as I safely shut the engine down, fired the extinguisher and circuited briskly to land. My second sortie with Ian had me teaching all the Lynx helicopter manoeuvres and for some reason ending up in cloud and then having to divert to the Westland Helicopters' airfield which had a relatively poor landing approach aid = a surveillance radar approach (SRA). Once back at Portland safely I fell out of the aircraft onto the tarmac with relief!

Phew! I had apparently survived my trap sorties.

The following day was given over to my 'oral' test. It just went on for ever. I was grilled about my knowledge of the Lynx and asked to draw diagrams of the fuel system, the flight control system and pretty much every other system. This gave me no fears. I taught this stuff and frankly had no qualms about presenting what I knew in an easy to understand format. The afternoon is where it unravelled. First up, I was extensively quizzed on something called 'vortex ring'. This is the situation where a helicopter is descending vertically with power applied. The airflow around the rotor blades becomes very confused and the aircraft can suffer a catastrophic loss of lift. Adding more power will make things worse. The solution, similar to recovering a stalled aircraft, is to push the cyclic forward and gain forward airspeed. This initially uses even more precious height, which helicopters often don't have, with the consequence that a crash results. Not good. Unfortunately for me my studies for ETPS had made me something of an expert on the topic and instead of giving the standardised explanation that a typical student would get, I said far too much … in fairness something my wife accuses me of frequently. The second topic that lost me points was raised by one of the A2s, who I later discovered was studying for his civilian licences. He pretended to be a visiting pilot from Brazil and wanted to know why it was raining all the time in the UK. What was wanted was a comprehensive explanation of the world's climatology. What he got was a shrug of my shoulders and, 'Well, it's England, it's winter, and yes it does rain all the time.'

My debrief seemed to take nearly as long as the oral. One of my flights was graded 'Exceptional' and one 'Just Exceptional'. My oral was of a similarly high standard generally – Phew! But I had stumbled on the couple of topics described above. So overall they decided I was only 'Just Exceptional' and since none of the three was an A1 they saw no reason to award me with such a category.

Bugger!

But, the good news was, I had achieved more than any other Lynx instructor previously, ensured my aircraft knowledge was as good as possible and being 'Just Exceptional' was, frankly, good enough for me.

Almost immediately after surviving my recat, we travelled to the States with our two children, Sam and Emily, then aged 4 and 2. Once the family was settled, with the children discovering the delights of *Barney the Dinosaur* on TV, I set off on my various adventures. First up was NASA as in, 'Houston we have a problem'. To this day I have no idea how I pulled off the coup of being hosted by NASA's head of astronaut training for a whole day. And what a fantastic day it was. I was shown around all the training aids including the swimming pools used to simulate low gravity. In the afternoon I got to spend a couple of hours in the Space Shuttle simulator. I was taught how to fly it and was invited to fly their glide descent profiles into numerous primary and secondary landing fields including RAE Bedford. The cockpit of the shuttle was laid out a bit like an airliner with relatively small windows. The instrument panel was fitted with eight flat-panel PFD/MFD displays that offered the usual Airbus/Boeing type of information. The traditional joystick had been replaced by a short-throw, fly-by-wire hand controller mounted on a pedestal. It looked conventional, but had the additional function of controlling the aircraft's yaw via thruster jets when in space. Once it had returned from space and entered the earth's atmosphere it became a gliding brick. It had short stubby wings and was a far cry from the optimum glider configuration which achieves glide ratios of better than 30:1; that is they fly 30ft horizontally for every foot lost in height. A light aeroplane typically achieves around 10:1. The shuttle's initial glide ratio was 1:1. The on-board computers would fly the aircraft to the overhead of the intended landing site aiming to arrive at 50,000ft. I was expected to take over just before the shuttle reached the 'heading alignment cone' that was located above the landing site. From there, I was required to fly the aircraft around an arcing pattern to final approach.

Pre-test pilot days my skill to fly numerous forced landings in various aircraft had not yet been acquired, however this task was made easier due to the head-up display (HUD) that was in my direct field of view. The HUD allowed me to look through the display at the runway and still receive visual cues of the approach. I was presented with a round, green flight-path marker representing the shuttle, and a guidance diamond. Theoretically, if I kept the flight-path marker on top of the guidance diamond at all times, the shuttle would glide smoothly to the required touchdown point. So should be easy eh? Passing 12,000ft, I roll out on final approach six miles out, about a minute from touchdown. I'm now flying a 20-degree glideslope at 10,000ft per minute which is seven times as steep as a normal ILS. Descending through 2,000ft, at roughly 300 knots glide speed, a pair of triangles began to rise from the bottom, one on each side of the HUD. These were the 'flare indicator' and were used to indicate when to start 'rounding out' for the landing. I felt the honour of the whole of the United Kingdom was now on my shoulders if I 'screwed up'. I crossed the hedge at 220–230 knots monitoring my height on the radar-altimeter or rad-alt. Monitoring rad-alt height was 'bread and butter' to a Navy Lynx pilot and finally I was back in my 'comfort zone'. Using all the information available and, tapping into beginner's luck, I managed to cream the main wheels onto the runway without ripping the tyres off.

Phew! I had survived another without embarrassment. Now please can I do it all again? And I did – several times.

How could I possibly follow that?

Next up was a longer drive up to Dallas, Fort Worth to visit Bell Helicopters. This visit was definitely aimed at my ETPS application and I had expressed a particular interest in the V22 Osprey tilt rotor aircraft which was early in its development as a new rapid ship-borne transport aircraft for the US Marine Corps. Again, I had a fantastic couple of days and was wined and dined like a visiting dignitary. I was given comprehensive briefings on all the various Bell products and was allowed to visit all the production lines. I was especially interested in getting to see the Cobra attack helicopters which had acquired an awesome reputation in Vietnam. Having learnt all about the beast I was again invited to fly the sim. What a great game. Wazzing low level around a fictional battlefield blowing up tanks and stuff. Later in my career I had chance to fly the real thing and was not disappointed. On the second day came the highlight of this trip. An afternoon in the V22 Osprey full-motion simulator. I had received comprehensive briefings about the programme beforehand, so I knew roughly how the aircraft was meant to fly. It had relatively short wings so that it could fit on the US Navy and Marine Corps carriers. Attached to each wing was a nacelle containing a turbine engine driving a very unconventional three-bladed rotor. Each rotor was cross connected with the rotor on the other wing. The nacelles could be rotated from the horizontal (for forward flight) to 85–96 degrees which was effectively aligned with the vertical. In forward flight the rotors could be considered as massive propellers and were turned relatively slowly at 84 per cent of their nominal speed. If rotated to be aligned vertically, the rotors became helicopter blades and at 100 per cent speed were able to provide enough lift for the aircraft to hover. Moving the nacelles was, as I am now aware, a conventional practice for Harrier pilots used to adjusting their 'nozzles'. As the nacelles were rotated the aircraft was deemed to be 'converting' and could be 'transitioned' from one mode of flight to another. As with the Harrier, the thrust could be used to support wing-borne flight at lower speeds.

Now the cockpit brief was a hoot. Again the instrument panel was fitted with four of the apparently obligatory PFD/MFD display panels. After the space shuttle I was learning fast. The flying controls were clearly unconventional. Thankfully, I was faced with a familiar cyclic control stick. In a helicopter this stick adds or removes pitch from the rotor blades in a cyclical fashion which changes the direction of thrust and, when hovering, allows the aircraft to be moved forwards, sidewards and backwards etc. Thankfully, that is how the set-up was configured in the V22.

Phew! Something familiar.

Additionally the aircraft appeared to have conventional yaw pedals. In a helicopter these would change the thrust of the tail rotor to control yaw. In an aeroplane they would be connected to the rudder to control yaw in forward flight. In fact, they were connected to the rudders in the V22 but also, through some fancy flight-control system, controlled yaw in the hover by using differential thrust on the main rotors. Finally I was briefed on the cockpit's more controversial controls. As a helicopter pilot I would normally operate a 'collective lever' with my left hand. This lever is usually hinged at the rear and moves in an arc in the vertical plane – that is if I move the stick up I add more power and climb up. If I lower the lever I reduce the pitch on the blades collectively and go down. In a Harrier the pilot's left hand rests on the throttle. As with any other jet aeroplane – pushing the throttle forward adds more fuel and gives more thrust and allows the aircraft to go faster. In the hover the throttle works in the same sense, and if more thrust is required the lever is pushed forward. So in a Harrier/V22 the pilot's left hand goes forward to go up – helicopter pilots pull the collective up and slightly aft to go up. You will note the potential for confusion and it certainly confused the heck out of me. Sinking towards the ground I found myself instinctively pulling the Thrust Control Lever (TCL) aft – and thus reducing power and crashing with a thump. Apparently Colonel Henry Blot, a USMC Harrier pilot and test pilot, had largely influenced the discussion on whether the pilot should be offered a collective helicopter control or a Harrier type throttle. As a result the control is often nicknamed the 'Blottle'. Even as I write this chapter, some twenty-eight years later, this is still a very controversial decision and the control laws for numerous battery-powered vertical flight aircraft are still being hotly debated.

In addition to the Blottle the aircraft had a knurled rotating device that fell under my left thumb. By rotating the knob I controlled the nacelle angle. Rotating forwards moved the nacelles from the vertical towards the horizontal, thus allowing the thrust from the rotors to be tilted more and more aft. Another whacky control was a beep function on the cyclic. If I want to move sidewards in my helicopter I would move the cyclic to the side and the thrust vector would tilt slightly and I would move sidewards. I found I could do exactly the same thing in the Osprey. But alternatively I could displace the stick sidewards and more thrust would be applied to one nacelle than the other and the aircraft would roll. With the whole aircraft tilted sidewards it would also start to move laterally. So I had options. Gosh decision, decisions!

First up I was allowed to fly the aircraft like a twin turbo prop. This was long before I'd been sent to 45 (Reserve) Squadron RAF at Cranwell to learn how to be a proper multi-engine pilot. But as I have stated repeatedly, flying around in a twin-engine aeroplane in the cruise is a heck of a lot easier than trying to hover a helicopter. And so it was with the V22. I was invited to fly as fast as I could; nearly 280 knots, if I remember correctly, and then flew as slowly as I could until I stalled. No drama. I then was invited to beep the nacelles into the vertical and try an autorotation. That is, I would close the TCL, reducing pitch on the rotor blades, and enter a rapid rate of descent. The airflow kept my blades turning and then just before I hit the airfield I had to slam the lever forward to try and add some pitch to cushion my touch down.

Bam!

The screens went red. I had crashed. I tried again.

Bam!

I crashed.

In fact, after three attempts I was improving but still had not managed to land this beast safely following a double engine failure.

Bugger! – I hadn't survived.

I went on to practice slow-speed manoeuvring and every time things got stressful I found myself moving the Blottle the wrong way and …

Bam! I died again.

There is a limit to the number of times I felt I should be subjected to my own death and having used up my nine lives I decided it was time to head to the Stockyards, at nearby Fort Worth, to drown my sorrows with a longneck beer or two. I have to say, as a non-TP, this experience proved invaluable and more importantly I was awarded a highly treasured V22 gold tie pin which I was able to wear at my ETPS interview.

Later on in the book I will talk about my various licences and how I got them. At the time of my visit to Houston I had both helicopter and aeroplane commercial licences. Before 9-11 it was very easy to get these UK licences validated by the Federal Aviation Authority (FAA) and then I could visit local flying schools and rent out aircraft. I checked out on a Cessna 150/152 and 172 and was able to take my family flying. I was offered a flight in an Enstrom helicopter which I felt I couldn't refuse. I flew down to the farm where it was based in a Cessna and enjoyed an hour or so in another type. The challenge came when I was to depart. Again, back then, my aeroplane experience was relatively thin and I had realised that the available take-off distance was very short. And it was a very hot day with no wind.

Yikes!

To gain the maximum length of runway we manhandled the aircraft and pushed it back so the tail was touching the hedge. Then I leapt in and gave the aircraft a very thorough power check before applying full power against the brakes. Sadly, releasing the brakes did not result in the punch-in-the-back acceleration I'd hoped for.

20mph … 30 … 40 … nose-wheel off … far end hedge approaching … 50 … just airborne … hedge just under the wheels.

Phew! Survived another and very glad of my decision to waste not a foot of available strip. I banked hard to overfly my anxious hosts who waved cheerfully – more out of relief I imagine than anything else. The following day I invested some hard earned cash in flying an elderly PA23 Apache twin. A type I was to re-fly just twelve months later when revalidating my multi-engine piston rating in Norfolk. The aircraft is a delight to fly. My final flight during my 'vacation' was to regain night currency. With hindsight this was probably a bonkers thing to do, but the aircraft was cheap to rent and convenient. Even then I was risk averse and had planned to get airborne in daylight at dusk so I could ease myself back into it. But the traffic was dreadful and an hour after sunset I found myself doing the walk-round with a torch. I was about to get lost – twice. At night the airfield was very confusing. Lights of all colours seemingly everywhere. I was told by Air Traffic Control (ATC) to follow a Malibu. Instead I followed a Piper PA-28 Cherokee – which looked the same in the dark. I was beginning to wonder where I was going when I got my first bollocking for being in the wrong place. Surely things couldn't get worse? Checks completed I was invited to line up on one of the runways and, with full power applied, trundled gently into the sky. After take-off checks complete … 500ft … gentle right turn through 90 degrees … a further right turn onto a downwind leg … looking for the airfield to make my radio call and …

Sugar! Where is the airfield?

I was now surrounded by more streetlights and shop lights and car headlights than you could shake a stick at, but what I couldn't see were any runway lights. I was lost within two minutes of take-off somewhere over downtown Houston. I could do nothing other than press on and hope. Guessing it was about the right time, I turned right again through 90 degrees, reduced power and started a descent to 500ft. On reaching, I turned towards where I thought I'd left the airfield and …

There it was!

I had not used unidirectional runway lights before. They are designed to only be visible when on the final approach path.

Phew! Another lesson learnt the hard way and I had survived without further embarrassment. Time to head back to our friends' house for a cold beer.

Once back in the UK I continued to research other simulators and flew across the channel to Brest and then Den Helder for a day each to fly their Lynx simulators. All this research had been a marvellous way to appreciate what various state of the art full motion training devices could offer. I believe I did the Royal Navy proud by making a very convincing case for us purchasing such a sim and then accurately specifying its required capabilities. Becoming such an expert was to create a huge problem for me in the future, but more of that in another chapter. For now I had to concentrate on my forthcoming ETPS selection process.

Chapter 2

ETPS Interview – Test Pilot Selection

> I was storming through the exam paper questions with confidence until I suddenly realised my paper was covered with blood ... my blood! What was going on?

Eventually the dreaded week arrived which would directly influence, for good or bad, the rest of my career. I was, frankly, bricking it.

There was another RN candidate for the possible one or zero places on the next course. If successful, the RN candidate would attend the 1994 course which would lead to being appointed to take over from Steve, based at RAE Bedford as an experimental test pilot doing lots of interesting research flying. As part of my prep I had spent a day at Bedford and even been invited to be a subject pilot in their highly modified Westland Wessex HC2. I decided this would be a great job for me. Lots of interesting work, interesting flying, and a very grown-up atmosphere. I would be *gutted* not to get this post.

Being the friendly chap I am, I found myself offering Martin, the other candidate, a lift up to Amesbury. Martin was a fellow Lynx pilot. He had also initially been selected to fly the Sea Harrier and done a fair amount of fixed-wing flying. Surely this would give him the edge over me? My confidence was low and, as I adjusted the passenger seat in my classic Mini Cooper S, my shaking hands slipped on the bracket and I badly gashed a finger. Fuelled with stress, anxiety and adrenalin I gave it little thought, and moments later we were blasting past Dorchester on the Salisbury road. We must have made for a very odd couple at the rather shabby Antrobus Arms that evening. Conversation was difficult as we were both keen to be selected ... pistols at dawn maybe?

After struggling to get any sleep we headed up to the Aircraft and Armament Evaluation Establishment (AAEE) Boscombe Down. The administrator of the school, a friendly RAF Sergeant, met all the aspiring students and, with suitable ID issued, it wasn't long before we found ourselves in a classroom being invigilated by Andy, an RN TP. Our first paper was Principles of Flight. Given my A1 recat research I was storming through the questions with confidence until I suddenly realised my paper was covered with blood … my blood! What was going on? My gash from the evening before had no doubt been subject to my unusually high blood pressure and I had sprung a leak. Hugely embarrassed and now running out of time I asked Andy for help – I received a withering response and elected to press on regardless. I completed the test with shaky blood-drenched hands, wondering whether or not bleeding on an exam paper was an automatic fail.

By the time we got to the dreaded maths paper I was starting to consider giving up. Not a good start. But I hadn't spent all my preparation over the last two years to be thwarted so easily. So, using lots of sellotape, I improvised a dressing of sorts and the second paper was remarkably blood-free on completion. With next to no time for lunch we were led individually into rooms with the academic and flying tutors. As expected, Andy and Eric quizzed me extensively about the Lynx, all of its systems, limitations and so on. Then they wanted to know what I didn't like about it. Compared to the Wasp it was a much more capable aircraft and, frankly, excellent for landing on the back of ships in stormy weather. So what was not to like? The flight control system was a bit whacky, the tail rotor was ineffective, giving problems in certain conditions and the avionics needed an upgrade. I did my best to give what I thought was an honest, balanced, but critical view, which it turns out was exactly what they were looking for. I was then quizzed about other RN helicopters and how they compared, followed by those of the other services. Again I had done my homework well, I think. But thereafter the questions became harder and harder. I tried to follow that pattern that so many cabinet ministers do when being interviewed by the media … that is steer the questions onto a topic I knew something about. It seemed to work and my intimate knowledge of the V22 Osprey and Space Shuttle filled up a good chunk of the hour long interrogation.

Phew! I had survived the first day. Back to the Antrobus for a quick beer with Martin in the hope of comparing notes. He of course oozed confidence. For a start, he hadn't bled all over the papers and apparently creamed the interviews …

Bugger!

Another night without any sleep followed by breakfast in my best parade uniform, my Number 5s. I had been advised that the events of the first day generates short reports and recommendations to the main board. This board comprised all the 'grown-ups' … the senior Test Pilots and experts of the establishment including the Chief Scientist, the Chief Test Pilot and the Commandant who was an Air Commodore. I wore my V22 tie pin.

Another one hour grilling commenced. In fairness this started out more light heartedly. I was being questioned about my reasons for wanting to be a test pilot and I was able to calm myself with what I thought was witty banter … in any event I raised a few smiles. Then it was back into exploring my knowledge, particularly about the job I would find myself in. I had done my research well and felt I had the edge over Martin, at last, who hadn't clocked up the road miles I had, dashing to Bedford and Boscombe and Yeovil. At last, one of the panel noticed my tiepin. It was clearly a strategy on my part to elicit conversation about something I now knew quite a lot about. Thankfully the panel of, mostly fixed wing, experts was really pleased to pick my brains on what I thought of the aircraft and its control laws. Had this helped? Well it certainly helped me feel slightly more confident. I had now given up on my plan to transfer to the RAF and I really had no plan B if I was not successful during this process. No pressure then.

We drove back to Weymouth both rather wrung out by our gruelling experience, and this wasn't the last hurdle. The ETPS panel would decide who would be acceptable, but if there was more than one suitable candidate from a particular service then it came down, in my case, to the Royal Navy Appointer. This was a Captain supported by an aviator Commander and a pilot specialist Lieutenant Commander. It was ultimately down to them to work out who could be made available set against a bigger picture backdrop. I will speak more of this system in a later chapter. But for now I drove my colleague home and pulled up outside my idyllic cottage in Broadwey wondering for how much longer this might be called home.

One morning some days later, I was at my desk when the phone rang. It was the Lieutenant Commander appointer.

'Would you like to attend 32 Rotary Wing Test Pilot course starting in January?'

'Sorry, say again?'

'You were successful at your interviews – I want to send you to ETPS next year.'

'Bloody hell! Yes please!'

I was sworn to secrecy until I had received both a letter from Boscombe and a further letter from him. Fair enough. I walked down the corridor to the office of Mike, the trapper.

'Mike, can I buy you a beer?'

'Sure, why?'

'I'm not allowed to say – but I'm in a really good mood after a call I've just had.'

Mike didn't need me to spell it out and by 1200 we were sat on bar stools at the O's Club (Officers' Club) quaffing pints of ale that have never tasted better. It was nice to be able to have that beer with Mike. In my new career path being an A1 or not would be quite irrelevant. I'd already phoned home but dashed back as soon as I could. We had not been willing to consider the implications of selection before – but now we could start planning. And I'd heard some news which, although professionally disappointing, was domestically helpful. That is that RAE Bedford was going to close its airfield by the end of 1994 and the aircraft were to be transferred to operate out of Boscombe. So although that would be frustrating professionally, it meant there was no need to move from Boscombe at the end of the course. Better for the children's schooling for sure. After what seemed like forever, the required letters landed on my doormat.

I had been selected for Test Pilot training – very exciting!

Work wise the next few months were rather tedious as my thoughts were now elsewhere. That said, I took great pride in my years running the sim. When I arrived it was seen as a place to locate tired and unenthusiastic aircrew. In my time, my attempts at recat had really raised the profile. I had insisted that all my staff were properly qualified observer instructors (QOI), or QHIs like me, or Instrument Rating Instructors (IRI). Overnight, I had transformed the professional atmosphere of the place. And I'd made sure that the Lynx HMA.8 sim was going to be procured to a very high specification. It had been a very good two years for me and had allowed me to pull my weight at home as my wife had been recovering from her two massive operations.

So, house hunting every weekend with the kids was fun. We found a good pub to lunch at with a massive slide and great bacon sarnies. Nice house found … offer accepted … our house sold … all looking good until about four weeks before Christmas when the chain began to look rather shaky. I took a very grey, rainy day off work and drove up to Boscombe to attend some of the helicopter preview presentations. More about this later, but teams of two or three students had completed end of course, formal assessments of all manner of aircraft and written huge reports. They then had thirty minutes to present their findings to all the senior staff who proceeded to grill them with a barrage of technical questions. Wow! It made my selection interviews appear tame in comparison. In fact I became rather depressed. How could I ever do this? I had been blagging. I had apparently managed to convey my broad knowledge but inside, knew I was a fraud. I would be rumbled on week one – oh heck! To add to my misery I had asked the nice RAF sergeant administrator to book me a married quarter in case our house purchase fell through. I went to visit the rather dilapidated council-house-type property and knocked on the door to be greeted by a very irate wife.

'This place is shit!' she said as I stood in front of her doorway as the rain came down like stair rods. I wasn't invited in and couldn't see much apart from what I could see from where I stood, getting soaked while she continued to complain, mainly about her shit husband in addition to the shit house and the shit neighbours. Oh dear!

I drove home, splashing through deep puddles in the dark, with my windscreen wipers working flat out, and did my best to put a more positive spin on certain aspects of my day to Ally, especially our new home in Romsey Road. The chain had indeed broken down … the quarter was accepted and I set about packing my office as I handed over to my replacement, Andy, a highly respected and experienced Observer Instructor. I had indeed raised the professional profile of the sim.

I arrived home late, tired, with a car full of books, with a plan to move house the following day. I turned the corner to be greeted by a scene from a typical Hollywood disaster movie. Lots of vans with flashing lights, cordon tape, cones and warning signs.

What on earth?

I was met by my father-in-law, Brian, who was down with my mother-in-law, Barbara, to help us pack. He looked sheepish – oh dear what had he done? Apparently he had smelled gas, called the emergency number and now I was surrounded by more gas experts than soft Mick. The first one accosted me as the property owner and began a series of sentences that all seemed to revolve around the expression of 'Effing Cowboys'. It would seem that both our gas fires in our two living rooms did not have any kind of flue. That's right … nothing to remove the lethal carbon monoxide from the room at all.

Bugger! How had we survived our three years there? How badly had we ruined our children's brains? And how were we going to sell a house without working fires?

Double Bugger!

I was knackered. This was a hideously busy time, and I needed this like a hole in the head. We couldn't delay the move. So the gas board removed our condemned fires. In the morning I dashed to the local antique shop to buy a couple of brass screens and returned to find half my house, including bins full of dirty nappies, already packed in a Pickford's removal truck.

We abandoned our lovely cottage, which had served us so well, to arrive dirty and tired that night at our new, less than idyllic, home. Uggh! In fact, we barely threw all our stuff in before we decided to head off to my wife's sister for Christmas. Between Christmas and New Year we fitted bunk beds into the kids' new bedroom and were planning to do some further tidying until we received a phone call one evening from our former neighbours. Broadwey had been flooded and our lovely, now empty, cottage was in the middle of it.

Hell's Bells! Give us a break!

The living room had been flooded with a depth of about a foot of water but thankfully the wooden floor was sorted after a good clean and rugs dried out etc. Christmas turned into New Year and finally the Taylor family set up in their new, rather characterless, home. The saving grace was a real open fireplace. No more gas fires for us. Stoked up high with coal and logs we settled in to our very tatty sofa I had bought with my first house and my thoughts turned to Monday when I had been invited to start my course.

Phew! We had arrived, in one piece … kind of, and although we had endured an exhausting and emotional Christmas, a defining chapter of my career was about to commence. I was about to begin my training to be an Experimental Test Pilot.

Chapter 3

ETPS, Class of 1994 – First Term

Initially all went well as I descended just outside of autorotation and then, all of a sudden …

I could see bugger all … !

The aircraft had been cooled to minus forty degrees or so and this very cold aircraft now encountered water vapour which instantly froze onto the bubble canopy. The interior misted up at the same time and I now could see *'the square root of nothing'*.

Yikes!

The third day of January dawned grey and foggy and damp, but I was thrilled. With a spring in my step I walked the few hundred yards to the main gate where, yet again, the kindly sergeant met us and we commenced the usual arrival admin. We were a motley crew. In this chapter you will find our course picture. We were from the RAF, RN and Army. We had French, Italians, Dutch, Australians, Canadians and Singaporeans. I was, by military rank, the senior student but custom was that the course leader was always a fixed wing pilot. Why? This division between the aeroplane students and helicopter people started on day one and never stopped. We were known as 'rotes' and we were, to some, a lower life form.

With identity cards issued, and numerous forms completed, we found ourselves in a classroom with Alan, the senior academic and fixed wing ground-school tutor. Before we had chance to catch our breath we were off studying the properties of the atmosphere leading to basic subsonic aerodynamics.

Aaaaargh! My brain hurts.

Fairly quickly we were issued with our flying suits and soon thereafter had name badges with our 'wings' sown on to the left breast. It turns out that both staff and students wore flying suits to work pretty much every day, unless it was a special occasion, like the course photo for example. This was quite a practical idea as it gave us all a common identity as well as appearance. Obviously we students were not allowed to wear the coveted 'graduate patch' or badge which I, for one, had now been lusting after for some time.

The first four weeks adopted a busy, but straightforward, rhythm. Little did we realise how much we would miss this relatively stable existence. We basically were back at school with five one hour lessons, followed by lunch in the officers' mess, followed by more lessons in the afternoon. Mostly we were all together and frankly, I had not yet realised that the 'rotes' were about to be split away from our colleagues for pretty much every activity apart from social events. Mixed in with the ground school we started to get lectures and briefs from the flying tutors, resplendent in their flying suits – and graduate patches.

Only two weeks in, we were lectured on our first real flight test activity, the 'cockpit assessment'. In fairness, we did have the initial 'phase brief' delivered by a fixed wing tutor who showed us lots of photos of Buccaneers, Phantoms and Hunters … cool! Sadly we were not about to be set loose on such aircraft. Rather, we were directed to one of the helicopters in our own hangar attached to the staff offices. We were split into teams, a pilot or two with a flight test engineer. We rotes numbered seven initially (although an FTE student resigned in the summer term), and were split into two pairs and a team of three. I was allocated the Gazelle. What's not to like? A nice Gucci cockpit with pretty dials and good field of view. We were still getting lectures throughout the day with associated homework and this task was our first taster of how much we would end up trying to achieve in parallel … spinning plates with one hand and juggling with the other seems an appropriate description. The aircraft were busy flying all day so we could only access them in the evening. First up was to document the Field of View (FOV). We were taught that we should first define where a typical pilot's eyes would be if sitting in the pilot's seat. We had all had our anthropometric measurements taken – so we knew whether aspects of our body such as torso, arms, legs etc. were of average or abnormal lengths. I was pretty 'run of the mill average' which made life slightly easier. Having worked out where my eyes would be, that defined the Reference Eye Position (REP), I hung a bob weight, by a piece of string, from the cockpit roof. This was then documented by taking photos and measuring at least three distances roughly 90 degrees apart. We then used a widget that was designed to measure angles and the like. Using a weird Mercator style piece of graph paper we were able to produce a monochrome plot looking very much like a photo taken by a very wide fish eye lens. In fact, I believe, students in recent years have been allowed to use a fish eye camera and achieve in seconds what can take hours in the traditional manner. Once the FOV was plotted we set about viewing, what was for me, a very familiar aircraft.

The Gazelle had been used as my basic trainer and again when I was taught how to be a QHI. But this time around I found the seat uncomfortable with limited adjustment. Doors were operated, and emergency egress practised, with required forces measured with a handheld force gauge. That done, it was time to assess all the instruments and determine whether they were 'fit for purpose' and frankly, they were not. No wonder I had found aspects of flying it difficult as a baby pilot. The dials were too small, badly labelled and some gauges were located incorrectly. How had this aircraft ever been approved by graduates from the school many years earlier I wondered? After a couple of evenings, working late into the night, we now had all the data we needed and had ideas about what we needed to be critical of within our flight test report (FTR). I know we hadn't yet flown, but it had been explained to us that normally we would follow up a ground-based assessment by some actual flying to determine whether our suspicions turned out to be correct in reality. Being able to write a good and clear FTR was, it was emphasised, an absolutely core skill of test pilots and FTEs. Anyone can find problems with aircraft, but it's trying to explain such issues – possibly to a non-technical reader – that is an essential part of the 'day job'. We were given lectures and a guidebook to clarify how we should format our reports. The results of our findings had to be explained in a series of paragraphs comprising seven parts. You will find flight test professionals waxing lyrical about seven-part paragraphs which, being written almost entirely in the past tense, took quite a bit of getting used to. While we were struggling with the Gazelle, our course mates were looking at the school's Westland Scout and Lynx. Our fixed wing mates were crawling over an Andover, Jaguar, Hawk and Hunter. Writing these FTRs took more midnight oil. I thought I was going to ace this first exercise. Many days later my beautiful report was returned completely covered in red ink. It was worse than my bloody exam paper. How could I have got so much wrong on an aircraft I knew well? This was a pattern that was to repeat itself constantly for the next eleven months. The theory was that by the end of the year we would have completed every single section of a full report that we would be required to write for our Preview Assessment.

Blige!

More ground school continued. When would we go flying? At last we were programmed for area familiarisation flights in the Gazelle and Scout; all we had to wait for now was the extensive drizzly grey murk and fog to clear. In the meantime on to the next exercise … but I haven't finished my FTR for the cockpit assessment. We generally had about five or six exercises overlapping at any one time. We would be getting the ground school for the first one … then we would be having 'phase briefs' from the tutors for the second … then we would be planning our assessments for the third … then we might be getting a dual demo with a tutor for the fourth before flying our own flight test sorties in our teams … then we would be analysing our results for the fifth … then writing the dratted FTR … and then receiving our debrief and red inked FTR back from the staff. It was hard to know what we were doing at any one time and I was glad I had years of experience under my belt as a QHI which also relied on good preparation, usually the night before any particular flight.

So what next? Another ground based assessment. This time flight control mechanical characteristics (FCMC) – what? I confess I had never heard of this expression previously. It turns out that, how flying controls are mechanised can directly affect the way an aircraft appears to fly. Controls suffer from a number of issues: friction, which is usually bad, but sometimes helpful; freeplay, which is bad; force gradients, which can be good or bad; and the ability to be trimmed, also good or bad.

At the time, the expectation was that all the helicopters we would encounter would have controls operated by hydraulic systems. So there would be no direct aerodynamic feedback from the rotors to the pilot. Instead, springs under the cockpit floor were used to give artificial forces. These forces could be measured with the aircraft on the ground with the rotors stopped. So, after the cockpit assessment exercise we were tasked with conducting an FCMC assessment of the same aircraft. Following a demo we again found ourselves working into the evening with our trusty tape measures and hand-held force gauges. This time there was minimal discussion in the FTR. It was more of a data presentation – this is what we measured etc., which was generally inserted into an Appendix in a typical full report.

My ETPS (1994) course:
Rear Row L-R: Me, Greg, Peter, 'Skin', Stu, Trevor, Dave, Sze, Geraint
Front Row L-R: Jeff, Keith, Crispin, Mark, Etienne, Quirino, Bert, Francesco, 'Scotty'. *(MOD)*

Two exercises in the bag and we had barely flown.

At last the fog and murk, so prevalent in Wiltshire in early February, cleared and suddenly the pace of the course shifted gear – slow down already! In addition to our ground school studies we started our conversion sorties to the ETPS aircraft fleet. Things have changed in recent years but, 'back in the day', every conversion was only two flights, totalling two hours or less. Yikes! It was a fantastically challenging but rewarding concept. Most military conversion courses took several months and countless flights. The philosophy was that, broadly speaking, all helicopters fly like helicopters, jets fly like jets etc. The crucial discipline, for the test pilot, was to determine the 'gotchas', or the differences that might catch you out. For example, the Gazelle was designed by Aerospatiale in France and, unlike most helicopters, the main rotors turned clockwise when viewed from above. This meant that the right yaw pedal was used for high power situations, as opposed to the left pedal used for pretty much every other non-French Western helicopter. I was lucky, as stated previously, I already had over a hundred hours of flying time on the Gazelle which, by most accounts, was a relatively easy helicopter to fly normally. So after just a single 'refresher' flight with the

Westland Gazelle XZ939. *(Tony Osborne)*

ETPS QHI, Bill, I was off solo flashing around the local countryside, with the collective raised to the Intermediate Pitch Setting (IPS), at 120 KIAS. Without catching breath I was off solo in the Scout after another single training flight. The Scout AH1 was effectively the same as the Wasp HAS1 on which I had cut my teeth flying in all manner of crappy weather. The biggest differences were that it had skids, rather than wheels on long stroke oleos, so sat lower on the ground; it had a seat that didn't contain a dinghy, so effectively was lower in the cockpit; it had no flotation equipment (so flew a little faster) and did not have a folding tail. Oh – and something that very nearly caught me out – a different rotor brake.

The rotor brake acted just like a car disc wheel brake. The Wasp was started on board ship with the rotor brake ON. Once the engine was running and some checks completed it was released, the throttle opened and the rotors spun up very quickly indeed, which prevented the blades sailing and flapping too much in gusty winds. The Scout however had a much less powerful brake which was only used for slowing the rotors when the engine had been shut down at the end of the flight. It was not allowed to be ON when starting, as the brake was not powerful enough to hold the rotors, which would start to turn, and very quickly burn out the brake pads. So this led the way to my first cock up on the course. On my first solo I leapt into this semi familiar machine, already looking forward to some low level 'wazzing' on Salisbury Plain. I started the aircraft from memory:

> I held the start switch to START with my left hand and opened the bright red handled HP Cock (High Pressure Fuel Cock) with my right. The Starter warning light was ON and the compressor rpm was rising steadily. All was going perfectly but … why was my internal warning system flashing an amber caption?
>
> Bugger! Rotor Brake!
>
> In the nick of time I released the rotor brake which I had inadvertently left selected ON during my pre-start checks. Thankfully, no damage done and a vital lesson learnt or so I thought …

My third conversion was on to the school's Lynx ZD560. This was one of a batch of three aircraft Westland had built for AAEE and RAE which

Westland Scout AH.1 XP849. ETPS Scout. *(Peter Van Polanen)*

were designated Mk5s. In fact they were pretty similar to the Lynx HAS 2/3 that I was intimately familiar with. Again, after a session in the local simulator (sister of the Portland sim I had run for two years) at Middle Wallop, I had another single flight 'conversion' and was sent off solo with my mate Keith, who was a Boscombe Down based FTE. Having cracked the normal training exercises in no time, I decided now would be a good opportunity to show Keith my Lynx air display routine. Remember the original *Top Gun* movie where Maverick decides it's a good time for a tower flyby? Well, this had a similar vibe. My display was well honed and relatively safe to fly.

'Max chat' applied (100 per cent Torque) running in to the display line in a gentle dive at 150 KIAS.

Far end of the line, an aggressive pull-up to 50 degrees nose-up, trying to ensure I made some 'blade slap' (wocker-wocker) to entertain the crowd; a rapid application of right cyclic with right yaw pedal to roll through a 'visually judged' (if you know what I mean) 90 degrees AOB turn. Accelerating back to 120 KIAS plus and then pulling up into a 'piggy', which looked a lot like a loop but was really a sustained wingover – a further wingover took me into an aggressive quickstop, which allowed me to show off some hover manoeuvres.

I concluded with a standard 'party trick', which was to climb aggressively from the hover at 'max chat' drifting backwards slightly, and, when at a suitable height, rotate the aircraft to 90 degrees nose-down followed by rapidly rolling through 180 degrees to allow me to depart away from the crowd as I dived on airspeed. In most other helicopters this would be a catastrophic manoeuvre, but not so the Lynx. The only issue was that at 90 degrees nose-down the gyros in the pilot's attitude indicator would topple – no drama as it would re-erect within a few minutes of level flight on the way home. Which is exactly what happened. It was then that my buddy, Keith – who knew a shed-load more about ETPS aircraft than I did at this stage – said,

'I wonder if that manoeuvre has knackered the gyro in the flight test instrumentation?'

'What?'

'The instrumentation in the back, which we turn on before every flight, uses an ancient gyro out of a Canberra bomber … I wonder what happens if that topples in flight?'

'Oh shit!'

I continued the flight home very gingerly, praying as hard as I could that the Canberra gyros were as robust as the Lynx ones.

Phew! Turns out they were – no harm done – and no embarrassing need for my sins to be confessed.

As this was all going on, my fixed wing student colleagues were grappling with the Hawk and Jaguar jets, the mainstays of the fixed wing course.

Westland Lynx 5.X ZD560. ETPS Lynx. *(Tony Osborne)*

This was when the fun flying ceased! From here on, our flying would be intensively occupied with learning flight test techniques or gathering the data required to write up our FTRs.

First up were some exercises that didn't require us to learn any particular test techniques. Amazingly we were trusted with assessing the Gazelle's operational ceiling. With an oxygen crate fitted in the rear of the aircraft, and briefings and hypoxia chamber runs completed, we were tasked with climbing a helicopter as high as it would go. Normally we were limited to 10,000ft due to the thinning oxygen at altitude, but armed with oxygen bottles and masks I 'slipped the surly bonds of earth' and commenced a climb to the west of the airfield. I had barely re-learnt how to fly the type but I was trusted with doing something most helicopter pilots never ever get to do ...

All went well on the way up and I was lulled into a euphoric sense of wellbeing. I was flying on a 'gin clear' February day at 18,500ft over Wiltshire and feeling pretty chuffed that all the preparation to get to ETPS had paid off. With the three French rotor blades thrashing at the ever-thinning air, it became apparent that I had all the data needed. The handling had definitely worsened with altitude and I was left with a minimal range of airspeed I could fly – too fast and the vibration would rise rapidly as I approached retreating blade stall. I wasn't going to climb much more before running out of fuel. So one last relaxed look at the marvellous once-in-a-lifetime view including both Bristol and the south coast before I gently lowered the collective lever to commence my return to Boscombe Down. It was on the way down that my problems began. Initially all went well as I descended just outside of autorotation and then, all of a sudden ...

I could see bugger all ... !

The aircraft had been cooled to minus forty degrees or so and this very cold aircraft now encountered water vapour which instantly froze onto the bubble canopy. The interior misted up at the same time and I now could see the square root of nothing. Thankfully, we had all received a quick instrument flying refresher flight following our solo flights. These sneaky tutors clearly knew what they were doing, I thought, and we had been asked to check the cockpit heater/demist was serviceable before we departed. So, without too much thought, I cracked the valve in the cockpit roof that fed hot bleed air from the Astazou gas turbine engine through some suitable pipework. It seemed to take forever, as I flew entirely on instruments despite the amazingly clear visibility outside the aircraft. Eventually, the Perspex started to clear and I continued my lazy descent towards home. It would be nearly twenty-five years later when, using oxygen, I next flew a helicopter to 18,000ft – an Agusta A109SP over Interlaken in Switzerland – what an awesome flight that was. (see 'Test Pilot').

With 'no rest for the wicked', that same evening, I was tasked with conducting a formal night-flying evaluation. I note with interest that, by the time I returned to the school two years later, this exercise had been dropped. I was teamed up with Greg, a Canadian Sea King pilot. Everything about starting up the Gazelle was harder in the dark. It was difficult to do the walk-round with just a torch. Finding the harness to strap in was more challenging. The internal lights did not illuminate the gauges evenly and then, if that wasn't enough, when I operated the start switch, the drain on the battery dimmed all the lights to zero. Thankfully Greg was on the case and held his torch at just the correct angle to illuminate the critical information. Phew! As fellow Navy types we were thankfully on the same hymn sheet, and managed to keep each other safe as we continued to stumble around the local area and circuit in the dark. We were tasked with assessing the aircraft's lights for effectiveness and the internal cockpit lighting. This had to be evenly balanced to allow all the instruments to be read and there should have been no glare or reflections. Unfortunately the Gazelle did not have the best of cockpits and we noted numerous deficiencies that would all have to be written up in dreaded seven-part paragraphs into yet another FTR. Before we had chance to start pounding away on our keyboards, we found ourselves being asked to measure and document the pressure errors of the Scout. In recent years this evaluation would almost certainly make use of the Global Positioning System (GPS), which effectively gives a reliable ground speed that can then be used to calculate a true airspeed. Back in the '90s we did not have this technology readily available, however the Gazelles were fitted with an extended boom, with various sensor devices that were placed well in front of the fuselage and rotor downwash that corrupted the data appearing in the conventional instruments and gauges. So in other words, the calibrated data from the Gazelle could be relied upon to be accurate, whereas the data appearing on the Scout's airspeed indicator (ASI) and altimeter could not. This formed the excuse for another interesting sortie. With one of my colleagues flying the Gazelle as accurately as he could, I was tasked to fly the Scout in formation. At each test point we compared indicated speeds and heights and 'Bob's your uncle', with a bit more analysis, we were able to surmise the errors. I had done a fair amount of formation flying and had recently led one of the biggest combined formation flypasts at RNAS Portland that had ever been seen with Lynx and Sea Kings and Sea Harriers all arriving over the airfield precisely on time at 50–250ft. The 'best ever' was the comment from the senior officer present. Anyway, I thought I could fly in formation, but this was really quite hard. As I closed up on the Gazelle I just didn't feel comfortable at all. I kept checking the 'slip-ball' to make sure I was 'in-balance', but it just didn't feel like we were flying parallel and then …

Kerching! The lightbulb in my head lit up.

Helicopters generally have tail rotors at the back end. They are designed to generate thrust laterally which opposes the tendency of the fuselage to turn in opposition to the main rotors due to a torque reaction. In most helicopters the rotor blades turn anti-clockwise which means the fuselage wants to turn clockwise so the tail rotor attempts to move the tail anti-clockwise, or to the right, to oppose the couple (turning). If the correct amount of thrust is applied the fuselage does not turn, but all this thrust tends to move the aircraft sidewards to the right. All conventional helicopters then suffer from 'inherent sideslip', which is a combination of their forward speed and this relatively small sidewards drift. Most operational pilots are almost totally unaware of it. However, I had just remembered the French Gazelle rotor blades turned the 'wrong way'. So while the Scout was flying to the right the Gazelle was flying to the left. So, if we had indeed flown exactly parallel to each other we would have collided.

Yikes! Who would have thought it? At least my sense of self-preservation had resisted my attempts to straighten up.

I realised that this was the first time I'd ever had to formate two such dissimilar types. Another lesson learnt.

Following this brief dalliance with night flying and pressure errors, we started the performance section of the training. With hindsight I wish I had paid more attention to the ground school aspects of this phase, but as far as I was concerned it was full of 'Greek flute music' and more bloody maths. The piloting aspects were easy to grasp. We had to fly the chosen aircraft incredibly accurately. Speeds had to be within 1 KIAS, heights within 20ft or less etc. This was very demanding and required massive concentration. In practice we would have to nail each test point or acquire datums and then call,

'On condition.'

As the data was gathered over seconds or minutes our attention had to be 100 per cent. Level flight performance was easy to understand and relatively easy to fly, but then came vertical performance, something our fixed wing colleagues did not have to grapple with. There were various ways of testing a helicopter's vertical performance. Close to the ground it could be hovered at different weights and potentially a range of temperatures. This could be achieved more quickly if the helicopter was tied to the ground.

What?

Yep … a helicopter could use a strop fitted to a force sensing hook. The other end would be fastened to a robust 'tie-down' buried into the concrete on the airfield somewhere. The pilot would lift into the hover until the strop was taut and data gathered. Then more power would be added. The aircraft's height would remain a constant due to the length of strop, but the pull force would be measured and effectively the helicopter had been made to appear heavier. This would be repeated several times with more and more power added up to 'max chat', with the force applied to the strop noted each time. This technique was OK but was influenced by the proximity of the ground which created a 'ground effect'. If you've read my first book you will already be aware that there is a cushion of air that forms between the helicopter and the ground which effectively means less power is required to hover. So data had to be gathered clear of the ground. The best way to do this was to use a low speed sensor. The ETPS Lynx ZD560 was fitted with a device next to the pilot's door frame that measured small amounts of horizontal movement which were then displayed on a gauge in front of the pilot. This was effectively a circular display with the aim being to drag the cross hairs to the centre which would then mean zero drift in any direction. Using the display a pilot could apply suitable control inputs so as to ensure a perfect hover. Again, then hover performance data could be gathered. On the face of it all these flights should have been dull, but were incredibly demanding to fly. Hovering a Lynx up at 8,000ft with no external references was another first. And quite surreal.

The final helicopter exercise for the first team was to assess the engine and rotor governing system of the Scout. A tutor gave us all a demo in the Gazelle, which happened to have an incredibly good rotor governor, and then we were let loose on the Scout – which didn't.

Sneaky!

For this exercise I was teamed up with fellow student Peter, who was a Royal Netherlands Air Force Alouette III pilot. His job had been low-level battlefield reconnaissance and, until he arrived at Boscombe Down, had done no instrument flying whatsoever which led to a very exciting few seconds when he first flew into cloud in the Scout – thankfully, Andy was alongside him to save the day and recover from the unusual attitude Peter had got himself into! He also had trained in a different way from most of us so I never quite knew what he was going to do next. Not to say that was bad, just a little disconcerting when he would often set off in a direction and manner that wouldn't have been my first choice. The Scout had the same Nimbus engine as fitted to the Wasp, with which I was intimately acquainted and, therefore, had a good deal of cautious respect for. It suffered from being prone to 'surge' at just the wrong moments. In summary, if the pilot was initially demanding a very low power setting and then with little warning asked the engine for 'max chat' or similar, then the engine would complain … and of more concern, initially fail to produce the requested power. This surging would be accompanied by some loud audio cues – namely banging!

On one occasion I was flying an air display as part of the 'Navy Days' weekend at Plymouth Dockyard. I was paired up with Steve, a particularly flashy 'Junglie pilot' displaying in a Wessex Mk 5. On one of our back-to-back routines I misjudged a manoeuvre and lowered the collective too much as I pulled up to about 60 degrees nose-up to conduct a 'torque turn'. This air display technique required the aircraft to be as nose-up as possible with a relatively low power setting. As the airspeed decayed to 'not-a-lot', the collective was aggressively raised and the massive torque reaction would rotate the fuselage around the rotor shaft. Once 180 degrees had been achieved, a sharp tail rotor input could halt the rotation and speed could be dived on ready for the next manoeuvre. On this occasion I lowered the lever a little too much. As I raised it again to commence the aforementioned turn instead, all I got was …

Bang! Bang! Bang!

Yep, I had caused the mighty Rolls Royce Nimbus to 'throw its teddies out of the cot'. I was 60 degrees nose-up, with no forward airspeed, and an engine that was refusing to play …

Bugger!

I am not a patient person; in this situation, however, there was no option but to do nothing and hang on. Which I did. And, just as I thought a rearward splash into the oggin beckoned, the turbine finally sorted its airflow over the compressor blades and the power returned with a vengeance. A flick later I was facing 60 degrees nose-down and gathering speed.

Phew! I had survived another – or so I thought.

On landing, the phone at my temporary landing site was ringing off its cradle. A very senior naval officer had been alarmed by my banging engine and felt sure there must be something wrong with it. I had to explain that the Wasp was 'kinda like that', and apparently the punters in the crowd had loved it. I really hoped he didn't phone my parent squadron to gain a more in-depth technical explanation. He didn't – Phew!

Needless to say, I discussed all the above with Peter. We had no intention of attracting too much attention so early in the course. So we did as briefed and moved the collective up and down aggressively – but not too aggressively. We performed jump take-offs by pulling to a pre-determined collective lever position – but worked our way up to the required rate very gently and incrementally. And all the time we observed the rotor speed decay and watched for any torque spikes and the like. Thanks to my prior knowledge and experience we achieved all we needed to in good time and with data gathered it was time to head to the bar – we could write up the dreaded FTR over our Easter holiday.

Phew! We had survived the first term.

That said, our livers had suffered. We had wholeheartedly all bought into the 'work hard, play hard' mentality. Initially we had 'meet and greets' where our wives could dress up and our children could wreck the officers' mess for an evening or two. The single guys had already established a 'frat house' for wayward fighter pilots and managed a local arrangement with the Wheatsheaf pub for regular lock-ins. The working day on Friday always concluded with much ale consumed in the mess bar. Wives would sometimes attend – mainly to carry their husbands home when their war stories had become not just boring, but incoherent. Most students would

RWTS Westland Scout XT631 outside ETPS. Used for our ERGA assessment. *(Mike Freer)*

write-off Saturday and return to their books and reports on Sunday. With church and young children to fit in I had to try and 'Keep Sunday Special', which meant most of my best and worst work was written while shabby. It turns out this was one of the most useful skills a test pilot can acquire for a successful career!

Chapter 4

ETPS, Class of 1994 – Summer Term

'Three … two … one … *now*,'

Now at 50 KIAS the appropriate height arrived and I commenced my flare …

Bugger! Nothing is happening – I'm still plummeting earthwards with the same rate of descent.

Yikes!

'Flare harder,' I say to myself and with an aggressive hoik of the stick, finally the 'ground rush' reduces somewhat, but the minimal flare has done nothing to spool up my rotor rpm so I now have less inertia in the bank to use for the touch-down. Suddenly my judgement became critical.

Bang!

If I had thought the pace of life and workload was hectic in the first term, it was nothing compared to the second or summer term. Within hours of restarting our studies, our Easter holidays seemed a distant memory. Needless to say, I was still trying to catch up on the outstanding FTRs from exercises completed in March. Quoted deadlines for the submission of our home-work were non-negotiable, however many cats we had that might have eaten it.

One of the highlights of my time as a student at ETPS was the many and varied visits we went on during the year. These visits included trips to various places in the UK including Rolls Royce in Bristol, Ferranti in Edinburgh, GEC/Marconi in Rochester, and a number of trips abroad. All such trips and visits included the drinking of copious amounts of alcohol which has numbed my recollection somewhat. I include all such memories within the next chapter which concludes with the end of term 'preview assessment'.

In order to blow the cobwebs away we started the term by flying 'refresher' sorties in the Scout and Gazelle and a famil trip in the Sea

King onto which we were all about to convert. We were also introduced to an aircraft which would become very dear to my heart over the next decade, Beagle Basset XS743. The Beagle Basset, which first flew in 1961, was designed by the Beagle Aircraft Company as a light transport aircraft. The RAF bought twenty aircraft, designated the CC.1, and used them in support of the V bomber force for ferrying crews around the UK when the bombers were dispersed. The majority were sold off in 1974 but Boscombe Down retained four examples, including XS743, which ETPS operated from 1967. In 1973 it was modified extensively by the Cranfield Institute of Technology to include a variable stability system (VSS). The left-hand seat (LHS) pilot retained conventional controls but had access to a bank of potentiometers, sited between the front seats, which were connected to an analogue computer. The right-hand control column was no longer mechanically connected to the flying controls. Instead it 'flew' the aircraft via the computer. This allowed the tutor in the LHS to use the potentiometers to alter the way the aircraft behaved. It could be made more or less stable in each axis, damping could be varied, and control quickening could be added to make it appear more agile and so on. In short, it was an absolutely priceless teaching tool and I, for one, wept a tear when the aircraft was pensioned off just a couple of years ago.

Our first introduction to the Basset was to fly a sortie dedicated to understanding the handling qualities rating scale. George Cooper was a test pilot who worked in the USA for the National Advisory Committee for Aeronautics (NACA) which was the predecessor of NASA, responsible for space flight among other things. George Cooper came up with a numerical scale for describing handling qualities (HQ) which was subsequently improved upon by another American, Bob Harper of the Cornwell Aeronautical Laboratory, now known as Calspan. Anyway, it came to pass that the Cooper-Harper Handling Qualities Rating (HQR) scale had become widely adopted by flight test practitioners, certainly in the Western world. So it was an essential requirement for we students to understand it and be able to apply it … and what better classroom was there for such a task than the Basset. Handling qualities could be altered with the flick of the tutor's wrist with satisfactory aspects becoming unacceptable in an instant. This actually was fascinating and fun, but challenging to try to determine which number from 1–10 should be allocated against each prescribed flying manoeuvre. And as someone

Beagle Basset XS743. Variable Stability aircraft used by ETPS. *(Chris Lofting)*

who has continued to use this scale for thirty years, I can honestly say, the task never gets much easier.

More helicopter training followed with the emphasis turning towards engine-off-landings … we were being prepared like lambs for the slaughter. But in the meantime, for light relief, we all needed to convert to the Sea King. A quick dash down to RNAS Culdrose in Cornwall (where I had completed my basic helicopter training some eleven years previously) and I found myself being given a thorough work out by some RN colleagues, many of whom I knew as a result of having just come from running another RN Simulator. We were shown no mercy, and despite barely having had chance to read the aircrew manual the night before we were subjected to engine failures and flight control and hydraulic system failures aplenty. Not having ever been a 'Pinger' (Anti-Submarine Warfare Pilot), I confess I quite enjoyed learning all about the various modes of the autopilot that allowed the aircraft to descend over the sea at night and establish a hover with minimal input from the pilot. Equally impressive was allowing the system to fly me away from the 'dip' following engine failure and appreciating it did it better than I could. We were given one malfunction to do with a failing gyro platform that had me ditching in seconds …

Dead again!

More alcohol required before dashing back to Boscombe the following morning for my first 'convex' sortie in Sea King XV371. At the time I didn't realise how attached to this particular airframe I was to become. And it turns out this wasn't a Sea King at all. It was really a Sikorsky SH-3D. Westland Helicopters effectively bought the rights to build the aircraft under licence at Yeovil. The first set of clones were called the Mk1 and fitted with Rolls Royce engines and a suitable sonar to look for submarines. XV371 was actually manufactured in the USA and shipped across to the UK as a 'kit'. In fact it still had 'Sikorsky' written on the yaw pedals.

I had two relatively short training sorties with Eric and then Bill, the latter including all the possible emergencies that could be practised in the real aircraft, which included the dreaded 'manual throttle'. I confess, not being a 'proper' Sea King pilot, this issue never really bothered me. In summary the control of each engine was partially managed by a very old analogue computer. This attempted to meter the fuel going into the engine to correctly match the power demands I was making with the collective lever … it was a glorified engine/rotor governor. However, it was more electrical than hydro-mechanical and could potentially fail. The failure could freeze the fuel flow or cause it to 'run up' or 'run down'. If the

Westland/Sikorsky Sea King XV371. First Sea King flown as a student and then subsequently flown on EFS as project test pilot. *(Public Domain)*

computer failed, a lever in the cockpit roof could be pulled to engage a manual throttle and now full control could be achieved on the dodgy engine. The only challenge was not having enough hands to move the throttle and the collective and the cyclic all at the same time. So it was normal practice to always fly the Sea King with a second person who was qualified to operate the throttles. In operational service this would be a second pilot or specifically trained aircrewman. In the flight test world we 'qualified' our FTEs to be able to fulfil that role.

However, as long as the other engine continued to work normally, dealing with such an emergency when operating 'ashore' was no drama and the drills were effectively the same as a Lynx. I would simply set an appropriate power on the duff engine and leave it alone. It would assist the good engine and as long as I remembered to throttle it back after touching down, all was well.

It wasn't the manual throttles that worried me on the 'Mighty King', it was simply starting it. Later on I would become very proficient in flashing up the aircraft in no time at all, having realised it could effectively be treated as a big Lynx, but as a student on ETPS, worry about starting the beast gave me sleepless nights. Having had my two conversion sorties and now fully converted to the Sea King (!) I was sent off solo with Peter, the Dutch Alouette pilot, acting as my 'stick buddy'. As we walked to the aircraft across the dispersal I immediately noticed that my worst fears had been realised. The blades were folded. My Wasp and Lynx both had folding blades which allowed the aircraft to be stowed in the ship's hangar, which was never much bigger than the aircraft's fuselage. Once the aircraft was 'spotted' on the flight deck my team of maintainers would spread the rotor blades so that I would walk to the aircraft ready to fly. Not so the Sea King. The heavy and large rotor blades were moved using a complex hydraulic system which was controlled by the pilot using a small electrical panel in the aircraft's overhead console. Lots of pilots before me had messed up either spreading or folding the rotors by getting the process wrong or not realising the system was faulty in time.

Yikes!

Walk-round complete we climbed aboard and worked our way laboriously through the checks which allowed us to get the first engine started which then was able to power the aircraft's generators and hydraulic pumps. Peter read out the check list one item at a time, to which I responded:

'Rotor Brake'
　'ON – and Caption illuminated'
'Number two firewall valve'
　'Closed'
'Flight Control System'
　'Disengaged'
'Collective Lever'
　'Down, Friction applied'
'Safety Valve'
　'Open'
'Master Switch'

I selected the Master switch ON and then began the onerous task of checking various lights that indicated everything was as it should be. Only months later I would be doing this in the pouring rain at night and would be faced with a failed system.

'Fold Power light ON, Number 1 Blade position light ON'
'Fold/Spread Switch'

This was it; the moment of truth. Would the blades spread? I selected the switch to SPREAD and waited. After what felt like an eternity the first blade began to move and the 'blades folded' light went out.

The 'Control Lock Pins Advance Light' went off, the Blades Spread light came on and we had spread the blades on a Sea King! I quickly turned the Master Switch OFF and, with hydraulic pressure now indicating, closed the safety valve which was indicated by the associated warning light being extinguished. With the spread/fold switch selected off it was back to starting a big Lynx again and we were able to eventually get airborne only slightly later than planned.

All went well for the first thirty minutes or so as I flew various circuits at Boscombe practicing all the required exercises. But …

Then it started to rain.

Rain? No drama surely? The Sea King had big-ish windscreens with very little rake or slope. So the rain just tended to sit there and very soon I could see – bugger all!

'Where the hell is the windscreen wiper switch?' I ask my mate.

'Dunno.'

'Great.'

Being able to see diddly-squat out of the front, I opened the side-window and slid sideways towards the ground so that I could 'land-on' and sort my life out. I plonked it on the ground – I selected the wheel brakes on.

Phew! Safe so far.

Now where on earth is the switch? I conducted an 'expanding square search' of the overhead console festooned with a myriad of switches and circuit breakers. I knew where it was in the Lynx – surely it would be in a similar location? Well – no it wasn't. And, after ten minutes of looking, I still couldn't find it. Thankfully my hour was up and I taxied into the rotary dispersal and quickly shut down. Now – should I tell everyone that I couldn't find the windscreen wiper switch? What do you think? No, I debriefed a very successful solo flight and then got a friendly engineer to point out the relevant switch – in fact it was a rotary knob, unlike anything else, mounted on the side of the inter-seat console. Why the heck was it a knob and why was it mounted in such a bonkers place? I have never found out.

So, now fully converted to the school's complete rotary wing fleet, time to get on with learning how to be a test pilot. The core subject matter for a TP has to be a sound understanding of 'stability and control' and the ability to use appropriate test techniques to assess an aircraft and gather appropriate data. First up was 'Longitudinal Static Stability' or LSS. Following extensive ground-school on the topic we were unleashed on the Basset and had chance to look at what strong and weak stability looked like followed by neutral and then negative stability. In simple terms, for aircraft to go faster, the cyclic or joystick needs to be moved forward, and once stable at a higher speed the stick should end up further forward than from where it started. In both aeroplanes and helicopters this change in displacement will most likely be accompanied by a force. This is further complicated by whether we talk about 'speed stability' or 'angle of attack stability'. In a helicopter, every control tends to effect the other controls. If we raise the collective lever the nose of the aircraft tends to pitch up, which requires the cyclic to be pushed forward to prevent it. So when trying to go faster – if we add collective/power to prevent a descent – we will corrupt our results as the datum cyclic stick position will change. Fixed wing test pilots end up talking about 'stick fixed stability' – where the displacement is noted, or 'stick free stability' – when the force required to hold a control in place is discerned. With the demo in the Basset completed we 'strapped on' the Gazelle for a demo before being sent off to gather data for the inevitable FTR. In fact I ended up in a team of three doing a formal assessment of the Lynx which, thankfully, produced 'satisfactory' results leading to an easier reporting task. We came to yearn for aircraft that were 'acceptable' rather than 'unacceptable' to keep our writing down to a minimum. I confess, this yearning has not changed thirty years later.

With the LSS flights barely entered into my log book we were straight into Longitudinal Dynamic Stability, or LDS. The same pattern repeated itself: Basset demo, Gazelle Demo, exercise flights in the Lynx followed by FTR. Conventional aeroplanes tended to have well-damped dynamic stability. It turned out that helicopters didn't. This suddenly started to make a lot of sense. Lots of situations in helicopters ended up being difficult to fly, especially when high power was applied for higher speeds or to climb. It transpired that even the trusty Gazelle was dynamically unstable in the climb. No wonder it had been so hard to fly when I was learning the trade on 705 Naval Air Squadron eleven years previously. I'm not sure if I can explain this easily ... but let me try.

The turning rotor blades create the thrust or lift required to get a helicopter off the ground. When the helicopter is subject to an airflow, possibly generated by the wind or its own forward flight, then the airflow increases lift on the advancing blades. Subject to more lift, these advancing blades start to flap up such that about 90 degrees later they have flapped up as far as they are going to. This means the whole rotor disc, like a dinner plate, is tilted up at the leading edge and the thrust vector is now leaning backwards. The pilot has to keep pushing the cyclic stick forward to overcome this 'flapback', which creates the apparent LSS. In situations where more pitch has been applied to the rotor blades, such as when climbing or flying at high speed, then the flapback is more pronounced and can easily create a divergent oscillatory response. This can be damped by the pilot, or a flight control system, but it does need to be dealt with. So a feature that improves static stability can make the dynamic stability worse.

Blige! My head is going to explode.

But we are not yet done with this phenomenon. April rolled into May as we found ourselves grappling with lateral and directional stability (Lat-Dir). For some reason lots of my colleagues, and later on my students, struggled with this topic. In essence, there are only two components. Directional stability is that of a dart. So if a dart, when it leaves the thrower's hand, is to fly straight it has to have tail feathers. Aeroplanes have tail fins as do most helicopters. If you can't get the dart concept, consider a weather cock that always tries to point into wind. So directional stability – *easy*. Lateral stability is exactly the same as LSS but shifted through 90 degrees or so. If the rotor disc experiences airflow from the side, the rotor flaps back and the rotor disc rolls away from it, shortly followed by the fuselage. A tendency to roll away from the prevailing breeze indicates stable lateral stability. Fixed wing pilots refer to this as a 'dihedral effect' as wings, which are cranked up slightly, tend to generate this response in aeroplanes. Perhaps the confusion comes because we have developed test techniques to generate the required airflows that use the non-intuitive control. For example; if I want to investigate lateral stability I can apply yaw pedal, which yaws the helicopter such that it experiences a sideslip or lateral velocity. By noting the aircraft's response to this airflow I can make a determination about its lateral stability. So I use a directional control to determine lateral stability. And to test directional stability I make roll inputs using the roll control (cyclic or joystick). So I guess this can be confusing!

Yet again Basset demo was followed by a demo, the following day, on the trusty Gazelle. Next we knew, we were in teams of three assessing the Lar-Dir of the Sea King. My friend XV371 was unavailable so we found ourselves flying another variant, ZB507 – a Mk 4X. This was a similar aircraft to those flown by my RN Junglie colleagues with fixed undercarriage (one less thing to have to worry about) but had been provided to RAE Farnborough with the radar dome normally fitted to the ASW variants. A conversion to a different mark of Sea King would take months in the regular armed forces … instead we each received a quick famil before being unleashed into the skies of Wiltshire to assess the aircraft without the flight control system engaged.

Those who know me are already familiar with my opinion of the 'Mighty King' – it was a Marmite aircraft, and I did not love it. Sure – it had some good points: it could land on a ship; it had proper wheels so could do running landings and take-offs; it was a stable hover platform, so good for ASW or Search and Rescue (SAR); and it carried a massive amount of fuel and could lift a commendable payload. But it just wasn't fun to fly. It was a bus. It was limited to just 30 degrees angle of bank, whereas I used to enjoy using at least 60 degrees in my Navy Lynx. Without the flight control system engaged – or Automatic Stabilisation Equipment (ASE) as it was called in this aircraft – the aircraft wallowed around like a semi-beached whale.

Teamed up with both Peter and Crispin (Army Lynx pilot) we set out to discern and document all aspects of the aircraft's lateral and directional stability. We had an immediate challenge. The Basset, Gazelle – and Lynx, for that matter, were all fitted with 'sideslip or Beta Indicators' (Greek letter Alpha is used to indicate angle of attack and Beta is used for sideslip). Our demo flights had been conducted being able to accurately set sideslip as indicated by a gauge in the cockpit. Sadly our test aircraft did not feature this additional dedicated flight test instrument. What to do? Well, it turns out that the best alternative was to attach a wool tuft to the windscreen. By then flying a series of manoeuvres along a conveniently located long straight railway line we were able to 'calibrate' the wool tuft and mark on the windscreen, with a china graph pencil, approximate sideslip angles. I had yet to realise that the vast majority of my future flight testing would have to be conducted with such examples of 'temporary instrumentation'. With the calibration in the bag, we went on to fly a series of dedicated test points, turning the aircraft using yaw pedals only or cyclic only, and then ending up flying what is delightfully known as a steady heading side slip (SHSS). Aeroplane pilots would have been familiar with using sideslips in order to adjust a glide angle when conducting a forced landing or for landing with strong cross winds. For helicopter pilots it seemed very strange to be deliberately forcing the aircraft to fly on a given heading which required it to fly with increasing angle of bank. But we knew that if, to achieve this, we needed to cross control (that is right stick with left pedal and vice versa) then we had demonstrated the aircraft had positive static stability in each axis. All of these academic tests confirmed what we already knew – it had weak directional stability and, depending on the power applied, weak lateral stability. No wonder it felt like flying a beached whale. But with the data in the can we could start the wearisome FTR while we turned our attention to more fun pastimes.

My wife, Ally and Me. About to head to the Boscombe Down Summer Ball 1994. We left Emily and Sam in the capable hands of Ally's parents Brian and Barbara. *(Author)*

ETPS, Class of 1994 – Summer Term   49

It will not come as a surprise that where many nationalities are gathered a long way from home, celebrating 'National Days' became an absolute imperative. Australia Day came at the end of January and the party laid on by Scotty (RAAF fighter pilot), dare I say it, set the tone and benchmark for every nation to follow. As Brits, we managed to celebrate Burns night twice – more of that in the next chapter. But it's fair to say the mid-summer period became a non-stop party. The two Italians, Quirino and Francesco, kicked things off with Festa della Repubblica on 2 June – I do really love Italian red wine and pasta! Canada Day (1 July) hosted by Stu and 'Skin' rolled seamlessly into 4 July celebrations with fireworks and Bud provided by fellow rote, Jeff. We always seemed to congregate at the fighter pilot 'frat house' for such big events. Bastille day was led by Etienne (French Mirage pilot) and I remember little due to the large quantities of fine Cognac which seemed to appear right on cue. How we had time to fit in the Officers' Mess Summer Ball I'll never know. Thankfully my parents-in-law descended to baby sit and staff, students and wives had a chance to dress up and dance the night away. And for those that couldn't dance there were the dodgems, which cost us nothing to use all night and provided the best way to get some revenge on our tutors for all the red ink that covered our painfully produced reports. Somewhere among all the student parties and socials we found time to have the annual ETPS Cricket Match … allegedly a sacred tradition, nearly as old as the Royal Air Force itself. It was another chance for staff, students, wives and children to mix and mingle in the English sunshine with copious amounts of chilled, tinned beer supplied regularly from the officers' mess. Needless to say the staff won – they always did. On top of this we had time to go gliding at Upavon. This activity fell on a beautiful summer's evening. I will never forget that first winch launch, when a long metal cable hawser was attached to the nose of my glider … seconds later a massive winch was given the OK to wind in the cable at an incredible rate, hauling my aircraft into the sky at a ridiculous nose-up attitude. Moments later the adrenalin rush calmed, as the cable was released, and suddenly we were gracefully floating above Salisbury Plain with the subtlest of wind noise to accompany our very lazy descent back to the airfield from whence we departed. And who knew we could do aerobatics at just 500ft above the ground? Wives and children came along. Back then, I was incredibly ignorant of how aviation was conducted outside of my blinkered experience to date. What a hoot,

Just about to go gliding at Upavon with Gerry. *(Author)*

Ally with Emily waiting to go gliding. *(Author)*

to find out that my wife could be taken for a quick 'jolly' in one of the training gliders. What a fun evening, but we were all glad to be home when the transport dropped us off at the married patch well after dark.

My duties for the day were not yet complete. All term my 5-year-old son, Sam, had been studying entomology – or 'mini-beasts' as they called it. The following morning he was expected to turn up dressed as his favourite insect, which turned out to be a stag beetle. As the clock chimed midnight, under Ally's patient direction, I was assisting her spray painting some clip-on reindeer antlers black and building the required beetle shell from cardboard, papier mâché and string. Used to working into the early hours anyway I was the proudest of dads as my son and my wife set off early to walk to school the following morning – it turns out stag beetles do not fit into children's car seats.

Somehow in this term we managed to blat off to Switzerland for a few days and more of that in my next chapter. Suffice to say – for every bit of fun there was always pain to be endured. For the fixed wing students, they embarked on their 'high risk' spinning exercises in the Hawker Hunter. For us rotes it was now all about engine-off landings.

If the engines fail on an aeroplane it will adopt a glide speed/attitude and, as long as a suitable piece of flat ground can be found, then an almost normal landing can be conducted. Not so with helicopters. If the engine stops then the blades are no longer being driven. The aerodynamic drag will very quickly slow the blades down to the point where they will no longer turn and the aircraft will plummet out of the sky = *very bad*. If the pitch can be removed from the blades, by lowering the collective lever, then the aircraft will enter a glide and the airflow coming up through the rotors will keep the blades turning. So it is critical for the pilot to lower the collective lever with alacrity.

This first aspect of the helicopter's high risk testing arrived promptly. We had to fly our trusty Gazelles at a safe height. We then had to close the throttle (in the roof) and then work out how much delay the pilot was allowed before the rotors slowed to their critical speed (known as Critical Nr). This immediately put all us rotes outside our comfort zone again. We were sent off in our student teams to go and gather this required data. Get it wrong and we could allow the blades to slow too much with catastrophic results. Later on, as a civilian test pilot, I would do this testing based on delaying our inputs and noting the response. At ETPS we adopted a more

Sam about to go to school dressed as a Stag Beetle. *(Author)*

'incremental approach'. We had fitted a very large, and accurate, rotor rpm (Nr) gauge to the instrument panel. The test technique was to determine a 'target Nr' at which point we slammed the collective to the floor to achieve a zero 'g' condition. Believe me – with the risk of catastrophic rotor delay we students really slammed the lever down …

Bam! And every time, dust and muck and maps would fly past us upwards.

After each successful test point we would mark the Nr gauge with a chinagraph for the next target Nr. Thus we progressively lowered the lever at a lower rpm working towards the theoretical minimum Nr. Each time we did this we timed the interval between 'throttle chop' and 'lever lowering' so we progressively worked our way up to a maximum 'delay time' that we felt appropriate for the test conditions. The manufacturer was required to ensure this was one or two seconds depending on the phase of flight. Civil helicopters only needed to achieve one second – which frankly isn't a lot. But at the end of half a dozen or so test points we reached our pre-planned minimum …

Phew! We had survived another.

This was just the beginning of this phase of the course. Once a pilot has successfully lowered the lever, the aircraft continues downward with the rotor blades being turned by the airflow which is known as autorotation. In order to safely land the aircraft the pilot has to do lots of things in rapid succession. He needs to slow the aircraft down from its optimum glide or auto speed. Then he has to reduce the rate of descent to a minimum otherwise a heavy or crash landing will ensue. Thankfully, slowing down by flaring the aircraft by pitching it nose-up also reduces the rate of descent. Landing successfully requires the pilot to manage the Nr carefully and build up as much as possible so that at the 'moment critique' pitch can be reapplied to the rotors to create lift to cushion the touch down. Raising the collective to reapply pitch to the blades then creates drag which immediately starts to decelerate the blades. So the essential lift lasts seconds at best. So this requires a good deal of judgement, skill and practice.

Blige!

The role of the test pilot is to determine the best combination of speeds and heights and technique to make such landings repeatable and easy enough for an average pilot to be able to fly. Thereafter the TP has to look at the implications of getting this technique wrong … Hells bells!

So, after what seemed like the briefest of practice sessions, we were sent off with a test card with lots of such landings to evaluate. In addition to the normal parameters we had to commence at airspeeds slower than, or faster than, the perceived optimum and at 'flare heights' lower and higher than the most sensible one.

I was teamed up with Alastair – he was the school's rotary wing academic tutor. So this was kinda the worst of both worlds. I was accompanied by a tutor, so had to be on my best behaviour, but not being a pilot he wouldn't be able to help if I screwed up.

Great!

I confess I wasn't sure what to expect, as previously I'd always conscientiously nailed the optimum conditions. With that condition nailed as test point 1, I moved on to flying 10 KIAS faster than I should.

So, 1,000ft over the grass strip alongside the duty runway, I advised Alastair to be ready to close the throttle in the roof.

'OK, on condition, are you ready Alastair?'

'Ready'

'Standby to close the throttle on my count of three – Three … two … one … *now*.'

Throttle closed we were committed to conducting an engine-off-landing. At 75 KIAS, as I commenced the flare, I realised immediately that I was going to need a good deal more judgement to slow down, without over-speeding the rotors. Easing the cyclic progressively aft it was important to allow the aircraft to continue descending towards the ground. It would have been far too easy, with all this speed, to flare too much, too soon, and end up running out of ideas far too high for a safe touchdown to be achieved – no pressure. My gradual and progressive flare seemed to be doing the trick but we still ended up running on to the ground faster than I would have liked. Test point 2 achieved …

Phew! Survived another.

Now to commence the whole thing with less airspeed. This meant my rate of descent would be higher and I would have less flare effect to reduce it. Oh well, here goes …

'Three … two … one … *now*,'

Now at 50 KIAS the appropriate height arrived and I commenced my flare …

Bugger! Nothing is happening – I'm still plummeting earthwards with the same rate of descent.

Yikes!

'Flare harder,' I say to myself and with an aggressive hoik of the stick finally the ground rush reduces somewhat, but the minimal flare has done nothing to spool up my rotor rpm so I now have less inertia in the bank to use for the touch-down. Suddenly my judgement became critical.

Bang!

We were down with minimal run-on. I was starting to see the pros and cons of using different speeds. Lots of speed gave more options but made it harder to judge the touch down point, and the run on speed was potentially too fast. But slow speed made the required judgement of the technique much harder … hmmmmmmm.

And what of height? Well starting higher was scary as I had to commence my flare very, very gently indeed to ensure I didn't stop going down. BUT commencing the flare lower than the optimum gate was even more scary. The flare had to be very aggressive and it had to stop the rate of descent entirely – if not, there was a risk that the back end of the helicopter would hit the ground as it was pitched more and more nose-up.

Blige! I was beginning to appreciate that my predecessors, who had accepted the Gazelle into service, had chosen the optimum 'gate' for such manoeuvres with a degree of wisdom. At long last my final test point had been flown and after a quick conference with my new best mate, Alastair, we decided beer would be in order …

Phew! Survived another.

However, ETPS had not yet done with forcing me to throw myself at the ground in a gliding Gazelle. The final phase of this critical aspect of helicopter flight testing was to do the 'avoid curve' … more properly referred to normally as a height-velocity curve. As you will have gathered from all of the above, a safe landing can normally be achieved if everything is done just right and the pilot is able to fly through a 'gate' at the optimum height and speed … typically for a Gazelle this would be around 65 KIAS at approx. 80–100ft above ground level. At this stage the aircraft needed to be into wind, without undue roll and with the rotor rpm safely within limits. So what if a pilot is flying slower than 65 KIAS when the engine stops? In that case the pilot would need to apply forward cyclic to accelerate the aircraft by converting height into speed. If insufficient height is available then the consequence will be a heavy landing or crash. A manufacturer will provide the pilot with a diagram. If the pilot is high enough then he can safely hover, knowing that he has enough height to regain the 65 KIAS or so required to complete a safe landing. As a rotary wing test pilot this topic was deemed a core capability so we all needed to know all about how to do this testing. If you have already read my first book *Test Pilot* you will know that I relied upon this aspect of my training a good deal. This was high risk flying and we were not allowed to do it solo. So we were teamed up with flying tutors. In my case I was teamed with Kevin, the newest tutor on the staff…

Great!

I think he was as nervous as I was! There was little room for error. If I messed up, Kevin would have to take control and do his best to sort things out before we 'totalled' the aircraft. The reaction time to such screw ups had to be near zero, so each test point was approached with caution and a brief reminder of what I would be expected to do. So for example, establish a hover at 700ft agl. As the throttle was closed I had to slam the collective down to the bottom stop and simultaneously apply forward cyclic to start accelerating towards a minimum of 60 KIAS before I reached 100ft agl…

'Are you ready?' asks Kevin before closing the throttle with the customary count to three.

And down we plummeted. I'm not a fan of roller coasters and this was, at the very least, many times scarier. Had I applied enough cyclic? Was I accelerating fast enough? Was the rotor rpm under control? What was my rate of descent? What was the rad-alt reading?

Blige! High workload or what?

Thankfully the 60 KIAS appeared as I approached 100ft with the rotor rpm nicely 'in the green' and I commenced a flare as on my previous exercise. The difference, with many of these test points, was that my rate of descent was a good deal higher than that of a steady state glide. So again my initial flare seemed to have little effect.

'More flare required,' I think, as my right hand is in 'survival mode' and is already applying the right amount of nose-up pitch rate. With helicopters you have to move all the controls at once and, as we pitched up, the rotor rpm accelerated viciously, so a large handful of collective lever was needed which my left hand thankfully applied instinctively.

Phew! So far so good…

Now floating to the ground, almost under control, all I now had to do, at just the right moment, was apply an aggressive 'check' by raising the collective a further couple of inches while levelling the aircraft before we bashed the tail and then, while keeping it straight with the yaw pedals, I was able to use the remaining amount of collective to cushion on to the ground which we now ran along at a brisk pace.

Phew! And that was the easy one.

I note in my log book this sortie lasted a hundred whole minutes … Hells bells! … that is an awful lot of adrenalin to use up. Thankfully this sortie marked the end of the high risk engine-off phase of our training and we just had time for a couple of fun sorties before the end of term.

I had been looking forward to flying the Wessex. I knew it was going to be a major part of my job, assuming I passed the course. A Rotary Wing Test Squadron (RWTS) RAF pilot, Jan, kindly brought across the squadron's elderly Royal Navy Wessex Mk V, XS509. I didn't realise it at the time, but this was another airframe that was going to feature frequently in my log book in the next couple of years. Thankfully, I loved the Wessex. Perhaps the biggest challenge for the ab initio pilot was climbing in, which required steps on the fuselage side, behind an engine exhaust and a large main wheel, to be navigated in a very particular order. Just like mountain climbing, get it wrong and a nasty fall was sure to follow. Thankfully I mastered the entry technique and like to think I didn't embarrass myself too much as I had the opportunity for a very pleasant potter around the local countryside. However, this trip paled into insignificance when compared to my last flight of the term. I was introduced to the British Aerospace Hawk T.1. As you already know, I was a frustrated fast jet pilot and could not believe I'd been at ETPS seven whole months before finally being programmed to fly one of the school's fixed wing trainers. I had not realised prior to joining the course just how divided the school was between rotes and fixed wing test pilots. But at last I was being briefed by Gordon on all the safety aspects of my first ever fast jet flight. Ironically we had done comprehensive ejection seat training at the beginning of the year and we all had 'G-suit' trousers which used high pressure air to apply constrictions to the pilot's legs when experiencing high G or high acceleration forces. So suitably equipped and briefed we walked to the jet.

Wow! How cool it looked on this sunny afternoon, resplendent in its red, white and blue 'raspberry ripple' colour scheme.

The helicopters all seemed to get covered in soot from their engine exhausts so never really glinted in the sun as this aircraft did just now. I was helped to clamber in and do up the various straps which took me forever. I was immediately in awe of the Tornado F3 fighter pilots who were on Quick Reaction Alert (QRA) at that very moment waiting to start up their engines and protect the UK from external nosiness. I was invited to start the engine which was easier than starting up a Gazelle:

    Engine Start Switches ON
    Anti-Collision Light ON
    Relight Button – Pressed and released
    GTS (Gas Turbine Starter) indicator GREEN –
    Engine Start Switch to START and released
    With the engine rpm 15–20 per cent Throttle to IDLE

In no time the hydraulic and electric system checks had been completed and we had called for taxi. Minutes later, lined up on the main runway, I was being invited to advance the throttle in my left hand to spool up the Rolls Royce Turbomeca Adour engine. With the engine instruments all indicating that the engine was apparently performing as advertised I released the brakes and …

Bam! We were off! Proper fast jest pilots would view this subsequent acceleration as leisurely – it blew my socks off.

Before I'd caught my breath, the airspeed of 90 KIAS demanded I rotate into a take-off attitude and almost instantly we were 'slipping the surly bonds of earth' and heading skywards. Passing 150 KIAS, gear up, flap up without hesitation and before I knew it we were heading through layers of cloud to that beautiful bit of the sky above 10,000ft which is invariably 8/8 blue …

Wow! This was the most fun I'd had with my trousers on in a long time!

Would I like to fly a loop? Whoosh – and a gentle application of aft stick had my trousers squeezing my thighs a tad as the ground became visible above my head.

Awesome!

Barrel rolls, and aileron rolls were performed with apparent ease and I realised I had fallen in love with this inanimate object. Surely it's not already time to go home? But all good things come to an end and with a quick demo of diving to Mach 1 (just so I could enter it into my logbook) we were descending through the murk to join downwind for the long south westerly runway. Throttle to Idle, slowing to 190 KIAS I dropped the gear and selected mid flap. Turning final at 150 KIAS I selected full flap and slowed to around 135 KIAS. As I approached 'the hedge' I slowed further to float over the piano keys at 110 KIAS. Ironically the hardest thing about the flight was keeping the aircraft straight after I'd landed. The brakes were very sensitive and I managed to achieve the customary 'first flight weave' without bother.

Phew! What a blast – can I transfer to the fixed wing course please?

Sadly not. At the time, I wasn't to know, that I'd end up getting chance to fly more fast jets than most fixed wing pilots ever do. For now I had to console myself with the knowledge that I'd ticked a box that might not have been achievable at all had I not worked so hard to be selected for ETPS in the first place.

As the term drew to a close there was just time to reflect on how chuffed I felt to have made it so far. During the last few months, three of our number (two FTEs and an FW pilot) had been 'chopped' or invited to leave the course. That was quite a high rate of attrition but I took comfort from the historical statistics that indicated most such departures were achieved before summer leave.

Fingers firmly crossed! Time to head to the bar for an end of term piss-up which all of us felt was richly deserved.

BAe Hawk XX342 landing at Boscombe Down. *(Jason Grant)*

Chapter 5

ETPS, Class of 1994 – Autumn Term

'What is the aircraft like in autorotation?' I had expected a discussion.

Instead the Swedish pilot in the left-hand seat promptly slammed both cockpit-roof-mounted engine throttles CLOSED!

'**** me!' I said, as I slammed the collective to the floor.

What is this bloke going to do next? No briefing … no three second countdown … no executive order of 'NOW'. What the heck?

Amazingly, we were given a whole three weeks leave … almost enough time to forget everything we had learnt so far. If the first day of the summer term was a shock to the system, then restarting our training immediately after the August Bank Holiday was ten times worse. We were thrown almost immediately into the Gazelle, Scout and Lynx to ensure we hadn't forgotten how to fly and then, without delay, we commenced our next exercise concerning power failures in multi-engine helicopters. Although not quite as exciting as all the engine-off landings we had done before our holidays, this had enough risk to grab our attention. A further treat awaited. In Germany there was a (sort of) equivalent organisation to Bedford and Farnborough based at Braunschweig and known as Deutsches Zentrum für Luft- und Raumfahrt – DLR. They had modified a Bo105 helicopter, a bit like our VSS Basset. They kindly flew it across to Boscombe Down for us all to have a couple of flights with various stability characteristics modified. Great fun and no report required. However, before we could blink, the Pilot's Assessment arrived. In fairness, this exercise was absolutely invaluable as it consolidated all the training we had done to date and provided an incredibly true-to-real-life flight test evaluation.

In recent years I have had to do literally hundreds of such assessments. The exercise was based around the concept of being offered a new, un-flown, aircraft for a single flight of just over an hour. During that flight we had to evaluate every aspect of the aircraft in the manner to which we had become accustomed. The immediate challenge was that the rented-in aircraft would not be fitted with any instrumentation. We had become used to our ETPS fleet, which were mostly equipped with gauges or 'desyns' to show us control positions, sideslip, angle of attack etc. How would we be able to gather the required data without such instruments? Well, we were then given perhaps one of the most important lessons of the course, as far as my subsequent career was to be concerned … that was how to design and fit 'temporary instrumentation'. Prior to this demonstration I had never heard of a seamstress tape measure … in fact I had not heard of a seamstress either. For some reason seamstresses needed cloth tape measures that self-retracted into their case using a spring mechanism. This meant that we could attach the end of the tape to a flying control and the case to a fixed part of the cockpit and thus, with some further maths, we could work out fairly accurately how much we were needing to displace the controls.

Hallelujah! – If we could measure control displacements, we could document all the static stability aspects. The other stuff we could assess from experience and make educated 'guesstimates'. With tape measures in place and a cunning plan prepared, over several late nights, we strapped into this new challenge with the 'real' aircraft captain alongside us to try and make sure we didn't break it. We had been specially selected, we were advised, to test the McDonnel Douglas MD520N single-engine helicopter, against a possible procurement contract for the provision of a new training helicopter to replace the Gazelle. Now this aircraft was, without doubt, rather whacky. It was fitted with a revolutionary system that removed the need for a tail rotor.

What? No tail rotor?

In fact, the system was known as NOTAR (NO TAil Rotor). The front end of the helicopter was very similar in appearance to the conventional MD500 helicopter. However, the tail was radically changed and a much larger boom fitted with two vertical fins/rudders at the back end.

'Well they must provide the directional stability,' I surmised correctly. 'And also a good deal of the directional control in forward flight also.'

The thick boom had a large fan fitted at one end connected to the main gearbox. Thus, as long as the rotors were turning, a large amount of air was blown down the tube to exit in a couple of different places. The air that reached the end of the boom blew through a slot in a rotating 'bucket' which was connected to the pilot's yaw pedals. By moving these pedals the blast of air could be directed to the left or right and thus cause the helicopter to yaw. But how was the massive amount of main rotor torque accounted for? Well this relied on another principle I learnt about for the first time … 'Coanda effect'.

Henri Coanda, a Romanian, had worked out that, by blowing air around a shape (like a tail boom), passing airflow was attracted to it. So by allowing air to flow out of the boom through some long slots, the downwash from the main rotors could be forced to attach to the boom and create a horizontal lift force which, amazingly, compensated for the torque. The best part was that, as more power was applied, this Coanda effect increased and automatically compensated for the greater torque – clever stuff! So I was looking forward to writing up the full flight test report that this exercise demanded as I knew that this system would clearly correct all the issues with such small helicopters and I was expecting it to be a joy to fly …

Mistake!

The MD520M was actually a bit of a dog, with a whole host of deficiencies that I had to write up as being unacceptable. Deficiencies were classified as 'unsatisfactory' or 'unacceptable', with the latter needing a stronger case to be made by much more robust seven-part paragraphs.

Bugger!

I can't remember if there were any good aspects, but the aircraft was unstable laterally, which was relatively rare, and the first time I'd seen it for real. The NOTAR system kinda worked as advertised, but with a massive lag. So the tail was always wagging the dog. The most unpleasant aspect was flying some engine-off landings. I flew them as I would in the Scout or Gazelle and commended myself on some smooth touch downs. But as soon as the airspeed over the vertical fins started to reduce it was impossible to keep the thing straight. Very alarming. Ironically, much later in my career I was required to formally qualify on the twin-engine version of the aircraft (MD902), which I flew extensively for Wiltshire Police and Air Ambulance and the National Police Aviation Service (NPAS). The MD902 was an improvement and I didn't have to perform engine-off

The author conducting the Pilot's Assessment exercise in the MD520N. *(MOD)*

landings in it, but the yaw control system was still poor when compared to having a conventional tail rotor.

The assessment was carried out individually rather than in teams, and required a full FTR, with all the various sections. I could not believe how much paper was required to capture all the information and my thoughts about just a single flight. But this was just the warm up act for our 'Preview' assessment exercise which was effectively our end of term graduation project. Although some Previews were undertaken in the UK, normally students were sent off around the world to be able to sample something completely new and outside their comfort zone. Thankfully ETPS included a series of external trips and visits throughout the year which, to a very limited extent, prepared us for the challenge of what was to come.

Early on in the year our visits tended to be UK based. We had a great day out at Rolls Royce, Filton. We were all flown in our (as we liked to call it) company jet (BAC1-11 ZE432) to the airfield famous for being the test centre for the UK Concorde: Filton. A thoroughly entertaining day was had with the company Chief Test Pilot, Andy, amusing us with numerous anecdotes of engines that did, and didn't, behave as they should do in Harriers and other types. His warbird experiences complemented the fast jet stories in exemplary fashion and, before we knew it, we were heading to a local pub for the annual skittles match. The loser of the game won 'the bone' trophy, which was a genuine ox bone that had a habit of becoming very smelly indeed in warm offices during the summer. Bob, the school CO, briefed us that losing was not an option – and with guile, determination and several pints of real ale, we reached the point where actually, we didn't care.

Having survived this baptism, only weeks later we were zipping up to Edinburgh, again in the company jet. We were off to visit Ferranti. Sadly the company had gone through a rough patch in the few months leading up to our visit and was in the process of being sold off piecemeal. I believe it was technically part of GEC when we all walked through the door, but as far as the staff and all the company signage was concerned this was still Ferranti – and they knew how to host a party. They were an old-school family company with a director's dining room. As the sun set we gathered for drinks before being seated. Our surprise for what then followed was jaw dropping. Swing doors crashed open and we were met with an onslaught of the skirl of the pipes as, not one but two, pipers marched into the room to the accompaniment of Scotland the Brave. Our astonishment was completed when we clocked the second piper as our own Stu, Canadian FTE, resplendent in all his Scottish regalia. Canada is full of Scots. Our deafening continued for a good couple of tunes and laments before we realised we were having a traditional Burns Supper. We were entertained by the Selkirk Grace before being allowed to sit and drink some more with our potato soup. I can't remember what we drank apart from the very nice single malt whisky that was generously left on all the tables. The dinner followed in traditional style with the pipers given free rein as the Haggis arrived with appropriate pomp and ceremony. The Haggis was addressed by a member of the Ferranti team, as tradition demanded, and more whisky was consumed. Well-fed and watered, we enjoyed a number of speeches after the meal. A good deal was said about the long-standing relationship between Ferranti and ETPS, and we students – now well the worse for wear – banged the tables in enthusiastic support.

Uggh! Shabby! The evening had finished early enough for the rotes to venture into the delights of the city. I'd like to say it was an unforgettable evening – well I'd like to say that, but too many brain cells were lost that night.

We rotes were to return to Scotland, shortly thereafter, to visit the helicopter operators in Aberdeen. The vast majority of civvy helicopters in the UK then and now earn their money ferrying oil workers out to the rigs and back. I remember little about the visit apart from being amazed at the take-off profiles of the Sikorsky S-61N helicopters. At the time I saw them as stretched Sea Kings. I watched them taxi on their wheels out to the duty runway. When cleared for departure, instead of doing a gentle running take-off as I might have elected to do, they lifted into a 10–15ft hover and then very aggressively pitched to over 20 degrees nose-down, to accelerate level just above the tarmac. How bizarre, I thought at the time. In more recent years I became aware that their public transport flights required them to use take-off profiles approved in their flight manuals. Sikorsky had not included a rolling/running take-off so a 'clear area cat A' profile had to do. All quite safe but must have been scary if sitting right down the back.

We were to enjoy the hospitality of GEC again – this time GEC Marconi based at Rochester. At the time, the UK MOD was in the process of trying to identify a suitable attack helicopter to equip the British Army. Many will know that they eventually decided on a version of the Apache AH-64D with the Longbow radar and Rolls Royce engines. One of the contenders was a version of the Bell Cobra helicopter, which I had been able to become acquainted with the previous year during my fact finding visit to Texas. At Rochester was a fully working, but fixed base, simulator of the new aircraft cockpit which, arguably, was far more advanced than the Apache and certainly the most advanced cockpit we students had ever seen. It had helmets with displays projected onto the visors and all sorts of glass cockpit screens and devices that allowed the battlefield to be displayed and enemy armour and other targets identified. Frankly, it was a real blast to pretend to be taking on the might of the Russian Army with an unlimited supply of Hellfire missiles. It was a great visit but sadly there was no more haggis to be had, which is probably just as well.

We were lucky to enjoy three different foreign visits during the course – Switzerland, Sweden and the French test centre at Cazaux, in the South of France. To some extent the visits had a good deal of commonality. They all involved flying new aircraft alongside people we didn't fully understand, followed by drinking copious amounts of alcohol to celebrate having survived the experience.

My first such baptism of fire was our visit to Pilatus and Emmen Airforce base, Switzerland. There were so many aspects of this visit that were 'broadening'. Lunch was taken sitting at long tables surrounded by numerous hosts. I was sitting alongside a consultant surgeon who was a reservist in the Swiss Air Force.

'So how does it all work?' I asked.

'What do you mean?'

'Well how do you get tasked to fly?'

'It's easy. I just look out of the window of my office and if it's a nice day I tell them to pull out my Hunter and I'll be there in thirty minutes.'

'Wow, you just get to fly a Hunter whenever you feel like it?'

'Yep.'

I was already feeling I was flying for the wrong outfit. With no time for dessert I was being sweated in the brand new Super Puma simulator. An expert on simulators, I was very impressed by the fidelity of this training aid, especially the visuals that were better than most I'd seen to date. But I wasn't there to enjoy myself, as emergency after emergency was thrown at me.

Phew! Didn't die.

Moments later I was in the real thing; Swiss Super Puma T-324 with Rolf in the co-pilot's seat. I was sitting in the jump seat as my fellow rote student, Greg, was being put through the mill on how to start the aircraft and do all the pre-take-off checks. I thought I had lucked out as the plan was for Greg and me to swap seats at a convenient time during the sortie. Greg did a splendid job of flying us around the local mountains and was finally invited to touch-down on a landing site which appeared to be situated on a near vertical slope – madness. Suddenly, I was very interested in my mate's abilities to fly this particular transport aircraft. With some coaching from Rolf we landed in a snotty heap in a very small area hacked out of the mountain side. With no warning to speak of, the large sliding cabin door was flung open and I was invited to step out of the relatively safe environment of the cabin. As I looked out of the door there was next to nothing between the cabin and a 2,000ft drop down the side of the mountain. I have never clung to the side of a helicopter with such tenacity before, or since, as I edged forward to the pilot's door. Poor Greg now had to face the same trauma I had just experienced and step out of his comfortable seat and become a mountaineer without any of the usual equipment, training or preparation. If memory serves, the adrenalin coursing through my body was unwilling to hang onto the side of the aircraft any longer so I literally hoiked my mate out of the seat, holding on to him to ensure he didn't immediately plummet to his doom. Once the seat was vacant I wasted no time in clambering in and fastening my five point harness. With Greg seated where I had been, I now had the problem of getting airborne from where Greg had put us. I looked left towards where the rotor blades or 'disc' could be seen. It looked bloody close to the mountainside. If I drifted left at all on lifting we would be eating bits of rotor blade in an instant.

Yikes!

Thankfully the aircraft had, for its time, a very good autopilot system and as I raised the collective to inch us into the hover, it was evident that this was a relatively stable helicopter and I was able to hold our position within a few inches of the starting datum as I scanned all the instruments to ensure both engines were working as advertised. They were …

Phew! 'Time to get the heck out of Dodge.'

As I pulled further power by raising the collective some more, I prevented the natural tendency to yaw to the left (it was a French helicopter) and then applied forward and right cyclic to slide smoothly away from all the hazards that might have killed us before tea time. Once clear I dived the punchy, but large, rotorcraft to achieve 150 KIAS and commence a low level tactical transit back towards where we had recently had lunch. What a blast! – Even Hunter pilots didn't get to have this much fun with their flying suits on.

Phew! I had survived my first ETPS foreign visit and had not had to face the thought of my wife being told I'd inadvertently fallen off the side of a Swiss mountain.

Next up was a quick cross-channel dash to the DGA Flight test centre in Cazaux, on the west coast, in the south of France where the French military did a good deal of air launched weapons testing. We arrived late morning and our RN Tutor gave us a very strict warning before we got off the company jet.

'There will be red wine served at lunch [yummy!]. Do not drink any! You may well be invited to fly in the afternoon.'

Sure enough, as we sat along long tables in the canteen, numerous carafes of the local vino were being sloshed back by our orange flying-suited French colleagues, especially by the chap sitting directly opposite me. These days my resolve is far less, but back than I was able to keep up polite conversation sipping beaucoup d'eau. Imagine my sense of indignity when, less than an hour later, I was strapping into a French AS365 Dauphin helicopter, only to find out that our safety pilot was the guy who had been sitting with us and slugging back the red at lunch. I was very happy to fly with a pilot who was well lubricated, but I definitely felt it was only fair that I should have been similarly disposed. Andy, I have never forgiven you!

It seemed only weeks later we found ourselves in Linkoping, Sweden. This was a successful visit from the point of view of getting to fly different types. First up was a Bell 204 which was effectively the same as a Bell UH-1, or 'Huey', helicopter. There can't be a helicopter pilot anywhere in the world that hasn't got a soft spot for this aircraft. Designed in the '50s, the type first flew in 1956 at Fort Worth. Since then more than 16,000 (yes 16,000!) have been built with the type serving with distinction in the Vietnam War. My formative years included watching black and white footage of these aircraft in US news bulletins. I had just turned 17 and been selected for a Royal Navy Flying Scholarship when I watched these helicopters pulling the last few members of staff out of the US Embassy compound in Saigon. Whatever your politics, this was still a 'tear in the eye' moment. So I was well chuffed to now finally be invited to fly one of these iconic military aircraft. I could not fail to be impressed. The rotor blades alone were both iconic and impressive. They were big. *Very big*. As they turned they just smashed the air out of their way. Sliding down my door window, my head was literally bashed from side to side by the air trying to get out of the way of these blades. The performance from a single engine was commendable and I was easily able to lift into the hover and depart the airfield very aggressively with *Ride of the Valkyries* (from the *Apocalypse Now* movie) ringing in my head. My safety pilot offered to show me one of the Huey 'party tricks'. As we approached the airfield he rolled the twist grip throttle on the collective firmly closed and ever so gently lowered the collective.

Had he not had the ETPS briefing on lowering the collective to achieve zero G?

But the rotor rpm did not decay as expected and we floated gently to the ground in a conventional but slow motion engine-off landing. But then my chum did something really bonkers. With the rotor rpm now gently decaying he raised the collective.

No!

We climbed 3ft above the ground as he fed in yaw pedal and we commenced a spot turn.

'But the throttle is still closed!'

But, sure enough, after 360 degrees, we were still 3ft off the ground with the rotor rpm still gently decaying as we landed on – to rapturous applause from me. Where was this aircraft last term when we students were being hurled at the ground in the Gazelle?

I barely had time for a much needed coffee before being thrown into the Bolkow 105 which was extensively used in Sweden and the rest of Europe as an anti-tank helicopter when armed with HOT missiles. The aircraft was in some ways a predecessor of the Lynx and had a rigid type of rotor head that made it very manoeuvrable. If you have seen the Bond movie *Spectre*, you will already have seen a Bo105 being rolled upside down repeatedly. This particular airframe has been flown by Red Bull for a number of years and managed to get approval to fly a variety of aerobatic manoeuvres normally prohibited for such aircraft. Anyway I was enjoying chucking the Swedish version around the sky when the ETPS TP student got the better of me and I asked, what I thought was, an innocent question …

'What is the aircraft like in autorotation?' I had expected a discussion.

Instead the Swedish pilot in the left-hand seat promptly slammed both cockpit-roof-mounted engine throttles CLOSED!

'**** me!' I said, as I slammed the collective to the floor – using the Gazelle rather than Huey timescales.

What is this bloke going to do next? No briefing … no three second count down … no executive order of 'NOW'. What the heck?

I started to search for somewhere to land. We were over a dense area of woodland with mostly 6ft tall 'Christmas trees'. Thankfully I spotted a small clearing. Would we fit? Could I manoeuvre this gliding helicopter aggressively enough to make it? I had to try. I had no idea whether I was being expected to fly an engine-off or not, but I had no way of re-advancing the engines so I got on with the best option available and was setting up nicely into wind and commencing a gentle flare to just clear the tree tops on the edge of the clearing ... flare ... flare ... flare ... check! As I raised the collective to check the rotor rpm I glanced a Swedish gloved hand reach up to the roof – and sure enough as I raised the lever to settle into the clearing I realised the engines had been re-advanced and instead of thumping onto the boggy ground I was able to manage a shambolic hover.

Phew! Survived another.

That was a heck of a lot of adrenalin used up that I hadn't expected. This escapade was repeated numerous times during my time of flying at ETPS. We spent hours comprehensively briefing our own training sorties, but then would leap into aircraft with strangers who didn't speak English as their first language and who made assumptions that we were not always privy to. Time for copious quantities of Absolut – the local vodka. And of course, plenty of toasts. Both the airframes I flew that day have survived the claw of the scrap merchant and are living a comfortable retirement in the Svedinos Bil- och Flygmuseum Automobile and Aircraft museum in Ugglarp.

For some reason our company jet had been unserviceable for our trip to Sweden and we had borrowed a very noisy C130 Hercules. Riding in the back with earplugs in, and heads throbbing from too much Absolut, our tutors suddenly started handing out envelopes.

'Que?'

This was very unusual but the noise prevented conversation and eventually I received mine. I tore it open to read ...

> A joint RN and USN test team had been requested to carry out a Preview Assessment of the Agusta Bell AB212 SAR aircraft as a possible short term solution for both our countries need for a combat search and rescue (CSAR) aircraft. We were to produce a comprehensive test plan over the next two weeks before being shipped off to Practica de Mare, near Rome, to conduct our evaluation.

It felt like the last twenty minutes of the *Top Gun* movie when Maverick and Iceman get their urgent assignments – well sort of. This was the expected announcement of our Preview Exercise. We had all hoped to be assigned to the very latest high-tech aircraft around the globe. The AB212 was not that. But I was very content. It was a twin-engine version of the Huey I had just had such a blast in. It had a very sophisticated search and rescue autopilot or flight control system – but, more importantly, we were going to get to fly around Rome in the autumn Italian sunshine; what was not to like? Meanwhile Greg and Keith had been assigned the Super Puma in France and, I confess, I was rather jealous of Crispin and Peter who would assess the Bell AH-1W Cobra in the States – the very type I'd so enjoyed learning all about eighteen months previously.

Having broken the news to my family, the next challenge was to produce the required flight test plan/schedule that my tutor, Andy, would be willing to agree to. I was teamed up with Jeff, who I hadn't flown with much previously. He was a USN Seahawk LAMPS (Light Airborne Multi-Purpose System) pilot and we decided he should be the expert on the AB212's complex flight control system, whereas I would deal with everything else. At the time it seemed like a good deal – like when you end up with a pair of browns on the Monopoly board but your mate has ended up with three reds.

We were not allowed to spend our working days on this prep though, as we still had a number of exercises to complete. One particular exercise

AB212 used for Preview Assessment. *(Brendon Attard)*

which was, for a number of reasons, to be crucial was our 'Simulator Assessment' training. Following the usual briefings we were despatched to the Chinook simulator which was at that time situated at Farnborough. We had been given a number of 'tools', so to speak, to assist us with trying to determine whether the fidelity of the simulation was suitable. The assessment commenced with a simple measuring of the cockpit. I was amazed to find that the cockpit wasn't an accurate replica of the real aircraft. How could that be when it would have been so easy to measure up the real thing? The fidelity of the performance and flying qualities was also not brilliant. It was to transpire that I would spend a good deal of my time in the immediate future assessing simulators and when I commenced work for the CAA some nine years later, this was a core aspect of my job.

With the simulator assessment complete there was time to get another handful of training flights in a Sea King. This was important, in that I would be flying the Sea King extensively when I joined Experimental Flying Squadron – but of more pressing concern was to get 'up to speed' on all the autopilot functions. As mentioned earlier in the book, the ASW Sea King was designed as a day/night, nearly all weather, submarine hunter. To that end it had to be able to establish a very stable hover in order to lower a sonar into the sea. Following investigation at one location it would have to 'jump' to another in order to chase or triangulate the position of a sub. At night and in poor weather this was best achieved by letting the aircraft system fly itself. I confess, it was impressive to watch this hefty aircraft being flown around 'hands-off', reliably establishing hover after hover. Suitably prepared for EFS and Preview, there was chance to squeeze in another fun sortie – a flight in the Army's experimental Airship ZH762 which was based at Boscombe Down for trials work. Airship Industries Ltd had produced a number of Skyship 600B aircraft. This example was being used by the Army with a view to possibly providing a surveillance platform in Northern Ireland.

The experience was amazing. This was a completely new method of getting airborne. Although incredibly slow, it pootled along quite well. The biggest challenge came when trying to return to Mother Earth. As the aircraft slowed down it became impossible to steer and equally, it was difficult to get the combination of ballast correct to determine its rate of climb or descent. If the aircraft was too light it would be reluctant to descend and vice versa. So the technique was to drive the aircraft quite aggressively towards a mooring tower while lots of Army ground crew rushed out to grab one of the numerous streaming ropes. If they were unsuccessful the aircraft had to be powered up and go round again which took forever. Thankfully all went well for my sortie, but only a few months later an Army test pilot screwed it up and crashed the airship damaging it beyond economical repair.

Yikes!

Eventually, Monday 24 October arrived and after a near dawn departure in the company jet we were unceremoniously deposited on the tarmac at Practica de Mare – the Italian military flight test centre. The base, opened in 1937, was the biggest military airfield in Italy and was less than thirty kilometres from the centre of Rome. We now had just ten working days to fly an AB212 for ten hours or so in order to discover all about its performance, handling qualities and autopilot functionality. We had no time to waste and promptly set about meeting up with the Italian test pilots who were going to host us. Thankfully we had been allocated a single aircraft for our sole use during the fortnight, which would make the report writing easier. My first flight was with Massimo who was a recent graduate of ETPS himself so knew exactly what we were needing to do. Over a beer, he later told me that he and his mate decided to evaluate a Bell 47 almost immediately after returning from Boscombe Down. The training had been done on the Lynx, but the Bell 47 had a teetering rotor head and was far less forgiving. They deliberately entered the vortex ring state at around 5,000ft and promptly tumbled earthwards for nearly 4,000ft before good fortune rather than flying skill caused the aircraft to fall into less disturbed air and two very white Italians were able to fly gently back to base!

Blige! Are we safe in their hands? I wondered.

That evening Jeff and I set about measuring up the cockpit, documenting the field of view and using external hydraulics to assess the flight control mechanical characteristics, just like we had been taught in the first term. The following day our testing commenced with the basic stability and control requirements. Our tutor, Andy, also flew the aircraft. The normal practice was for each team to have a tutor allocated. They would attend for the first few days to ensure that all the logistical issues were in hand and that things were going smoothly. They would also fly the subject aircraft themselves so that they would better understand our comprehensive report

AB212 with the author conducting the Preview at Practica de Mare. *(Author)*

when it landed in their in-tray. One of the challenges with having a tutor around was keeping him entertained. Once he had flown his single flight he inevitably became rather bored and wanted to head out each evening to sample the local taverns and pizzerias. Needless to say, Jeff and I were working our socks off to ensure we had captured all the required data from the day's flying and then plan ahead for the following day. Despite that, Andy convinced us to head into town that evening.

'I'll drive,' says Jeff. 'I'm used to driving on the right so it will be safest!'
Wrong!

Having missed the chosen restaurant due to some inept navigating, without hesitation Jeff commenced a U-turn and, without slowing, started to turn the steering wheel ferociously. Given the super-wide highways he was used to in California this might have been forgivable up until the point when …

Bang!

The outer front wheel made a resounding contact with the huge kerbstone – and all of a sudden there were just 'three wheels on our wagon' – well three wheels that were still round with inflated tyres that is.

Bugger!

So out we all get – tired – grumpy and desperate for copious amounts of vino and food – but instead found ourselves jacking up a rental car. Thankfully there was a spare, and I was talked out of my desire to string up my mate from the nearest lamppost by his private parts! Fortuitously, the Italian rental company was relatively content when we finally returned the car, with only one trashed rim – not unusual in Italy apparently.

We had organised an away day for the morning after. The AB212 was used by the Italian Navy for search and rescue and we had been invited to visit 604a Squadriglia SAR at Grosseto which was 200 kilometres north along the coast from Practica. Even better, we were going to fly ourselves there in two 'company aircraft' – an MD500E helicopter (81272) and an S208 Siai Marchetti aeroplane (61969). Sadly the Marchetti was written off in a fatal accident less than three years later. I flew the MD500E for the outbound leg and then the Marchetti on the way back – what a blast. Our hosts at 604 Squadron could not have been friendlier or more helpful. They explained how the AB212 was deployed and used and talked us through the various modes of the flight control system. The following day it was back to work – well kind of. The role we were evaluating the aircraft for was 'Combat SAR' rather than just over the water rescue. I had heard there was some fun flying to be had in some mountains near Rome. If we could gather our level flight performance data en route then I convinced myself and Jeff this was an essential use of three hours of our precious allocated ten. Whether it was or wasn't I'm not sure, but the memories of wazzing around the mountains in a souped-up Huey are priceless. We even did some ad hoc landings and took some photos. On return to Practica we were met by some bad news. On one of my landings the skid had rested on a rock which had taken most of the weight of the aircraft … and I'd damaged the skid.

Bugger!

There was no spare AB212 and changing the skids was several days of effort. I had a sleepless night awaiting an engineer's report the following morning.

'Still Fit to Fly,' he had surmised.

Phew!

I was banned from further ad hoc landing sites, but I breathed a sigh of relief as we were able to conclude the first week on a high. So what should

Author flying the AB212 in the mountains near Rome. *(Author)*

some young chaps do after their tutor leaves when situated just down the road from one of Europe's more exciting cities…? Exactly!

Leaping into the rental we roared northbound for some sightseeing and copious amounts of pasta and red wine. Being American, Jeff liked to eat early and I had to work hard at trying to introduce him to a Mediterranean lifestyle. After my efforts, at least when we ate, there were others in the restaurant, albeit we were definitely on all the 'early bird' offers. The 48-hour pass was barely enough before we had returned on Sunday afternoon to prep for our second week. This week was mostly 'Jeff stuff', which included the flight control system testing and some more performance. As mentioned earlier, I had not paid enough attention when performance was being taught and I had assumed Jeff would know more than me.

Another mistake! Hmmmmmmmmm …

While we were swotting up on our ground school notes I arranged to do some winching, a primary requirement for a CSAR aircraft. It was a warm day with no wind. The Italians had a dedicated winch dummy which weighed an artificially heavy 400lbs. Undeterred, I started up the AB212 – at which I'd now become quite accomplished – and lifted into the hover. We had ballasted the aircraft to be at Maximum All Up Weight once I'd picked up my 'survivor'. I picked the aircraft up into a nice tidy hover and, with checks complete, flew a gentle circuit to position over the calibrated weight. Once established in the hover my crewman lowered the strop which was arranged around the 'shoulders' of my survivor. I then prepared to do what I would have done in my Wasp or Lynx – that is I would respond to my crewman's call, 'Up ten feet.' I raised the collective gingerly until I reached the maximum torque allowed and …

The square root of nothing happened. My survivor remained firmly on the ground. I asked my crewman to 'raise the winch' and, as he did so, my helicopter was progressively hauled lower and lower. I had hoped that, when I had sufficient 'ground effect', I would be able to inch the 400 lbs airborne, but it was not to be. Time for Plan B, as I ensured we were disentangled from the load before landing on to off-load ballast and try again. Although I had been planning to conduct a role relatable evaluation I had stumbled upon a perfect way to assess the hover performance of this aircraft. Eventually I had off-loaded enough ballast to just raise the survivor off the ground. Instantly I had the numbers of available hover weight at that outside air temperature. And sure enough the numbers tallied with the performance in the aircraft's flight manual – great. I then off loaded even more ballast so I could get on with some more realistic winching which the AB212 was able to do well.

I'd had my fun for the day and handed over to Jeff who set about assessing the aircraft's flight control system. This was an old aircraft with a good deal of limitations, but the FCS was amazing for its day. It was able to automatically fly us down into the hover over a located survivor. Initially I was critical of the performance in that, at Max All Up Weight it struggled – but in reality at normal weight it performed very well and effectively had an overload capability to allow more fuel to be carried to give it a commendable endurance. We completed some night flying and flew our final flight on the final Thursday of our fortnight, before the mandatory 'thank you' drinks laid on for our hosts who had remained incredibly helpful and good humoured throughout our 'amateur hour' evaluation attempts. The BAC 1-11 arrived right on time the following day and whisked us off to Boscombe to start our report writing.

In some ways I feel we had been too keen. We had gathered a massive amount of data about the aircraft which now needed to be fully analysed and plotted into colourful charts and graphs. If I remember rightly the completed FTR had to be handed in at 0800 on a Friday morning. Jeff and I had completed everything on our computers using the state of the art WordPerfect 5.1 software by around 1600 the previous afternoon. All we had to do now was print it off, give it a final proof read and hand it in. It will not surprise many of you to learn that the process took sixteen hours. Every time we printed a section the formatting would run amok or we would find major spelling errors or grammatical mistakes. How could this be? It had looked so good on our computers. It hadn't helped that we had written different sections and Jeff's American software was subtly different to my UK version. We did not sleep a wink. My wife thought I had been abducted by aliens and I even missed seeing my children, who had already gone to school before I got home.

Thank goodness it was a Friday and we had almost nothing to do as Andy, our tutor, commenced documenting our numerous errors. Amazingly, he called us in to debrief us on Monday morning. He clearly had worked through the weekend and, perhaps for the first time in twelve months, I realised he had needed to work even harder than us. Overall it could have been worse. But we had missed out discussing the aircraft's low speed handling qualities which would clearly be a black mark and count against us. For the first time since the course began we had become aware of the prizes that would be awarded at the end of course 'McKenna Dinner'. In addition to the Westland Trophy for the best RW student, we were competing for the Patuxent Shield for best RW Preview. I had discounted the notion of being the best RW student already and had hoped for a shot at the Preview prize, but now I wasn't sure. A glimmer of hope had come during our late night proof-reading session. All three RW teams were in exactly the same boat with the air hanging blue due to various Army, Navy and Canadian expletives. Greg and Keith had been to France to test a French Super Puma. Their report was all but complete when they started to produce a table showing all the various configurations they had test flown and at what weight and centre of gravity (CG). After a good deal of grumbling there was an almighty collective …

Oh Shit!

What's going on? Keith, my UK FTE mate, explained … it turns out that for every flight, the aircraft had been loaded outside the permissible weight/CG limitations.

'Bloody hell!' That's going to take some explaining. More than that. The following day, ETPS tutors were busy contacting their opposite numbers at EPNER to try and determine if any harm had been done.

Phew! It turns out all was well and the French helicopter squadron, which was entirely responsible for the aircraft's loading, was also very apologetic for not spotting the numerous mistakes. Anyway – I thought – maybe that will blow the Super Puma team out of the running for the prizes?

With the report debriefed we had another few days to prepare our oral presentation of our findings. We had thirty minutes exactly, followed by thirty minutes of questions. We had to present in the 'cinema', which was the poshest briefing room we had back then. Everyone from Boscombe Down was invited, along with interested parties from industry and the like. The senior team (that had interviewed me) were joined by my future colleagues from Bedford and Farnborough – no pressure then. Thankfully I don't usually have a problem waxing lyrical about stuff I know about and the hour flew by without too many embarrassing silences. We got chance to sit through all the course previews including the fast jet ones which, I have to confess, did have me rather envious.

Previews completed, and a quick famil in a piston-engine helicopter accomplished, it was time to dress up in our best bib and tucker for our graduation dinner. The arrangements were somewhat bonkers. Wives were not invited to our end of course McKenna Dinner and in previous years had complained. So on the Friday beforehand we had a 'Graduation Dinner' with our better halves and all received a certificate from the famous Bedford and BAe test pilot, John Farley, who entertained us with a speech about his time testing the Harrier which probably made more sense to the fast jet guys than us rotes. Less than a week later we were at 'the McKenna'.

It is tempting to add yet another account of the history of ETPS at this point; instead let me refer you to the excellent book *Learn to Test,*

Author receiving his graduation certificate from John Farley. *(MOD)*

Test to Learn by John Rawlings and Hilary Sedgewick. Suffice to say, the school was formed at the behest of Air Marshal Sir Ralph Sorley, the then Controller of Research and Development. Ralph was also nicknamed 'Eight-Gun', as he had insisted that Spitfires and Hurricanes were armed with eight, rather than four, machine guns which made all the difference when trying to shoot down a German bomber or an ME109. For some reason, Ralph donated a Headmaster's mortar board hat to the school, which was then, and is now, known by the forties' slang term 'titfer'. The first boss of the school was Wing Commander Sammy Wroath and he was known as the 'headmaster'. After successful completion of the first ever course in 1944 he handed on the baton to Group Captain J.F.A McKenna AFC and the training flight became formally the Empire Test Pilots' School with the word 'empire' allowing the school to be opened up to a more global student intake. Sadly, during the second course, Sam McKenna was killed when test flying a Mustang Mk IV during a high speed dive test point. As a result of this tragic accident a trophy was donated in his honour and awarded each year, at the end-of-course

McKenna Dinner, to the best student. In 1963 the first rotary wing course was run and Westland Helicopters provided an additional trophy that would be awarded to the best RW student and the McKenna trophy then became the FW only prize.

The Mckenna Dinner finally arrived. It was to be a fitting end to an absolutely life changing twelve months. We students felt like we had not slept properly for a year but continued to 'power through' on a mixture of alcohol and adrenalin. Of course, we started the evening with a student gathering for a few sharpeners – now known as the 'pre-lash'. Pre-dinner sherry was gulped, as if by drowning men. I have no idea what we ate because, frankly, we didn't much care. The dinner differed from our graduation dinner in a number of areas. Firstly our wives were not

The McKenna Dinner 1994. *(MOD)*

invited, secondly the rest of the establishment was, so my future boss and colleagues were there. Additionally, it served a dual purpose: in addition to the prize-giving it was utilised to thank people from industry that helped achieve the TP/FTE training. So representatives from Rolls Royce, GEC, Ferranti and the other test pilot schools were present. The top table was heaving with lots of 'grown ups': the other school commanding officers, our own Commandant and Chief Test Pilot and Chief Scientist, and the military attaches for all the embassies that represented all the various nationalities of my course mates. We students could not have been happier to be there. We had a humorous grace, three courses accompanied by some splendid wine, before a series of toasts with port, including the Royal toast. In a wardroom I would have remained seated but it appeared to be the accepted norm for the senior service to go with the flow and stand alongside everyone else. After a quick pee break, Bob, our boss, donned the aforementioned titfer and explained that this had been donated by Ralph Sorley for this very purpose. Bob's speech concluded with the prizegiving. There was the Dunlop trophy for best FTE, and Hawker Hunter trophy for best fixed wing 'pair of hands' – I'm not sure why rotes were not eligible for this particular prize. Then came the Edwards trophy for best FW preview and now, finally, the Patuxent Shield for the best RW preview. I eased forward into my seat to ensure I didn't miss what was being said … and the trophy is awarded to … the Bell AH-1W Cobra team.

Crispin and Peter had undoubtedly done an excellent job – so I applauded, just as losers do at award ceremonies – loudly and enthusiastically. Time for another glass of port. I wasn't listening when the boss went on to tee up the award of the Westland trophy. Something was said and Colin Hague, Westland Helicopter's Chief Test Pilot, arose to his feet and looked at me. In fact all my mates were looking at me. What had the boss said? The mist cleared as I recollected something about hearing my name. No time to lose, I thought, and leapt to my feet to boldly stride towards where Colin was standing with an outstretched hand. Colin was definitely a hero of mine. A fellow RN Wasp pilot, he had graduated from ETPS in 1972 and ended up as Westland's CTP in 1988. He had been a key player in the development of the Lynx and more recently the Merlin. My hand was warmly shaken and with due regard for the photographer hovering to one side, I grabbed firm hold of the trophy which was not dissimilar to a football cup.

Acquired as new build aircraft in 1978, the Westland Gazelle HT.3 was the core teaching vehicle for the rotary wing course. During my time as a student XZ936 had a straight, rather than 'cranked', pitot boom. *(Chris Lofting)*

XZ939 was a sister aircraft of XZ936. During my own course we flew both XZ936 and XZ939. *(Chris Lofting)*

Gazelle ZB625 was acquired by MOD Boscombe Down from RAF Shawbury (No2 Flying Training School) still in its RAF colour scheme as an additional resource and first flown by me for ETPS training in March 1998. Initially the aircraft was flown without instrumentation but by 2002 was instrumented and took a full part in the teaching programme. *(Tony Osborne)*

Acquired as a new build aircraft in 1987 as a Lynx AH.5X ZD560 was the mainstay of the twin-engine training fleet during my time as a student and as a member of staff. It was upgraded to an AH.7 and ultimately was fitted with the reverse direction tail rotor and composite rotor blades with BERP tips. The Lynx were troublesome at ETPS as it was an operational aircraft and ETPS was bottom of the priority list for spare parts. *(Tony Osborne)*

Lynx ZD559 first flew in 1985 and was operated by RAE Bedford until moving to Boscombe Down as part of EFS in 1994. I flew the aircraft for a number of trials including when fitted with the 'balsa-wood rotor blade'. After the demise of EFS the aircraft became part of the common user fleet and I then flew the aircraft extensively on ETPS alongside ZD560. *(Tony Osborne)*

Lynx ZD285 first flew in 1984 and was allocated to RAE Farnborough and then transferred to Boscombe Down in 1994. I flew it for a number of trials including the field of view trial. It was extensively modified inside and out and sadly no longer flew after the demise of the DRA tasking in 1996. *(Michael Fisher)*

ETPS did not have a dedicated Sea King during my time as a student or a member of staff. Its own aircraft had been destroyed in an accident in 1993. We used ZB506 extensively. *(Tony Osborne)*

ZB506 was a 4.X aircraft fitted for the provision of a radome on the rear fuselage. In 1994–5 it carried the Blue Kestrel Radar which I flew a few times and later had a modified nose to allow various sensor turrets to be fitted. *(Adrian Balch)*

As with ZB506 I flew this aircraft for various trials during my time on EFS but when the DRA tasking dried up the aircraft was converted to a more standard Mk 4, painted green and flown as a regular Junglie aircraft. *(Adrian Balch)*

This is me flying XS509 in April 1995 following a period of maintenance. I flew XS509 extensively in 1995 and 1996. The aircraft was cleared to routinely fly touch-down engine-off landings and was the largest aircraft cleared for this in the UK. *(Chris Lofting)*

My Wessex photographed in 1992 before the tailcone was replaced. *(Don Gilham)*

This is me flying XR503. Sadly, she was fitted with a replacement tailcone in a standard Junglie green colour. For the whole two years I operated XR503, the tailcone was never repainted in the correct colours. *(Mike Freer)*

This Scout SP849 was operated by ETPS for many years and was flown by me as a student and member of staff on ETPS – right up to when I crashed it in April 1997. *(Adrian Balch)*

As you will have read, acquiring this aircraft was my initiative. It was a second-hand aircraft on a lease. Originally G-NEXT it was placed on the military register ZJ635 in 1999. *(Alan Cordina)*

I test flew a couple of Sea King 3As during my time on RWTS including ZH542. *(Gary Beale)*

On RWTS I tested a couple of Pumas including XW233. *(Gary Lakin)*

During my time as a tutor on ETPS I engaged with FAST Helicopters of Thruxton and flew G-BXKL extensively in support of ETPS flight test courses. *(Robin A Walker)*

The Basset XS743 was one of an original batch of aircraft operated by ETPS which was converted by Cranfield to have a Variable Stability System fitted which made it an ideal airborne classroom to teach handling qualities. I flew this as a student but then flew it extensively as a tutor for seven years. The aircraft is now part of the Boscombe Down Aviation Collection at Old Sarum *(Jason Grant)*

One of a batch of ETPS aircraft that was converted by Cranfield to have a variable stability system fitted. Unusually the ASTRA Hawk was flown solo from the rear cockpit as the front seat occupant could only fly the aircraft through the VSS system. It was in this aircraft that I suffered my first Mayday following engine flame-out over Devon. *(Michael Fisher)*

I flew this ETPS Jaguar XX145 with John who had been the Chief Test Pilot during my first year on EFS. *(Chris Lofting)*

I flew this ETPS Jaguar ZB615 with Laurie, the then CO of ETPS in my first year as a tutor on the staff. *(Chris Lofting)*

I flew this Jaguar XX835 with Trevor during my time on EFS and couldn't find the oxygen switch. *(Scott Rathbone)*

This was one of the RAE Hunters transferred to Boscombe Down and was used for numerous trials. I flew WV383, with Jon, the CO of EFS just before the squadron folded. *(FAST)*

I flew a number of sorties on EFS using Andover XS646 for various sensor trials. *(Scott Rathbone)*

Andover XS606 was built in 1966 and allocated to ETPS and was used by the school until 2012. I flew the aircraft a number of times as co-pilot when we used the aircraft for various visits if the BAC1-11 was unavailable. It was sold to an African operator in 2013 and was sadly destroyed in a crash in 2015. *(Scott Rathbone)*

My flying of XS606 was usually at high level when using the aircraft to get to and from various 'visits'. *(Tony Woof)*

HS-748 XW750 flown on a trial with Trevor. *(Adrian Balch)*

The ETPS BAC 1-11 was used primarily for training the fixed wing test pilots to operate big commercial aircraft but additionally was the primary method of transport to get students and staff around Europe for various visits. I was formally qualified on the aircraft as a co-pilot and enjoyed pretending to be a proper airline pilot. *(Chris Lofting)*

XS235 Comet 4C - the very last surviving airworthy Comet at the time – flown with course mate Mark. *(Adrian Balch)*

The Tucanos were acquired just before my time as a student and equipped ETPS to take over from the Hunter for the spinning exercise. I flew ZF511 as a student with Brian and again in March 1997 with Dave. I found the seating position to be quite uncomfortable. *(Paul Massey)*

The AlphaJets were purchased from the German Airforce by QinetiQ to support ETPS training as hours on the Hawks became more difficult to achieve. I flew ZJ645 in 2003 with our USN exchange pilot. *(John Allen)*

I flew the VAAC Harrier in July 1999 with Tom while on the staff of ETPS. It was without doubt one of the most exciting flights of my time at Boscombe Down. The aircraft was originally based at Bedford and flown by my EFS colleague Dan for a while. It was used to develop the control laws for the F35 Lightning jet. *(Jason Grant)*

Bloody Hell! I had won the Westland Trophy! I was the best RW student of 1994. Wow!

I returned to my seat in stunned euphoria, with the cup placed safely in front of me. Seconds later the winner of the McKenna trophy was announced as Trevor, my mate and senior fixed wing student.

Good result!

We could not yet adjourn to the bar as we had to listen to a formal, and completely forgettable, speech by our guest of honour, who none of us can remember! With that accomplished it was time for more drinking. Before I had chance to make the bar Colin Hague reappeared with a bottle of champagne. What I hadn't realised (and why would I?) was that the company bought the winner a bottle of fizz which was then drunk from the cup. Tradition had it that I passed it around to previous winners thereafter, including one of our tutors, Eric, who had won the trophy himself a few years earlier. Eric went on to explain some less well known historical detail. When he won the trophy he ended up on the top of a human pyramid holding the cup aloft. The pyramid collapsed and a dozen heavy blokes landed on top of a relatively soft trophy.

Blige!

Eric had the good sense to get the cup to a jewellers the following morning. The shape of the cup was fully restored but in the process all the engraved names on the cup were suddenly a good deal harder to read. Who would have known? In fact I was able to attend nearly all of the following McKenna dinners, one way or another, for nearly twenty years and took great pride in taking my entitled swig of the fizz and sharing this story with the new winner. (I was able to attend the dinner again a couple of years ago as part of a twenty-five years' reunion of my course. I was really looking forward to finding out who would be the recipient, only to discover the school had for some unknown reason stopped awarding this prize.) When eventually we were all partied out, and all but a handful of us remained, it was time to stroll home. I slept for barely minutes before both my children were on our bed demanding to know what this huge silver trophy was for. I was delighted to tell them.

What a great ending to this particular year. The dinner was, as usual, held on a Thursday and the following day we commenced a family tradition which was to last two decades. We went into town, complete with my throbbing head, to buy the best Christmas tree I could focus

Author receiving the Westland Trophy from Colin Hague. *(MOD)*

on. And that was before I had to sow all the sequins on my daughter's red robin costume for the dance performance she had to take part in that evening. No rest for the wicked.

I had passed the course. I was a test pilot – an experimental test pilot. I was as chuffed as anybody could be about anything. But actually, the real task of learning how to do flight testing had only just begun.

Chapter 6

Wessex

Author flying Wessex XR503 at Boscombe Down. *(MOD)*

'We're on fire!' I shout down to the boffins hoping they would grab the fire extinguisher but the reply I got was surprising.

'No, we're not …'

'I can smell burning,'

'That's just us.'

'What the hell are you talking about?'

I simply loved the Wessex! I'm often asked what my favourite aeroplane or helicopter is and I always find it a very difficult question to answer. There is no one aircraft that is perfect, it depends on what the task or role is. Of course, all military pilots will always have a soft spot for their first operational type. Towards the end of our flying training on 705 NAS at RNAS Culdrose we were made aware of the various 'slots' that were available for our course. I had been in love with the Wasp, and the concept of flying a single pilot aircraft off the back of small ships, for some years. I was delighted to learn there was a single Wasp place which turned out to be one of the very last direct entry opportunities for this aircraft as its days in operational service were already numbered. So on my wish list I put WASP HAS MK1 in large letters – but there was also a Wessex V slot available. When I was just 16 I was a member of my school Combined Cadet Force (CCF) and I had been selected to attend a junior leadership course based near Thetford, Norfolk. The course taught me nothing about leadership but did convince me that yomping around the countryside carrying a GPMG (machine gun) with ammunition was far too knackering a way to spend several days and I had deleted 'Infantry Officer' off my career options. But, after a few days, we had slogged several 'clicks' to RV with some support helicopters, namely Wessex HC.2s. While waiting in our 'sticks', to be transported on to the next exercise location, I was accosted by a young Flight Lieutenant:

'Are you from Bury Grammar School?'
(What had I done wrong? I wondered.) 'Yes, indeed!' I responded nervously awaiting the inevitable bollocking.
'Well, that's my old school.' He says and we immediately struck up a lively conversation about my desire to be a helicopter pilot.

Clearly he felt it was his duty to convince me to join the 'light blue' rather the 'dark blue'; he reallocated me to his 'personal' Wessex, and after a word with the aircrewman/loadmaster I found myself seated in the doorway as we flashed up the first, then second engine. Moments later we were airborne. I say airborne, despite the fact that I don't think we ever got above 50ft for the entire flight. We flashed between trees, along dirt tracks and hedges, we turned, when we had to, using 60 degrees angle of bank as a minimum and, when it was finally time to land, the aircraft was flared from 100 KIAS to stationary in a heartbeat.

'Bloody Hell! That was awesome,' I shouted to the loadmaster as I was sadly returned to my earthbound role of GPMG operator. But the seed had been sown and I had a real hankering to, one day, emulate this fellow student from BGS and fly a Wessex myself.

By the time I was filling in my 'wish list', this was a type close to retirement from the RN with only a handful of further chances to fly it. I confess I was slightly torn, but I knew that only the best pilot on the course would be offered the Wasp slot due its uncompromising challenges and its remote operating environment. So I put Wessex down as second choice and awaited the outcome of our 'scores on the doors' so to speak. I was both delighted and disappointed that I was chosen for the single Wasp place. I thought this inevitably would mean I wouldn't get to fly the Wessex and I was right. It was retired from the RN in 1988 and there were no new Wessex pilots trained after 1985, when I was still busy flying the Wasp.

Bugger!

But I was about to get a second chance. One of the main duties of the 'Bedford' rotary wing test pilot was to fly Wessex HC.2 XR 503. This Wessex was built in 1963 and taken on charge by RAE Bedford in 1982. It had been highly modified to undertake and support a number of research and development trials and activities. The left-hand instrument panel had been mostly removed to make way for a very novel first generation glass cockpit. Equipment racks and wiring had been added to allow various experimental flight control systems to be fitted and, despite its age, it was used to conduct cutting-edge, state-of-the-art technology research. I was to be her final project pilot, which was a great responsibility but also an amazing challenge.

The training received at ETPS was seen to be of a suitable standard to qualify a pilot on type. So I arrived at Experimental Flying Squadron (EFS) on 3 January 1995, qualified and current on the Gazelle, Scout, Lynx and Sea King, but sadly not the Wessex. My new Flight Commander, Charles, had already given this some thought and had arranged for me to go to RAF Shawbury just a few days later. I reported forthwith on Monday 30 January to 2 (Advanced) Flying Training School who were using the Wessex HC.2 to train RAF pilots how to fly and operate multi-engine helicopters immediately after award of their 'wings' on the Gazelle. As always, I had spent the previous night rereading and swotting up the Wessex notes I'd already borrowed, and my session in the fixed base simulator first thing went well enough such that I was programmed to fly my first sortie in the afternoon. I confess, I walked out for my first proper flight as a Wessex pilot with a sense of excitement. I was about to tick off another item on my 'bucket list'.

The aircraft (XR521) looked splendid in the sunshine of a late January afternoon, adorned with a scarlet red nose and band around the tail on top of its standard RAF camouflage. The Wessex was derived from an American

Sikorsky H34 or S58 aircraft. The type, powered by a rotary piston engine, had seen extensive service with the French in Algeria and with the US Marine Corps in the Vietnam War. Westland Helicopters bought the rights to manufacture the type but promptly fitted it with a Napier Gazelle turboshaft engine and christened it the Wessex HAS1. The aircraft was developed into a better anti-submarine aircraft as the Wessex HAS3 and it was, in this single-engine variant known as 'Humphrey', that a previous boss of mine (Ian) had rescued numerous hypothermic SAS troopers off South Georgia early in the Falklands war. The single engine didn't quite have enough power to make use of the potential for the aircraft so two Gnome engines were squeezed under the bonnet and fed the original drive shaft via a coupling gearbox. This variant was the Wessex HU Mk.5 in naval service, or the HC. Mk.2 in the RAF. The two versions were very similar, the main external difference being larger windows in the cabin of the naval version to assist with emergency egress. Because of its heritage, the pilot sat high in the aircraft above the engines which drove the gearbox via a drive shaft running between the two pilots' seats. I clambered up the side of the aircraft cautiously. Compared to the Wasp and the Lynx that I was more used to, this was a very different cockpit environment. But, now a test pilot, I started to concentrate initially on what was similar to other helicopters. There was Westland's heritage plainly on view with a dash of Sea King and Wasp evident. Starting was relatively easy:

> Battery ON
> Booster pump ON
> Port Computer (like a Sea King) ON
> Starter (selected) ON
> Speed select AFT
> Starter pressed.

And, with the compressor rpm rising, the HP cock was opened and, whoosh, the Gnome burst into life. The second engine was started just as the first, with the rotor brake able to hold the rotors as per my Wasp and the Sea King, so the flight control system and hydraulics could be checked. For some reason the FCS was known as Automatic Stability Equipment (ASE) and gave some basic damping to make flying easier, but also provided a rudimentary heading and height hold. With the ASE checked, rotor brake released, I advanced the starboard speed select to 1000lbs ft torque and the rotors steadily accelerated to a nominal speed of 233 rpm – a good deal slower than the rotor speeds of other helicopters I had operated. With MAIN drive selected I advanced the left-hand engine to match the right and before I knew it I was completing my pre take-off checks, which were very similar to every other set of helicopter checks I'd come across. With radio calls made, chocks removed, I taxied forwards to clear the dispersal before finding my spot to depart from. The Wessex had a massive collective lever with a beautiful wooden handle at the end. With trepidation and adrenalin in equal measure I raised the collective and lifted 13,600lbs of war machine into a 10ft hover.

Wow! I was flying a Wessex.

By close of play Tuesday I had amazed my instructor and had completed the entire conversion syllabus in just three sorties which is just as well (as you will read about later) as I had to dash down to London, via home, that evening for a critical meeting on Wednesday regarding my future as a TP. Having had little sleep I was back at Shawbury on Thursday morning and I distinctly remember a difficult conversation in the office of the 2FTS Commanding Officer. I had asked for my logbook to be signed to indicate I was indeed genuinely qualified on the aircraft, and so I would have some form of evidence to show my colleagues. My instructor was a nice chap but definitely more used to ab initio students rather than qualified TPs. Most of his students would have been flying the aircraft for several weeks before this topic of 'qualification' was even considered.

'So,' says the Boss, 'are we happy to sign off Chris as qualified on type?'

'But he doesn't yet know his checks!' states my instructor, which of course was normally a requisite for his conventional students.

In fairness, I had planned to learn them during my homework evenings, but the need to dash to London had put an end to that. Thankfully I outranked him by a considerable margin and was of the same seniority as the Boss. I explained that at Boscombe Down we were actually forbidden from trying to conduct checks from memory and we were required to use flight reference cards (FRCs) or printed checklists. With this statement duly noted on my docs I was deemed fully qualified and offered a further three flights on the aircraft 'solo' in order to consolidate the training I'd done and fill up the remainder of the week that was felt to be the minimum period required by the RAF to instil within me their Wessex operating doctrine before letting me depart south for Wiltshire on Friday. I have to say, those extra three flights were a real bonus. I was now qualified and could relax and enjoy the aircraft and by the second such flight decided to demonstrate my helicopter air-display routine to my instructor since I was now the aircraft captain. He hadn't flown wing-overs or torque turns before and was suitably shaken and stirred on completion.

Another couple of weeks would pass before I was finally invited to fly XR503. I was excited. At last I could get on with what I was being paid to do. It was the first in a series of trials looking at using GPS as a source of guidance. What is absolutely routine now, as I write this chapter, was novel and radical back then. After a comprehensive briefing with all the boffins I walked downstairs from my office. The helicopters of Rotary Wing Test Squadron (RWTS) had for many years been located on the south side of the airfield and the squadron enjoyed its own dedicated hangar and dispersal. When the aircraft of EFS had been moved to Boscombe a few weeks earlier, it had been decided that we three helicopter pilots of 'B Flight' would be accommodated in the same office block as RWTS, and our helicopters would live in the same hangar. 'A Flight' and our aeroplanes were all accommodated on the airfield's north side. This inevitably made life difficult for numerous administrative matters – but I digress. I made my way downstairs to the engineer's office in order to have a thorough read of the MOD Form 700. This was the military equivalent of a Technical Log and held all the relevant aircraft information. In particular, the first few pages were red and included any defects or limitations that the aircraft had. These were followed by green pages which included 'Acceptable Deferred Defects'. It was not unusual for there to be a good handful of the latter. But there were remarkably few entries and nothing to note in the red pages at all. Great! In good time I strolled across the dispersal, in a similar fashion to, as a teenager, walking to my very first car which I'd inherited from my grandfather. The sun was high in the sky and glinting off the red, white and blue colour scheme (although the olive drab tail, which had been added recently, was still awaiting paint in the correct colour scheme). Following my professional external walk-round to check for anything untoward, I climbed up the starboard steps to clamber in through the right-hand window. All of this I accomplished with the dexterity of someone who had been flying the Wessex for years and as I slung myself into the seat I commenced a rapid scan of what was about to be my home/office for a good deal of the next two years.

'Holy Moses!' I remarked to no one in particular.

'What are all these holes in the inter-seat console?'

'Where is the ASE?'

Where the black boxes with associated switches, knobs and warning lights should have been there was nothing apart from some loose wiring.

'What the hell?'

So, back out of the starboard window, down the steps and now a brisk walk back to the engineering office.

'I've just been in 503,' I state. 'What's going on?'

'What do you mean?'

'Where is the ASE – the autopilot?'

'What autopilot?'

'Well – the usual autopilot that should be fitted to every Wessex HC.2.'

'It hasn't got one.'

'Why not?'

'It's out being repaired.'

'How am I supposed to know that? There is no mention of this crucial defect in the MF700.'

'Did you look at the local RAE Bedford form at the back?'

'What's one of those?'

'Bedford have their own way of doing paperwork and because this aircraft is constantly being modified, and the fit changed, then the various configurations are just listed on a single form at the back of the folder.'

'Now I find out! – So what works and what doesn't?'

'Well nothing works. You have no autopilot so you'll have to fly the aircraft without it.'

'Bloody hell!' The ASE provided damping and other functions that made the aircraft easier to fly. I was now faced with flying, at least my first few sorties, with none of the assistance that all Wessex pilots would expect unless they had suffered from an inflight malfunction. Thankfully, I had practised this mode of flying at Shawbury and I knew I could cope okay. So another long stroll back across dispersal to be met by my load of boffins. They already knew all about the ASE – it had just not crossed their minds to mention it.

Great! A good start to my new life as 503 Project Pilot.

The main research work that 503 was used for, during my tenure, was to continue working towards an auto-land system for helicopters to recover to frigates and destroyer-sized ships. I don't think it's much of a spoiler to say that over twenty-five years later this is still an ambition rather than a reality, although the technology has assisted with the recovery of drones. So my flying of the Wessex had various phases, when one aspect or another of the overall system was being developed and trialled. The critical component was a highly advanced automatic flight control system that would be able to fly the aircraft with sufficient fidelity and aggressiveness to ultimately land on the back of a moving ship in all weathers and sea states.

The flight control systems being researched were mounted in equipment racks in the rear of the aircraft that couldn't be seen from the cockpit and were usually manned by two or three boffins who would be monitoring their performance and recording data for subsequent analysis. It is fair to say I was always on a steep learning curve on these sorties as a baby-faced newly qualified TP. On one of the very first such sorties I was flying along with my hands off the controls as this experimental flight control system flew me along, closely following the contours of the ground.

'Does the system prevent over-torque?' I ask innocently as the aircraft is constantly being invited to climb and descend, needing varying amounts of power. If too much power was demanded the gearbox would be damaged.

'Oh yes, the system prevents over-torque.' I was assured.

Only moments later, as we approached rising ground the collective lever started steadily rising with more and more torque being demanded. As the torque gauge approached the red line of 3,200 lbs-foot. I instantly intervened by physically forcing the collective to stop rising …

'Shit! What's going on? You said the system would prevent over-torque,' I yell to the boffins.

'Yep, it worked,' they say.

'No it bloody didn't.'

'Yes, it did. The pilot is part of the system. It's your job to intervene to prevent limits being exceeded – and you just did.'

'Now you tell me!' It would have been nice to have been told about this as part of my lengthy before flight briefing. Shortly thereafter we were again flying along, testing the experimental FCS. All was going well I thought.

'Chris, is it OK if we change the FCS control laws now?'

In my innocence I had expected a switch or two to be flicked or reset. Moments later there was a very strong and intrusive smell of burning in the aircraft.

'We're on fire!' I shout down to the boffins hoping they would grab the fire extinguisher, but the reply I got was surprising.

'No, we're not …'

'I can smell burning.'

'That's just us.'

'What the hell are you talking about?'

'We are just soldering-in the new black box.'

'Holy Moses!' Yet again I had been caught out by an apparently conventional Bedford practice that, by any other set of airworthiness standards, would have been deemed bonkers. Still, once the new black box was in place we completed yet another successful sortie.

Experimental Flying Squadron was an amazing working environment. We had a relatively small number of test pilots and a lot of flying to do. Very often we needed both an aircraft captain who needed to be qualified on the type, but in addition, we would need an evaluation pilot to fly in the other seat. This was a huge amount of fun and a really broadening experience. During my two years at EFS I managed to fly in the Hunter, Jaguar, Hawk, Andover, HS748, Comet and Harvard. Equally, my evaluation pilots were my fast jet or transport pilot mates. The squadron boss was a fast jet pilot but, as was the RAF way, he had been qualified on the Gazelle in order to be able to supervise RW operations. I took him flying in a Gazelle when I had the chance but had to keep a close eye on him, especially if we decided to fly an engine-off landing. Thank goodness I was already an experienced instructor. Anyway, early on in my time in the squadron I asked the Boss to join me in 503 for an evaluation on a Friday afternoon. I have come to learn that flying on Friday afternoons, or the last day of term, seems to throw up more challenges than any other days. This was one of those days.

After a successful flight, where my boss had enjoyed flying from the left-hand seat, we landed on RWTS dispersal just before 4 pm, which was when the airfield was due to close. I applied the wheel brakes, ensured the flight control system was off and started the shutdown:

Pitot heater –OFF
Rad-Alt – OFF

Author flying Wessex XR503 at Boscombe Down. *(MOD)*

    Radios/Avionics – OFF
    Booster pumps OFF
    AC Power OFF
    Anti-Icing OFF
    Speed Select Levers – 'Ground Idling'

I was now monitoring the rotor rpm gauge closely as the rotors slowed. Like the Sea King, the Wessex had centrifugally operated flapping restrictors, which limited the movement of the blades at slow speed to minimise blade sail. These effectively provided droop stops which the blades would rest on, as their centrifugal force of rotation ebbed away. The Lynx didn't have droop stops but the Wasp did, which were chunks of metal. Many of my fellow Wasp pilots came unstuck when landing in high sea states. If the cyclic was pushed forward just as the deck was tipping the aircraft backwards, then the rotors would hit the droop stops with such force that they would be physically knocked off. This was a known problem and my ground crew were always listening for the distinct sound of four of these bits of metal flying off in all directions. If this happened, and the engine was shut down, the blades would drop as they slowed and strike the tail boom. A very similar occurrence to my Scout accident which I talk about later in the book. The only way to prevent further damage to the Wasp was to fill the fuel up, via a rotors-running refuel, and then a ramp of mattresses was built over the tail boom to catch the drooping rotor blades as they stopped. This took some time and left the pilot having to shut down knowing that bad things might happen. I sat in the Wessex as the blades slowed to:

130 … 120 … 115 … 110 rpm

These centrifugal droop stops should engage by 110 rpm and my eyes were glued to my marshaller who I expected to raise both hands with his thumbs inwards indicating the droop stops were engaged and I could then close both HP cocks – but it was a Friday afternoon and I was flying with my boss …

And sure enough I did not get the thumbs-in indication I needed.

'Bugger!'

I had no idea what the implications of this snag were. I immediately invited my boffins to leave the aircraft, while they could do so safely, and I got on the blower to RWTS Ops. We had a private radio channel so I could call them directly and I asked to speak to anyone with Wessex experience. It was now nearly 4.30 pm and I could hear the tumbleweeds blowing against a backdrop of stony silence …

'Double Bugger!'

So I explained the situation to my illustrious co-pilot and given that he was my boss, thought I'd do the decent thing. I invited him to leave and walk to a safe distance, which he did. I then stop-cocked the engines and allowed the blades to slow as much as I dared before immediately applying the rotor brake to try and stop the blades as rapidly as possible.

Phew! The blades stopped. Nothing had been struck. Aircraft and pride intact I breathed an enormous sigh of relief and clambered out. Time to head home for a large beer.

Many months later I was at a drinks do when I overheard my boss narrating his version of events. Apparently I was 'risk averse'. He meant it as a negative attribute I'm sure, but it has stood me in good stead for nearly three decades of test flying to date, so I'm not complaining. In October I flew my last flight with this boss. This time the tables were turned and I was flying in his highly modified (RAE Farnborough) Hunter WV383, which was used for research into experimental head up displays and night flying systems. We had a great flight and as the sortie concluded he invited me to fly a one-in-one forced landing pattern which was required should the engine flame out. In fairness most of the hard work was done by the radar controller who had to drive you around the sky when you were losing 1,000ft every mile. The challenge for the pilot was that the engine powered the boost to the flying controls, so this exercise simulated this by me having the system turned OFF to force me to fly unaided. The controls were indeed heavy, but not ridiculously so, and I was able to line up nicely with Runway 23 and float gracefully onto the tarmac.

Phew! Risk Averse maybe – but not such a bad pilot by all accounts.

Less than two weeks later, Experimental Flying Squadron ceased to be. Very sadly, it appears the funding for a dedicated research and

The RAE/DRA Farnborough Hawker Hunter WV383 Cockpit. *(FAST)*

development squadron was insufficient and three new squadrons were to be formed each taking on some aspects of the EFS portfolio. So Fast Jet Test Squadron and Heavy Aircraft Test Squadron came into being, and B Flight EFS was merged into RWTS … although for accounting purposes and a whole bunch of other reasons, the R&D experimental test pilots continued to be dedicated to the R&D task and we remained mostly autonomous of our new parent squadron, but it did now mean I could be asked to fly any of the other RWTS trials that came along. And it meant my chain of command had changed which was to have consequences a few months later.

Apart from testing various flight control systems the aircraft was also used as a test bed for various approach aids. These used a variety of sensors in combination but were blazing a trail of using GPS and subsequently differential GPS systems. Very ahead of the times, the team had come up with a pretty reliable system that could drive the aircraft towards a fixed point on the ground. The next challenge was to do this to a moving target which ultimately would be a ship. Ships are complex, expensive to operate and are committed to numerous operational commitments at sea. What we needed was an interim platform to progress development of various concepts. Of all the various options, the boffins elected to acquire a clapped-out ex-Civil Defence van. Sure enough, it was big enough to mount all the required racks of equipment in the back, and sure enough, its flat sides and roof made it easy to mount various antenna – but it was a knackered old van. After much planning and briefing the day finally arrived when we would use this asset in anger. We had closed down Boscombe Down so that we could have exclusive use of the airfield for a couple of hours. Additional gear had been installed in 503 and after an extremely comprehensive briefing we staggered airborne at our maximum allowed weight with the intent of positioning on long final for Runway 23 (the main south-westerly runway). We had exclusive use of the airfield and I was chatting directly to the 'bread van'.

'Bedford Mobile – This is Gauntlet 70. We are one mile final – commence Run 1.'

'We can't!'

'Say again.'

'We can't.'

'This is Gauntlet 70 – half mile final – *Commence Run 1.*'

'This is Bedford Mobile – the van clutch has packed up – we can't move.'

The whole point of this very expensive trial was to build on all the work we had successfully achieved to date, where we had demonstrated being able to successfully recover to a stationary target. We now needed to see if the same technology could be used to find a moving target – for example a warship. Our test plan required the 'bread van' to move at increasing speeds along the two mile long runway from 2 mph to 35 mph.

'Bugger!' We had a serviceable aircraft airborne full of boffins, we had a dedicated airfield with a two mile runway for the next two hours, we had acceptable weather and had spent several hours briefing and many weeks preparing.

'Double Bugger!'

I don't know why it fell to me to sort this out, as I was busy flying a Wessex around in circles – but somehow it did. Apparently I have a 'red personality', which is task-orientated – and it definitely was on this occasion.

'Slam it into second.'

'Say again?'

'The van clutch and gearbox can be fixed tomorrow – we can't reschedule this trial for months – just do it!'

And so I observed a very tired 'bread van' leap forward, with rubber from the rear wheels scarring the taxiway, BUT – we now had a moving 'bread van' with a top speed of 38 mph – Hurrah! In fact, the next two hours proved to be a great success and the kit worked as advertised. Thank goodness Vauxhall had built strong gearboxes.

So we had a system that could get the aircraft back to the ship, even if the ship was flat out at over 30 knots. What was needed next was a system that could then drive the aircraft over the flight deck from a position adjacent to the ship. I'm not quite sure of the technology – I just flew the airplane – but I think some form of infra-red tracker was used. If the system knew exactly the diameter of my rotor blades it could work out where the helicopter was. As an interim step this guidance was projected onto a cross-like display of lights. The lights indicated how close to the landing spot I was. The project had this cruciform display mounted on a metal tower on the south side of the airfield. I was to spend many happy hours in 503 hovering in front of this tower in all weathers. It turns out it worked rather well. I could easily be guided to land exactly where I was supposed to.

The next challenge was to see if all this kit worked on a ship – underway at sea.

Trying to get hold of pussers' warships for trials at sea was problematic. They tended to be rather busy exercising with NATO allies and fending off the Russians from time to time. However, an opportunity had been identified, and I can't quite recollect which bit of the jigsaw puzzle fell into place first. RFA *Fort Victoria* had only recently been built and commissioned as a combined fleet tanker and supply ship. She had been subject to a deck trial in order to clear her flight deck for Sea King operations. The outcome of this trial was that one of her landing spots suffered from excessive turbulence and downwards flowing air from the surrounding superstructure. So another trial was needed once the position

Author landing Wessex XR503 on RFA *Fort Victoria*. *(DRA Bedford)*

of the spot was changed. A cunning plan was concocted where I would lead a detachment consisting of me and a whole bunch of boffins and 503. Meanwhile RWTS would embark with Sea King HAS.6 XZ576 in order to clear the new spot for Sea King operations.

The Sea King needed two crews, hence four pilots, and I sometimes needed a co-pilot. Someone with more clout than me decided we could pool resources and I would be both a Sea King and Wessex pilot for the detachment, and one of the Sea King crew would ride shotgun with me if required. In some ways this was a golden moment in my military flight testing. We had all the RN TPs from Boscombe and were not diluted by our khaki or light blue brethren. The down side was that the RWTS Senior Pilot, who was the same rank as me, had documented himself as the 'Detachment Commander'. When this was proposed I politely deferred – I had no axe to grind. However, once on 'the boat', even though we were always just a few minutes' flying time away from a dedicated Coast Guard SAR Sikorsky S61N, he declared that we could provide twenty-four hours search and rescue capability. I had limited experience of such operations and zero experience of flying the Sea King for SAR. Despite my reluctance I found myself on a duty roster and denied my usual after-flight drink from time to time. In my experience, then and now, after dicing with death doing flight test, the best way for me to calm the nerves is with a beer or a glass of vino. Being denied this release mechanism was counter-productive. His name has also been added to the list started in France by Andy who had denied us vino with our French colleagues.

My trial went very well. The sea was almost as still as a millpond and the daytime weather gorgeous. We flew through the weekend and on a beautiful Sunday afternoon I was returning to the ship and asked my boffins if they would like me to show them my air-display routine. There was a unanimous 'Yes' vote as I applied 3,200lbs torque and accelerated to 120 KIAS. I centred my display on the flight deck and was aware of an audience of those in Flyco and my ground crew. Wingovers, torque turns, quick stops and my infamous nose-down bunt – all were stitched seamlessly together as I finally hit the brakes to land on.

'That was simply awesome,' says the bloke in Flyco. 'Would it be OK to put out a pipe and get all the ship's company to watch another one? – it is a Sunday.'

Author landing Wessex XR503 on RFA *Fort Victoria*. Taken from the Sea King. *(DRA Bedford)*

I took a quick review of my potential career-limiting prospects for carrying out a flying display without formal briefing and authorisation and quickly declined. But it was definitely one of my better displays to a ship to date.

One of the upsides of now being part of RWTS was that I was able to take part in the non R&D flight test activities and it was a really useful experience to be fully involved in the deck clearance testing – which is arguably a core skill for an RN TP.

With over twenty hours of Wessex flying and six hours of Sea King flying to the deck I was feeling suitably refreshed as a Fleet Air Arm pilot and it was time to head home. A very pleasant all-day flight via Prestwick (home of 819 NAS) and the RAF Shawbury (where I had completed my Wessex training) achieved the aim.

I arrived back at Boscombe to discover a couple of things. I was now the de facto RWTS expert on the Wessex. And second, Wessex HU Mk 5 XS509 had just reappeared from a long period in maintenance. The Wessex Mk.5 and the Wessex Mk.2 were very similar and I was instantly at home in the Wessex 5 conducting the required maintenance check flights.

Wessex XR503 with the DRA based scientists. *(DRA Bedford)*

Now I really was making up for the lost time of missing out on the Wessex immediately after 'wings'. My recent deck time and now my Wessex 5 qualification had ticked all the boxes. And one of the really nice things about XS509 was that it was allowed to do engine-off landings – yes indeed. It was the only twin-engine helicopter, that I was aware of, that was routinely allowed to conduct EOLs. And, as apparently I was the expert, I instantly set about building my experience before I could refresh the other RWTS pilots.

The Wessex had four quite large, relatively heavy, rotor blades and so was relatively well placed to achieve safe touch downs. In addition it had mainwheel oleos designed to be thumped onto moving decks at sea and the tail wheel could cope with being banged onto the ground as the aircraft was still rotating to the level attitude. The only really difficult aspect was that the secondary hydraulic system was driven not from the main gearbox, but from the coupling gearbox, which combined the drive of the two Gnome turbine engines. Since we were simulating a double engine failure it was only right and proper to fly the aircraft with the secondary hydraulics selected OFF. Without this system we also lost the ASE and any hydraulic boost to the tail rotor and all the control loads were higher, just what you needed when trying to finesse a gentle touch down. But the Wessex coped with such abuse admirably. Another bonus of flying the Wessex was that I was suddenly adopted into the RAF support helicopter clan. So in addition to testing the Wessex I was soon a Puma pilot, which included needing to be an NVG expert in order to sign off certification mods to the cockpit. In reality I think my invitation to this 'club' within RWTS was partially driven by needing others to do some of the night flying.

Following some more flying, to improve the cruciform landing indications, things were starting to reach a climax for both me, as an Experimental Test Pilot, and my worthy steed, XR503. Trial Avalon had been years in the planning and all I had done so far with the aircraft was leading up to this point. That was to take the Wessex to a Type 23 frigate operating in rough sea states and evaluate all of the various systems that we had been progressing to date. The idea was that we would detach to RNAS Culdrose and station our mother ship, HMS *Marlborough*, in the Atlantic and we could then ask her to motor into deeper sea to get rougher weather if required, or into the Western Approaches if we needed calmer weather. No such plan survives contact with the enemy – or in this case, the Met Man. The weather for our trial turned out to be dreadful. A massive storm had motored gently across the Atlantic and, only slightly less severe than a hurricane, it arrived almost as soon as we needed to start flying. In some ways this was a Godsend, as a large part of the trial requirement was to assess operating in rough weather and I had borrowed a Lynx HAS.3 (XZ234) for some aspects which I will write about in a later chapter. Day one, we were already experiencing sea state 3 maybe 4, which is starting to get bumpy. The normal maximum for operational Lynx ops was sea state 6. It was at this stage that the weakness of my pre-embarkation planning was worrying me. My predecessor Steve, who was now on exchange in the US, had managed to land 503 on sister ship HMS *Iron Duke* previously.

My thinking had gone along the lines:

> 'Anything he can do, I can do better!' However, he had operated in pretty calm seas. Anything I achieved this particular week would be more difficult.

Wessex XR503 on HMS *Iron Duke* 1994. *(DRA Bedford)*

I started by asking HMS *Marlborough* to make ground towards Portland – for two reasons. First, I had been based at Portland for ten years which would put the whole game on my home turf and, second, Portland Bill would potentially provide some protection from the stonking westerly winds – a good decision.

23 October 1996 dawned wet and windy, but with my load of boffins on-board I set off southbound to try and find 'Mother'. And find her I did, looking very impressive crashing through the surf, into wind, to accept me for my first landing. There was to be no incremental approach this time. This was no simulator where I could stop the ship from pitching, rolling, yawing and heaving. I was very grateful that, by then, I had clocked up nearly 2,500 deck landings on frigates of this size. To some extent, landing on a moving deck is more of an art than a science and, there is absolutely no doubt, it is a specific type of helicopter operation for which experience really counts. I confess, I was anxious. There was an awful lot riding on this trial and if I couldn't pull off landing my Wessex in a difficult sea state, my reputation would be in shreds.

Setting aside my nervousness, with my leather gloves hiding my sweaty palms, I approached the port quarter on the left-hand side of the ship. I had asked for a Red 15 wind. That is, I had asked the ship to steer a course that put the relative wind at 15 degrees on the port bow.

HMS *Marlborough* during Trial Avalon. *(DRA Bedford)*

Author hovering XR503 waiting to land on HMS *Marlborough*. *(DRA Bedford)*

My experience had taught me the benefits of this particular relative wind. It reduced the ship motion to some degree; it reduced the turbulence due to airflow over the superstructure as much as possible, and yet gave me a wind that I could fly into which reduced the power required to hover. It was the 'optimum' wind. I arrived alongside the flight deck. The ship was moving a fair bit, which was to be expected. The challenge now was to monitor the motion – I was relying on my experience to understand the movement of the ship/deck. It was crucial to actually land-on when the deck was as close to level as possible and, just as importantly, not heaving up to meet me or rolling to try and throw me off. This was not for the faint-hearted. Also crucial at this stage was to assess the amount of power I was using. At this point, I was in clean air of around 30 knots or so. This was reducing the amount of power the Wessex needed to hover, BUT I knew that as soon as I moved across the deck the airflow would be extremely turbulent and most likely down-drafting; both factors which could massively increase the amount of power required to stay aloft. The normal practice was to position myself relative to the 'bum line'. This was a white line which ran athwartships across the deck with the idea being that, if I hovered with my backside over this line, the aircraft would be positioned correctly fore and aft to be over the landing spot. All well and good for the Lynx or Merlin it was designed for BUT – not so fast, Quixote! The Wessex was a good deal bigger than the Lynx with larger rotor blades and, even more crucially, had the tail wheel at the back, towards the end of the tail. From the front of the rotor blades to the tail wheel I measured over 55ft. The length of the T23 flight deck was 70ft. This was capable of coping with a Merlin helicopter but the Merlin, like the Lynx, had its undercarriage under the main cabin area and did not have a tail wheel. This was going to require very precise flying, even on a good day and I had no desire to do what my mate did in the Falklands war. When landing his Wessex on Type 21 frigate HMS *Arrow*, he had managed to drift too far forward and all four of his main rotor blades struck the ship's hangar – Ouch!

With all of this in mind I sat alongside the ship waiting for a quiescent period and then briskly commenced my sidewards motion. Had I been in an RN Wessex I would have had an aircrewman hanging out of the large sliding door conning me across the deck. Sadly I wasn't flying an RN Wessex and as I edged over the deck I realised I had no idea whether my precious tail wheel was over the deck or over the ogwash. If it was the latter I would have bashed the tail cone into the back of the ship and written the aircraft off. Not ideal. I was already as close to the hangar superstructure as I felt brave enough to be and it was then that one of my boffins, with a sense of self-preservation, became aware of the potential disaster and offered to look backwards out of the door for me. Thank the Lord! With his encouragement I inched forwards until he had convinced me we were over the deck and I smoothly eased nearly six tons of aircraft and boffins onto the salt sprayed deck – and promptly lowered the collective fully to prevent 'ground resonance'. Proper RN ratings from the ship's flight dashed out with nylon lashings.

Phew! I had survived my first Wessex deck-landing on a Type 23.

I shut down and investigated the domain that was to be my stomping ground for the next seven days. First up was to see exactly where the rotor tips were in relation to the hangar door – bloody close.

Then I strolled casually around to the tail of the aircraft to note my tail wheel was almost a full twelve inches onto the flight deck. Easy peasy then! This wouldn't suffice for my future landings – I would have to land a further 2ft or so nearer the hangar.

Yikes!

I made my way up to the bridge to introduce myself to the Captain and instantly recognised him as one of the warfare officers from HMS *Newcastle* where I had served four long months of my training time and where I had handed in my resignation three times. A long story which I will recount in my next book. Thankfully this colleague was one of the nice guys I'd got on with and he was already impressed by my prowess as a Wessex pilot – I didn't like to tell him just quite how hard I had been working and how under-confident I was with myself. I flew two further sorties to the ship and clocked up some more landings to build my experience before dashing back to Boscombe Down to swap 503 for a Lynx so I could carry on into the night looking at some night landing aids. The following day, even with *Marlborough* cowering in the lee of Portland Bill, the sea state was at least 5. Proper Navy weather. I was incredibly glad it had been slightly calmer the day before as this was now no laughing matter. I had to employ all my ability and rely heavily on my extensive deck landing experience to continue with all the required test points. In all I flew the Wessex for fourteen hours over four days and completed thirty deck landings,

Author about to get airborne in XR503. Note position of bum line. *(DRA Bedford)*

which was no mean feat in the conditions. I went on to operate the Lynx for two further days, clocking up over twenty hours with over 180 deck landings, of which 40 were at night – mostly on one sortie. I had definitely earnt my flying pay – which I will discuss more in a later chapter.

Unfortunately, my acquaintance with 503 was coming to an end. Just as when I had been a Wasp, and then a Lynx Flight Commander, this aircraft had been all mine for two years. It didn't go anywhere without me. After Avalon she deserved a well-earned rest so it fell to her sister, Wessex XS509, to provide my last ever flight on RWTS, and last ever Wessex flight just before a well-earned Christmas leave.

Sadly XR503's days were numbered; with a shortage of funding for any further trials, and with her work successfully achieved, she was pensioned off the following year. I had hoped she would be sold to a wealthy collector who would preserve her in a climate-controlled hangar, but no. She was to suffer the ignominy of being despatched to the MOD fire-fighting school at RAF Manston where she resides to this day; a burnt out shadow of her former self.

Rest in Peace Westland Wessex HC Mk.2 XR503.

(HMS *Marlborough* was sold off to the Chilean Navy in 2006).

Chapter 7

Sea King

I gently slowed to establish a hover over a large field and then the radio burst into life …

'Gauntlet 70 this is Gauntlet 71 – whatever you do, don't slow down. We can't see you but we're right behind you!'

'Bugger!' I cried out as a warning to my crew, as I pulled the collective aggressively to 'max chat' and rotated expeditiously around the nose sensor to accelerate as quickly as this poor aircraft was able to.

The Sea King, or the 'Mighty King' as its many fans described it, was one of the core types for B Flight EFS and it was to provide my mount for my very first flight on the squadron with Charles, Flight Commander, alongside me. Now, it's probably fair to say, Charles was a 'proper' Sea King pilot and fan of the aircraft. Prior to attending the United States Naval Test Pilot School (USNTPS) he had been an RAF search and rescue pilot operating

Sea King Mk4X ZB506. *(Chris Lofting)*

the Westland Sea King Mk.3. During one of his more harrowing rescues, in the North Sea, he picked up some survivors from a sinking boat ... and then the winch-wire managed to fly up into the main rotors doing a massive amount of damage to the rotor blades. He had to choose between ditching, which might well have drowned the already embarked survivors, or try and make a safe landing somewhere. He managed to nurse his stricken aircraft to a nearby oil platform and achieved a safe landing. On shutdown he noted that at least one of the main rotor blades had been almost cut clean in half – but it had not failed, and his decision not to ditch no doubt saved the lives of most of his passengers.

So my first flight with my immediate boss was in Sea King Mk.4X ZB506. Two very similar aircraft were built by Westland Helicopters in 1982 and were both designated Sea King Mk.4Xs. They were almost identical to the regular Mk.4s and, in 1998, ZB507 was, in fact, converted to a standard Mk.4 and served as an RN 'Junglie' aircraft until being pensioned off. ZB506 was nominally the RAE Bedford aircraft with its sister based at RAE Farnborough. By the time I started to fly them they were each used as required, with ZB506 fitted with the capability of mounting an experimental Blue Kestrel radar on massive longitudinal beams.

Anyway, my first flight in 506 went well and I wasn't sacked on the spot. So I was immediately reintroduced to good old girl, XV371 – the Mk.1 Sea King I had flown the previous year on ETPS. I have already mentioned that this was the last surviving example of a batch of four aircraft originally shipped to the UK from Sikorsky. The aircraft now had a modified nose which included a reinforced area in front of the cockpit and a cut-back lower fuselage. This allowed numerous sensor turrets to be bolted directly to the aircraft. A big part of my work for the next two years was to be flying around these airborne test platforms with a variety of sensors fitted. Often, the final versions would end up as missile seeker heads or similar. So my first revenue-earning sortie was to be in 371 with a Passive Identification Device (PID) mounted on the front. I met up with the boffins the day before the trial commenced. All the chat was going fine until they announced I needed to descend vertically over a target at over 1,000ft per minute ...

'Say again?' I say.

'We need you to position directly over this target, hover, and then descend vertically at 1,000ft per minute.'

'Well that's going to kill us all,' I replied nonchalantly.

'What do you mean?'

'Have you heard of vortex ring?' I ask my wide-eyed audience. They hadn't and, as you know already, I had become something of an expert on the topic. And I had learnt, anecdotally, that the Mighty King was particularly unforgiving in this matter. So my boffins looked very glum indeed.

'What exactly is it you need to do a vertical descent for?' I ask

'Well. We need to have the target in view and generate a vertical rate – we need to be moving.'

'Could we moving up rather than down?'

'Isn't that even more difficult?'

'Not if we're not too heavy; in fact it's a lot easier to achieve and a hell of a lot safer!'

Turns out the boffins were trying to be helpful but had no inkling about helicopter performance. In fact this was one of the more pleasurable aspects of the job. That was trying to find out what the boffins needed to achieve and then work out how we could deliver to our 'customers' exactly what was required – safely. The following morning we manned up in 371 with Charles offering to be my co-pilot and we nailed every test point.

Phew! Credibility restored.

The following day I found myself back in 506. The aircraft no longer looked anything like it had done just a few days before. On either side of the aircraft were some massive beams painted in the correct blue to match the raspberry ripple colour scheme. Held out in front of the aircraft, like a butler carrying in a very large terrine of soup, was the Ferranti Blue Kestrel radar designed to be mounted in the EH101 Merlin helicopter. I was tasked to fly the aircraft and a cabin full of radar experts down to the Isle of Wight where we would use ship targets of opportunity – which meant ferries mostly. Flying the Sea King with this massive dinner plate on the front was strange indeed. At low speeds there was little difference, but as I flew faster the airflow started to push the nose of the aircraft down. This meant I was starting to use more aft cyclic the faster I went. The astute of you will realise, from my earlier explanations, this was an aircraft that now had unstable or negative longitudinal stability. And as you can imagine, with all that area up front, the directional stability or weather cock effect had not been improved any. But the Sea King was a forgiving old lady and up to around 90 KIAS coped well enough. This speed was as fast as I could have mustered in my trusty Wasp and certainly fast enough to get down to the coast and back. In fact I was fortunate to catch the last few trial flights of the Blue Kestrel radar. Obviously my excellent flying skills were all that was required to finally complete all the required data gathering before the radar could be installed in an EH101. So ZB506 was wheeled to the back of the hangar and wouldn't fly again for a while.

So, back to being the 'pilot of choice' for XV371. On one of the trips in February where I needed to operate out of the Army training area at Chertsey I borrowed another 'proper Sea King pilot' from RWTS. Steve was a Junglie and had flown a couple of tours in the dark green Mk.4s based at Yeovilton. The meteorological report for the day was poor and the outside temperature was very cold. As we briefed Steve asked;

'So, we can't fly then!'

'What do you mean?'

'Well Yeovilton are forecasting freezing rain so we aren't allowed to fly the Sea King.'

'Why not?'

'It's not cleared.'

Now this was a concern as I'd been flying my 371 in some pretty shitty weather for over a month. I scanned my FRCs limitations section and dusted off the very thin Mk1 Aircrew Manual and started to scour the limitations section for anything relevant – nothing.

'Here you go Steve, you have a look!'

Sea King ZB506 equipped with Blue Kestrel radar. *(Scott Rathbone)*

He did and found nothing at all similar to the limitations he was used to for the Mk.4. So it's probable that the limitations had never been reviewed after the HAS.1 stood down from operational service, but that wasn't formally the position and a whole can of worms would have been opened if I'd started to investigate thoroughly. So I decided we would fly anyway, but I did get Steve to keep a closer than usual look out for any real ice that might ruin our day. Nearly four hours of flying time later we landed safely at dusk and walked across a very cold and windy dispersal, glad that the potential for freezing rain had not required us to land in a field somewhere en route. February turned into March which turned out to be one of the busiest months of my flying career ever – over sixty flying hours, of which half were in the Sea King. We were flying three sorties a day, often in three different types with different crews on quite different tasks. Ironically, not being shy of hard work, I loved this frenetic pace. It felt like we were really achieving a great deal – getting the job done efficiently and safely. I thought my life on EFS was always going to be this busy until I realised that this pattern was typical of experimental flight testing where the annual budget had to be used up before the end of the financial year. No doubt, due to this manic workload, I had not been following all of the stuff going on in the background and, on the evening of Thursday 30 March, I was briefing for yet another sortie in XV371. We had pretty much finished the briefing, and all knew what we were about to do, when Al, the RN Air Engineer Officer (AEO) I would be using as my LHS crewman remarked:

'It's a shame …'
'What's a shame?'
'Tomorrow is the last ever flight of XV371 before she gets scrapped.'
'What? They are scrapping the only remaining member of that first 'gang of four' SH-3Ds?'
'Yep.'
'Well that can't go without some form of remembrance!' says I, and I promptly got on the phone to start organising a departure fit for a king.

I spoke to RNAS Yeovilton and Westland Helicopters and arranged we would do a final 'fly-by'. I then chatted with Charles and he agreed to fly photo-chase in one of our Lynx helicopters, so a cunning plan was hatched. In the morning I flew with Al in my trusty Wessex before we reconvened to fly 371 – and guess what? The weather was dogshit. Low cloud, drizzle, very low freezing level and, as I've already mentioned, I had to be particularly careful about icing with this unique veteran. But we briefed for success and I got on with flying around Boscombe as the boffins gathered their required data. At the appointed hour the Lynx started up and as the formation leader I pointed westward and set off at an appropriate pace. The weather at Yeovilton was apparently just about flyable so I grobbled along beneath the cloud but, as the ground rose up, the gap of clear air was becoming more and more crimped. Behind me were Charles and Bob (who was to be my future Boss on RWTS). As a Navy pilot I was used to this kind of pseudo VFR flight and had been there before and 'got the T shirt' as a Wasp and Lynx pilot, but even I was starting to feel I'd been beaten and when I thought I could press on no more I gently slowed to establish a hover over a large field and then the radio burst into life …

'Gauntlet 70 this is Gauntlet 71 – whatever you do, don't slow down. We can't see you but we're right behind you!'

'Bugger!' I cried out as a warning to my crew, as I pulled the collective aggressively to 'max chat' and rotated expeditiously around the nose sensor to accelerate as quickly as this poor aircraft was able. Thankfully the Lynx didn't rear-end me and the A303 provided a suitable IFR (I follow roads) cue. Fortunately, the cloudbase lifted just enough for us to find Yeovilton and Yeovil as a formation and get some good photos of 371 returning to her roots. For the return to Boscombe I decided not to repeat the VFR option and, as soon as I was able, I called up Boscombe to get a bespoke IF service. I should have climbed higher but did not want to risk an encounter with real icing. All worked out and I have a super picture of me flying this retiring lady over RWTS dispersal, late on a Friday afternoon.

Phew! Survived to give XV371 a suitable send off.

In fact, the aircraft languished in the hangar for a while before being sent to HMS *Sultan* in Portsmouth where she was upgraded to look more like a proper Sea King and used for training engineers. She was then transferred to Fleetlands and then the School of Flight Deck Operations at RNAS Culdrose and, very sadly, in 2017 she was lifted by a Chinook to the fire pits at Predannack where, just like my lovely Wessex, she has been used for fire-fighting training.

Rest in Peace Sea King XV371.

With Bedford aircraft XB506 languishing at the back of the hangar, and XV371 retired, we were left with the Farnborough aircraft ZB507 to continue our trials flying tasks. This aircraft was fully equipped with an NVG cockpit so we did a number of trials in the dark using various sensors that were supposed to help us 'see' better. (It was on one of these night flights I couldn't get the blades to spread as I mentioned earlier.) One of the benefits of these 4X Sea Kings was they were equipped for procedural instrument flying like civvy helicopters. That is we could fly ILS or NDB approaches so some time in 507 was spent progressing these procedural instrument flying skills. It wasn't long before the demise of 371's unique capability for mounting sensors on the nose was realised and ZB506 was promptly dusted off and a very similar modification embodied. This required a 'proper' handling qualities flight-test programme, which I was invited to plan and conduct. It was my first such requirement to use much of what I had learnt the previous year at ETPS and was, therefore, quite enjoyable.

Only a few weeks later I was to have one of my more memorable trips in the aircraft. As I mentioned earlier we flew as co-pilots for each other across the whole squadron and I was asked by my mate Tim to assist him flying an Andover trial. This was a really great day out, not least because it also

Author flying Sea King XV371 on its last flight. *(MOD)*

involved another colleague, Dan, formating on us in his Jaguar. Tim was an F4 Phantom pilot by trade and it's probably unfair to comment on the one-on-one air combat we had to do, where – not surprisingly – we lost. Was it Maverick that said: 'It's not the aeroplane, it's the pilot?' Well he wasn't flying an Andover versus a Jaguar! Still, it was good to be flying as fast as we could with Dan alongside doing his best to prevent the jet stalling. At a party at Tim's house a few days later he dug out the video of him and his mates low-flying Phantoms in the Falklands. The footage was very impressive and, as a result, deemed fit for 'mate' eyes only'. The payback came when I invited Tim to join me on some ZB506 trials. First up I had to qualify him on use of the emergency throttles. By now I was qualified to instruct on all the ETPS and EFS fleet of helicopters so this was relatively easy to do. A couple of days later we had a full day of flying trials at Chertsey. I let Tim fly and I relaxed. A good crew resource management strategy. For lunch we were going to drop into Fairoaks where we could get a sarnie and fill up with fuel. I let Tim fly us in. As we swept over the runway threshold in a sporty style I was reminded of the fact that this was the home of Alan Mann Helicopters Ltd, who were a traditional recruiter of RN helicopter pilots. With my future career prospects in mind, clearly I did not want to blot my copybook; just as that thought crystallised, I realised Tim had not started to bring the aircraft to a controlled hover and we were now sliding sideways across the grass at 90 KIAS …

Hells bells!

Time to protect my future career options I surmised as I took control and brought the majestic beast to a halt just in the nick of time to stop where we needed to be to get fuel – almost like we'd done it on purpose … clever I thought. The fuelling of both crew and aircraft achieved, we continued to complete our trial flying before heading back to Boscombe in fading light. I already knew a frontal system was approaching from the west and, based on all the forecasts I'd checked, had set off in order to get home before the bad weather arrived. The Met man had lied. As I tuned in to Boscombe's ATC approach frequency we were party to the efforts of ETPS tutor, Dave, trying to land in a Hawk. He had a couple of attempts using a Precision Approach Radar Approach (PAR). On each approach he descended to 200ft (and might have been a smidge lower) and each time he failed to see the runway and had to go around.

'If Dave can't get in no one can,' says Tim, as I started negotiating with Air Traffic to be vectored for a similar approach. It was the middle of October and we were in thick cloud with a freezing level just above us. As already explained this was not a helicopter type that could fly in freezing conditions which meant I wouldn't be able to climb high enough to give myself a safe margin above some of the surrounding ground. So I had no great wish to have to try and divert when bumping into the ground or encountering ice were both strong possibilities, so I briefed Tim accordingly … we really did need to get in to Boscombe and I really did need his help. I would be flying and he would be looking out of the windows with a mandate to shout when he saw anything at all. Ironically, unlike so much of what I'd been doing of late, I was now slap bang in the middle of my comfort zone, as flying in shitty weather had been part of my day job as an RN pilot for many years – but no time for complacency, I thought, as I told myself to sharpen up. I established on the centre line at 100 KIAS and turned on the instrument panel lights and all the external lights the aircraft had.

'You are on the centreline approaching the descent point. No need to acknowledge further transmissions unless requested,' advised ATC. I was already on the dedicated PAR talk-down frequency and given the lack of any circuit traffic had already been cleared to land, although I could tell from the stressed tone of the controller's voice, she wasn't optimistic.

'Commence your descent NOW for a 3 degree glideslope.'

I smoothly lowered the collective and checked that my flight control system had remained engaged and that my rad-alt was reading a sensible height above the ground. And it was then I began to cheat. Normal practice was to fly a set approach speed of 90 or 100 KIAS. This allowed the helicopter to fit in with fixed wing traffic and was an easy speed to fly at. Instead I lowered the collective further and, monitoring my rate of descent and rad-alt height, I commenced a very gentle flare to a more decelerative attitude.

'Nicely on the centre line, slightly above the glide-slope, correcting nicely …'

'On the centre line, on the glideslope …'

By 1,000ft I was at 80 KIAS, by 600ft I was flying at 60 KIAS and as I descended though 400ft I continued to slow to 40 KIAS. With a smidge of headwind, my progress over the ground was now a snail's pace.

'Can you see anything yet?' I ask.

'Not yet … not yet … not yet … nope nothing … what was that?'

A wisp of thinner cloud?

'Can you see the lights?' I called, as I was about to reach my legal 'decision height' of 150ft (50ft lower than the fixed wing height), which meant I had to decide whether to land or go around. Time for another cheat methinks, as I commenced the now legally required go-around but raised the collective at the most leisurely pace I could manage.

'There!'

'What?'

THERE! – are they the approach lights?' – Time to concentrate on looking out and sure enough, out of the gloom appeared very pale diffused patches of light.

Decision made! – *continuing* – as I washed off more speed … 30 KIAS … 20 KIAS as we arrived in a perfect hover over the runway 'piano keys'.

'Welcome home Gauntlet 70.'

My Phantom pilot friend was lost for words, as he had already been planning on a night in the bar at our diversion airfield. I landed and, with a huge sigh of relief and release of adrenalin, released the tail wheel lock before taxiing back to RWTS as the sun finally set and turned the grey to black as the airfield closed, having recovered all its birds for the day.

Phew! Survived another.

Trials flying in ZB506 continued for the rest of my time on EFS and RWTS and, I note, I was still hard at it in December 1996. However, that wasn't to be my last flight in the old girl as I used her in my next job as an RW tutor at ETPS. Sadly ZB506 has now been scrapped and the last I heard she was at White Waltham being used as a prop for some filming.

Rest in Peace ZB506.

One of the advantages of merging B Flight with RWTS was that we got to fly on regular 'certification' or 'release to service' test flights. Soon after the merger I was tasked with flying a Sea King Mk.3A (ZH542) on a trial for a UHF homer clearance. It was quite a lengthy flight as I had to fly around in circles a good deal. I did not have a co-pilot so had to train up my RAF navigator in how to manipulate the throttles should we have a computer problem. During my briefing of my sidekick I had said:

> 'And after leaving the circuit I'll bring the gear up.'
>
> 'Bring the gear up?'
>
> 'Yes – the gear retracts on an RAF SAR Sea King, so I'll select it UP as we leave the circuit.'
>
> 'None of the other pilots I've flown with have done that,' he says.

And I realised that many of my brethren were Mk.4 pilots, which had fixed undercarriage. One of them had inadvertently landed a trials Sea King with the wheels up some years earlier, so I guess there was more than a tad of concern about not doing it again. The 3A had a very sophisticated autopilot and I spent most of the sortie trying to work out which switch did what. I must have worked it out as, the next thing I knew, I was responsible for flying an FCS trial on the aircraft. As you will have read in the previous chapter, I also got roped into flying Sea King HAS.6 XZ576. For some reason it fell to me to do all the check flights to get her serviceable so we could fly her out to RFA *Fort Victoria* for a deck landing trial to clear a revised landing spot.

I used my trusty Wessex to get out to the ship but once there flew over six hours and thirty deck landings as part of the flight test programme assessing the ability of the Sea King to operate to the spot. For this type of flight testing the aircraft was comprehensively instrumented so all my control inputs were recorded, along with the amount of torque being used and engine temperatures etc. So Big Brother was definitely watching. We were given special approval by Westland Helicopters to pull more torque than the normal limits, which allowed us to gather the necessary test data with some margin for mishandling. Principally, as an experimental test pilot I was there to comment on the handling qualities I had encountered for each landing, which is another way of trying to assess the difficulty, or pilot workload, of the task. To make this easier we had developed a mini-questionnaire which allowed us to numerically define the difficulty of each landing, like the Cooper-Harper HQR scale.

Because my Wessex flying was all done by day I managed by default to get most of my Sea King flights at night. I confess I was glad to always fly these sorties with another RN TP. The chance of disorientation at night is much greater, the Sea King was less forgiving than my usual mount (Lynx), and again I was working my socks off to achieve the required test points (landings) in an expeditious fashion – not least so we could get to our beds before it became too late. Crucial to a safe landing was not to 'over-torque' (pull too much power and damage the gearbox), not to land with any drift which might have ripped the tyres off or worse, and to ensure that the firm contact required on touchdown was not so firm it trashed the undercarriage – no pressure then. And at night it is a good deal harder to judge ship motion, especially if the flight deck is heaving vertically upwards just as you are allowing the helicopter to descend. This has caught out a good number of my colleagues over the years, often resulting in a heavy landing, causing damage. Acceptable landing after landing was achieved and ticked off as we sought stronger and more challenging winds. Eventually we had done all that was asked of us. I would like to say we celebrated with a beer – but we were still under the cosh of our party-pooper leader!

So I concluded my TP tour after working extremely hard to get scores and scores of very demanding flight-test sorties completed and having come to respect, if not fully enjoy, flying the 'Mighty King'. It had proved a worthy deck landing aircraft, capable of flying well in the worst of weather and a very stable trial/sensor platform. It had coped with having the huge Blue Kestrel Radar strapped to the front and had demonstrated its SAR capability – especially in 3A guise with a modern autopilot. But, at the end of the day, it still had a punitive 30 degree angle of bank limit and, with the best will in the world, flew like a bus.

Landing Sea King XZ576 on RFA *Fort Victoria*. Steve in the LHS. *(Author)*

Chapter 8

Lynx

'Ground – Gauntlet 70 standby for my next test point; right cyclic with right yaw pedal this time.'

'Ground – Roger – Cleared to continue.'

'Three ... two ... one ... *now*.'

'F*** me!'

In less than a blink of an eye I was rolling at a phenomenal rate past 90 degrees. I wasn't to experience this rate of roll in a helicopter ever again!

As you will have gathered, I am a great fan of the Lynx. It had exceptional manoeuvrability due to its semi-rigid titanium rotor head and the naval version was, in my humble opinion, the very best helicopter to be flying if you had to land on the back of a ship. There were two Lynx operated by

Author about to fly the Lynx HAS.3 from HMS *Marlborough*. *(Author)*

EFS. Farnborough Lynx AH.5X ZD285 first flew in 1984 and Bedford Lynx AH.5X ZD559 in 1985. ZD560 was the third of the batch and joined ETPS in 1987. The 5X resembled an Army AH.1 but had more powerful Rolls Royce Gem (41) engines similar to those fitted to the Lynx HAS.3 I had flown operationally. All the aircraft were eventually upgraded to AH.7 standard with better tail rotors and 559 and 560 ended up with BERP rotor blades.

The Farnborough Lynx was associated with, and supported, a number of trials concerned with future battlefield or attack helicopters. The two years I worked as an experimental test pilot at EFS were vital to the future of the UK Army Air Corps as decisions had to be made over the purchase of a suitable attack helicopter. ZD285 was extensively modified and had a state-of-the-art night vision goggles (NVG) compatible cockpit. It had a modified nose which accommodated a sensor turret which could host numerous development FLIR and low light TV sensors. Additionally, it had powered system racks, so could accommodate various black boxes. A good deal of time was spent developing helmet mounted display (HMD) technology. The concept evolved from the Head Up Displays (HUD) of fast jet aircraft. In a helicopter the idea was to project vital information onto a pilot's helmet visor. This included crucial instruments such as attitude, altitude and airspeed. Additionally, power or torque would be displayed and then additional flying information would be included, like the 'flight path marker' or 'lolly-pops', which showed the pilot where to fly to achieve certain waypoints. Further symbology gave the pilot additional cues in order to hover, even without being able to see the real world outside. All of this technology is now relatively commonplace, and even finding its way into civilian certified aircraft of all shapes and sizes. Because the 'evaluation pilot' would fly the trials looking entirely through a helmet visor it was possible to simulate night. This enabled the trials to be flown in daylight which allowed the safety pilot to be able to keep the aircraft safe and take over should the subject pilot mess up. I flew a number of such sorties without incident.

Another major research topic of the time was using active noise reduction (ANR) in pilot headsets. A mini-computer generated sound in the helmet earpiece completely out of phase with the surrounding noise. Now it is possible to buy a Bose or Zulu or David Clark ANR headset over the counter for less than £1,000, but in the '90s this was very innovative technology. The three of us on B Flight were all issued with new earpieces for our helmets which were powered by battery boxes containing three PP3 9V batteries which, when wired in series, gave the 24-28V required to power the ANR circuitry. I am now badly deaf as a result of exposing myself to loud aircraft noise throughout my career and wished I had been given access to this technology more. One of the problems with these experimental units was that all the electronics had to be built into each ear cup, so all the foam used to add passive attenuation was removed. When the batteries started to lose their voltage they would issue an ear-piercing screech through the earpieces which was deafening in its own right. Once failed, the aircraft noise reaching our ears was worse than ever and, frankly, intolerable. So we all were equipped with two battery boxes so we could swap over when required. We burnt through three PP3s every three hours or so, therefore had to always be aware of when we expected to need new ones. I ended up with several boxes of green batteries that powered my kids' toys for years after the trial ended abruptly!

The major task using 285 during my two years at EFS was a Field of View trial. The use of NVG had become commonplace for night-time military helicopter use by the '90s, from early use in the Vietnam conflict followed by the UK's use during the Falklands war. NVG comprised two tubes that could be fastened to the front of a helmet like a pair of binoculars. Each tube, powered by batteries, contained sophisticated electronics which looked at the outside view through a low-light TV device and then amplified the image intensity so the pilot was presented with a green monochrome image of the world into each eye. The devices amplified light, rather than generating it, so there had to be some moon or starlight available to work with. Prior to flying using NVG we would check what the forecast amount would be. These tubes had a very limited 'field of view' (FOV), typically around 40 degrees laterally and vertically. It was like trying to fly with two loo rolls strapped to your face – doable, but not easy. Pilots had to compensate for this poor field of view in a number of ways including rapid and frequent head movement. Work was afoot to try and improve the offered FOV, but bizarrely no one had ever done any work to find out what FOV a pilot actually needed to fly. Or more importantly, how the workload varied with increasing or decreasing angles. There was no point spending millions of pounds on improving the NVGs' FOV if it didn't actually help the pilot any.

So the boffins at Farnborough, working with their counterparts in industry, and the USA (NASA) and Australia, devised an international trial using subject experimental test pilots from all of the above. We would use ZD285 with the evaluation pilot wearing a specially modified Apache helicopter helmet. These helmets were fitted with a custom-made inner lining that was moulded to an individual pilot's head. The helmet was modified to artificially constrain the pilot's FOV. By dropping in different apertures, we could vary the FOV incrementally from very small to almost normal. Each sortie the helicopter was required to fly around a series of set piece manoeuvres called Mission Task Elements (MTEs) which I will explain later. The evaluation pilot would then be asked to complete a mini-questionnaire like a Cooper-Harper scale and award scores for how difficult or easy a task was. The task was repeated by the same pilot with several different FOVs. This allowed a huge amount of data to be gathered. The B flight pilots all had a go at acting as evaluation pilots and then moved on to being the 'safety pilot' for a number of other candidates, and it was a fascinating experience to watch a number of different experimental test pilots from a variety of nations working their absolute socks off to achieve these flying tasks. One of our subject pilots was Dave from the Australian Army. He was a graduate of the ETPS course of 1993 and therefore was chums with a number of my colleagues. So we had a few very sociable beers during the week he was in the UK and even squeezed in a flight to Helitech (a helicopter trade conference) using Sea King ZB507. The following week I was teamed up with the Deputy Chief Test Pilot from Westland Helicopters who was to be a key player in their development of the UK spec AH-64D Longbow Apache. Knowing I would be looking for a job after leaving the RN I had to be my most professional and friendly – I couldn't afford to pick up any black marks with this chap – no pressure then!

Bedford Lynx ZD559 had been used predominantly for researching handling qualities. It had been heavily modified to be able to record hundreds and hundreds of bits of information from around the helicopter. This included the usual control positions, engine and gearbox parameters and numerous strain gauges to assess if any part of the fuselage was being fatigued. What was unique though, was that the aircraft could be fitted with two experimental rotor blades, one of which was equipped with a balsa-wood 'sheath' which covered the main rotor blade. Embedded

Author flying Lynx ZD285 wearing the Apache FOV helmet. *(Author)*

within this sheath were scores and scores of pressure sensors. Each sensor was able to measure the pressure of the air immediately around it. All this info was fed back to the blade hubs and then down through a very sophisticated system into the main cabin where it was all recorded for further analysis. Additionally, the aircraft was equipped to work with a telemetry ground station so that a whole bunch of boffins could stay safely on the ground and monitor in real time what was going on.

I worked with telemetry when I was engaged on a particular trial that was investigating the effect of tail rotor failures in flight. As losing a tail rotor is often catastrophic, a package of work was put in place to investigate further. In order to progress incrementally, a cunning plan was hatched to use the Advanced Flight Simulator (AFS) at Bedford but the 'model' to make the simulation as real as possible needed to be produced. So enter yours truly and 559. I was despatched time and time again to fly to a safe height and then, with either the AFCS engaged or disengaged, asked to make measured control inputs of increasing size so that the boffins could work out how the aircraft actually responded to such inputs. Of particular interest were 'step inputs' into the tail rotor, which to some extent were simulating the aircraft's initial response to a tail rotor failure. The flying could best be described as 'very exciting'. Although the Lynx was very forgiving and had demonstrated its ability to fly briefly upside down, this wasn't within our plans. The semi-rigid rotor head ensured that the aircraft's response to a control input was both crisp and instantaneous. My TP colleagues at Westland Helicopters had helped develop an AFCS which damped the aircraft's response to pilot inputs making it easier and safer to fly. However, I was asked to make control inputs with this system disengaged. All went relatively well with me becoming more confident in both the aircraft and my own ability to recover it from the unusual attitudes in which it often found itself. On the last flight of the trial I was invited to apply full lateral cyclic inputs. That is, move the cyclic stick, which was the main flying control, very briskly sideways until it hit the stop. I could bet my last pound that I'm the only Lynx pilot outside of Westland Helicopters that's ever done that deliberately – maybe the only pilot ever? Without the AFCS the aircraft's roll rate was eye watering. I started each of these test points in a 45 degree turn in the wrong sense, with the hope that I could commence recovery when we had achieved 45 degrees the other way and stop the aircraft exceeding 90 degrees or so, as we had decided we shouldn't deliberately fly upside down.

With the pure cyclic inputs in the bag I chatted to telemetry:
'Ground – Gauntlet 70 how was that?'

'Rate of roll was within limits – you are cleared to the next test point – using yaw pedal.'

So we had discussed this testing at length – I was trying to avoid going upside down and starting by being in a turn which inevitably meant I was flying with a smidge of into-turn yaw pedal to 'balance' the turn. This meant the roll response away from the turn was very uncomfortable and I thought the yaw pedal might be corrupting the 'roll due to cyclic' data.

'Ground – Gauntlet 70 standby for my next test point right cyclic with right yaw pedal this time.'

'Ground – Roger – Cleared to continue.'

'Three … two … one … *now*.'

'F*** me!'

In less than a blink of an eye I was rolling at a phenomenal rate past 90 degrees. I wasn't to experience this rate of roll in a helicopter ever again!

Gingerly applying opposite cyclic and centralising the yaw pedals and checking down on the collective to prevent an over-torque – as the milliseconds passed, I re-established control.

Yikes!

'Gauntlet 70 from Ground – are you alright?'

'Yep, I think so.'

'Well we would like you to come straight home – very gently.'

'Oh, OK'

I didn't need any further details, clearly my eye-watering recent test point might have put undue strain on more than just the pilot. I pottered gently back to Boscombe and landed on at RWTS dispersal as carefully as I could. Time for a pee, a cup of tea and a long chat with the boffins in that order. By the time we started our debrief, they had had chance to analyse the downloaded data more thoroughly and the upshot was that thankfully no damage had been done – apart from to my nerves. The good news was that they decided this sortie formed an 'end point' in their data gathering requirements – so no need for me to rush off and do it all again. Praise the Lord!

Phew! Survived another.

Not long later I was to fly with the 'balsa blade' for more data gathering. As always, we had a comprehensive briefing and it was stressed that the blade could not be exposed to rain. I am guilty of being task-orientated – there is a small part of 'Maverick' in me that remains to this day. On this occasion I was keen to get this sortie done, despite a very low risk of an isolated light shower later in the day. I thought I had exercised due diligence regarding protecting the blade so off we set to the west of Boscombe. The weather was forecast to deteriorate from the west so I was very confident that if the sky did darken I would be able to scurry home ahead of it. Which was mostly true, and at the appointed hour I pointed east to return to the airfield. The weather had remained pretty much as forecast but I was experiencing a small element of doubt and I now wanted to be on the ground and shut down as soon as possible. Having chatted to the approach controllers and then transferred to stud 3 for 'tower', I negotiated a rapid descent and expeditious downwind join directly over south-side. I turned final, washing off speed, and was about to congratulate myself when I saw just a handful of drops of rain on the windscreen.

'Bugger!'

Just a few drops – not real rain I thought optimistically as I landed and shut down briskly, to be met by: 'What part of "do not fly in rain" did you not understand?'

I looked at the precious balsa cuff to see a dozen pit marks like you might find on the surface of the moon.

'Double Bugger! Can it be fixed?'

'Dunno.'

'Expensive?'

'Maybe *very*.'

'Oh shit!'

I didn't sleep that night knowing I had been too much 'Maverick' and chanced my arm and been caught out. The following morning I found a very nice certificate on my desk – 'The Michael Fish Award of 1996'.

Very funny!

The better news was that the pit marks were not as bad as they first appeared and, after some very deft finessing, with a piece or two of wet and dry, all was nearly as good as new.

Phew! I had survived another, reputation still intact, and morale restored all round.

One of the major projects that DRA Bedford and thus EFS had been involved with immediately before and during my tenure was Aeronautical Design Standard 33 (ADS33). Traditionally an aircraft's handling qualities had been defined in terms of its 'stability and control'. Most of my year at ETPS had been focused on understanding this topic and learning to employ a variety of test techniques to gather appropriate data. It is fair to say that most of the current civil certification requirements for aeroplanes and helicopters are still based on this traditional methodology. However, in the 1980s it was becoming increasingly evident that future battlefield helicopters in particular would be difficult to assess against such traditional criteria. The major catalyst for improvement was the US Army's Light Experimental Helicopter programme which led to the RAH-66 Comanche – an aircraft I was fortunate enough to see, despite it being shrouded in secrecy, on one of my visits to Sikorsky at West Palm Beach.

This generation of rotorcraft was to be flown via computers using fly-by-wire or fly-by-light technology. Novel controls were to be used such as sidesticks and inceptors that could potentially do away with the need for a collective or yaw pedals or both. Clearly, acceptance criteria that were based on stick position, or displacement forces, might not be appropriate. Additionally the 'frequency domain' was becoming more important and it was realised that the visual cues or environment were relevant as to how easy an aircraft was to fly. In 1982, the US Army Aero Flight Dynamics Directorate (AFDD), then assigned under the US Army Aviation Systems Command (AVSCOM), began development of a new handling qualities specification for military rotorcraft. This effort resulted in the US Army's initial Aeronautical Design Standard–33 (ADS-33A), 'Handling Qualities Requirements for Military Rotorcraft', published in May 1987. This was to go through a couple of upgrades internally, but by the early '90s the US research effort had started to become more international with a number of similarly interested parties becoming involved, including the National Research Council (NRC) in Ottawa, Canada, and DLR in Germany, who both had variable stability trials aircraft.

The DRA contribution was the highly instrumented Lynx ZD559. So, much of my time during my two years in EFS was to help develop the crucial Mission Task Elements (MTEs) which formed a core part of the ADS33 philosophy. In simple terms a number of very prescriptive flying tasks were defined and flown. There were very precise accuracy criteria chosen and the manoeuvres were flown against the clock, with some incredibly tight timings. This inevitably meant most of the manoeuvres were flown as aggressively as the experimental test pilot and aircraft could manage which, frankly, was highly demanding and very hard work, but a lot of fun. The MTEs needed various airfield markings to be produced. For example, one MTE was a very rapid acceleration followed by a quick stop. This had to be achieved in a given distance, in a given time. It involved commencing over a start line with a stable hover, promptly applying 'max chat' while rotating aggressively around 30 degrees nose-down (!) to accelerate level (along another marked line) rather than climb. As soon as the target speed was achieved the collective was lowered, entering into autorotation, and again the aircraft pitched 20 to 30 degrees nose-up to prevent the aircraft climbing or descending while trying to control the rotor rpm that would rise alarmingly. The final 'coming to a halt' before the end marker was extremely challenging as the collective now needed to be raised, the aircraft levelled with cyclic, and the aircraft kept straight with the yaw pedals – all without exceeding the aircraft's torque limits.

Yikes!

As you can imagine, these MTEs took considerable practice and our piloting skills needed to be kept current. Our input to the process was greatly appreciated by the international community and led to ADS 33D being issued in 1996. I was to teach all the MTEs to my students when I became a tutor at ETPS. As I write this chapter, I am involved with two companies building electric/battery-powered flying taxis, or EVTOL as they are known. It has been decided by the major regulators that a version of ADS 33 and selected MTEs will be used to evaluate the handling qualities of such complex aircraft which, again, are flown entirely through the cleverness of computers and fly-by-wire technology. I have to say – such outcomes are very pleasing – to know that my hard work and efforts have genuinely made a difference.

One of the stranger tasks, but ironically most enduring, was my involvement with the rolling deck or Rolling Platform as it was officially known. Part of DRA Bedford's research into operating helicopters from ships at sea led to Frazer-Nash being contracted to produce a facsimile of a Type 23 frigate flight deck which could be powered to resemble the movement of the deck experienced when at sea. This rolling platform was installed at Boscombe Down and used for some Merlin 'drop testing', and to some extent there was a hope that the facility could be used more extensively. So, with that in mind, I was tasked to fly ZD559 to get some publicity photos. Ironically, I was not allowed to land on the platform – but had to make it look like I had. Actually, the photos of this sortie are still in use today over twenty-five years later and I have to say they are impressive – and everyone that has seen them thinks I really did land on it! But the rolling platform was not done with me. The next step was to see if the platform could be used for some real 'deck landing' flying. As 559 was an Army configured aircraft, with skids, it wasn't suitable, so I got on the phone to my mates at RNAS Portland and borrowed a Lynx HAS.3 (XZ699). It was going to be fun, flying my former operational type and, even better, I was teamed up with my FTE mate from my TP course, Keith. The platform was a flat plate measuring 16 x 12m, could accommodate a 15 tonne aircraft and was fitted with a grid compatible with the Lynx harpoon system. The harpoon was a grabbing claw under the aircraft that could be activated on landing to grab onto a specially designed grid. This would hold the helicopter in place temporarily as the ship was pitching and rolling before more substantial nylon lashings could be attached. The top of the platform weighed 40 tonnes, but using a powerful hydraulic system, very rapid roll rates could be generated with the platform rolling to +/- 30 degrees.

We had developed a comprehensive and incremental test plan and worked our way through the test points with increasing amplitudes and rates of motion. I was, by most definitions, a very experienced deck landing pilot with over 2,500 landings in my Wasp and Lynx in some pretty poor weather. As I've already stated, the key to a successful landing in rough seas is to build up experience of a ship's typical motion in any given conditions. The aim is always to land the helicopter when the deck is as close to level as possible and, even more importantly, is not heaving vertically upwards, which could make the normal downwards velocity of a landing helicopter unacceptable for the undercarriage.

Although the platform resembled a ship's deck in some respects, it was not the same in two crucial aspects. Firstly, there was no superstructure like the hangar or horizon bar to provide necessary visual cueing, and secondly, the motion was a simple sine wave oscillation and nothing like a real ship's motion. This meant that the roll rate of the deck was at its fastest as the deck was level, which was not the same as real life. Anyway, it made landing on this moving platform a real challenge. On a number of test points I would position over the platform, commence my descent to land when it was level, only to find I'd misjudged it and I ended up landing when the platform had reached an extreme amount

Author flying Lynx HAS.3 Landing on Rolling Platform at Boscombe Down. *(MOD)*

of roll. While this started to convince me that the platform as presented was not a realistic representation of a ship underway, it did illustrate just how accommodating the RN version of the Lynx was. But what to do and what to say about this very expensive facility? I had so wanted it to provide useful training or be valid for ship operation flight testing, but sadly it really wasn't. A long FTR outlining the problems followed and I'm not sure whether the platform was ever used in anger again, although it remains a facility offered by QinetiQ.

In my second year as a TP, I borrowed an RN Lynx a few times for various reasons. I managed to get assigned to a trial of the Lynx HMA.8 which was taking over from the Lynx HAS.3. I was teamed up with a former RN Observer colleague, Phil, and we did some extensive testing on the Sea Skua helicopter-launched anti-ship missile system which was fun, not least because we did some of it out of RNAS Portland, my original stomping ground for ten years. This missile was great and as I write I wonder just how much havoc I could create in the Black Sea right now given a Lynx armed with such missiles.

But the highlight of my two years – as the experimental test pilot responsible for the UK's deck operations research – was undoubtedly Trial Avalon. If you have read the Wessex chapter, you will know something of the trial. The folks at DRA Bedford had borrowed a real life RN Type 23 frigate, HMS *Marlborough*, in order to conduct a whole host of different deck ops trials. We

134 Experimental Test Pilot

Author flying Lynx HAS.3 Landing on Rolling Platform at Boscombe Down. *(MOD)*

HMS Marlborough during Trial Avalon. *(DRA Bedford)*

had wanted some high sea states and by golly did we get them with sea states 7- 8 (Violent Storm, Wind 50–60kts, 30ft waves) on the penultimate day. The highest sea state is 9 which is associated with a Hurricane.

Hells bells!

I'd flown the Wessex out initially to look specifically at the various guidance systems which had been originally set up for 503. This included the cruciform I mentioned earlier which, in its current guise, used a series of lights to indicate how close the helicopter was to being directly over the landing spot/harpoon grid. This worked really well and I asked for it to be switched ON all the time as I needed all the help I could get operating in conditions well beyond the normally accepted limits. Another of the aids we needed to evaluate was the Landing Period Designator (LPD). This was a fascinating bit of kit. It was programmed with the finite limits that the helicopter could cope with on touchdown including the pitch and/or roll of the deck and the touchdown velocity. Then it would be programmed with the mass of the ship. Using some very clever computed maths and the laws of physics, it would be constantly calculating the time it would take for the deck to go from being IN limits to OUT of limits.

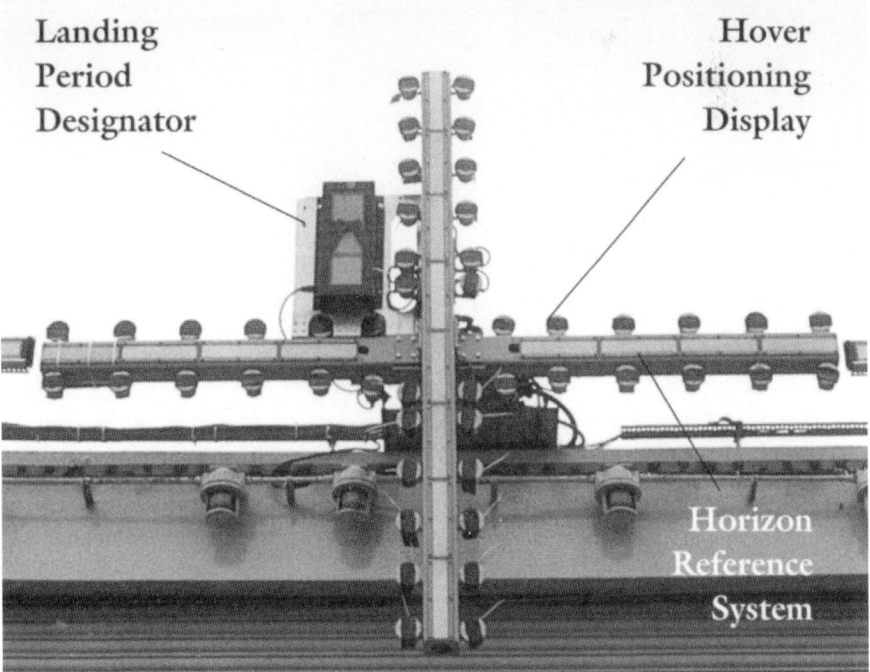

Fitted Visual Landing Aids for Trial Avalon. *(DRA Bedford)*

If this period was within a normal pilot's ability to land that type, then a green light would be illuminated in a traffic light display. Amber was 'risky' and red was 'don't even think about it'.

One of the bizarre aspects of the logistics of this trial was that my initial flight each day was out of Boscombe Down with a full load of boffins. I also carried two dummy torpedoes on the aircraft. The idea being that if an engine failed I could jettison the torpedoes and immediately reduce my weight – hopefully allowing me to avoid ditching on the one remaining engine. This combination put me at near max weight when I approached the ship for my first landing of the day. I would have a hundred test points in order to formally evaluate the above landing aids – but guess what? I always insisted they were both turned ON for my first arrival. They were definitely helpful and in the storm force weather I needed every ounce of help I could get. The weather deteriorated as the trial continued and by the penultimate day it was officially a 'violent storm'. As I mentioned earlier, I had gained a huge amount of relevant experience operating my Wasp and Lynx worldwide in some pretty bad weather, but we would usually avoid operating if the sea state was too high to launch the 'crash boat' to recover us if we ditched. Typically, that meant sea state 6 was a normal operating limit. I flew out to HMS *Marlborough* already aware that I would be facing some of the roughest seas of my flying career. On sighting the sleek grey warship cutting gently through the foam-topped green waves I was not disappointed. I could see the two propeller screws completely out of the water. For the uninitiated – that is not normal!

Blige!

I again requested a Red 15 wind for my landing (with a very high all up weight) and approached the 'port wait' to hold alongside the ship until I perceived the deck was within limits. I had launched my Wasp from HMS *Diomede* in the Bay of Biscay some ten years previously in order to take some photos of the ship for PR purposes. Seeing the bow of my Leander class frigate with its classic 4.5 inch guns crashing through the waves gave me perhaps the most awesome photo of a warship at sea ever taken. But then I had to get back onboard in time for tea and medals! I had hovered alongside my flight deck for nearly thirty minutes as I conned the ship onto a variety of headings in order to get the motion within acceptable limits to allow me to land – I nearly ran out of fuel. This time I had the LPD to augment my own judgement.

HMS *Marlborough* during Trial Avalon – stern out of the water. *(DRA Bedford)*

Pulling around 90 per cent Torque.

Wipers ON.

Side window open to get a view despite the spray.

'Is it steadying?'

LPD … Red … Amber …Red … Amber … *Green*!

As the LPD flicked to green momentarily I aggressively applied right cyclic, adding collective so as not to sink, and left pedal to keep straight.

The cruciform lights moved rapidly to the middle as I applied left stick to stop the sidewards movement – and wasting no further time, I initiated a brisk but acceptable rate of descent, preventing any drift as I dropped 15ft or so with the LPD now showing Red.

Bang – all three wheels on deck.

Harpoon engaged with a button under the collective and a hurried 'thumbs up' to the deck crew to get the lashings on.

Bloody Hell!

That was effing difficult. And that was just my arrival to start the day's flying. I had three sorties and five hours flying to do before I could head home for a beer. Each landing was equally exciting. This was, without doubt, the very worst sea state a helicopter could operate in with a frigate.

The final aspect of the trial was to assess the landing aids at night. In addition to the cruciform and LPD I was to evaluate the use of electro luminescent panels (ELPs). These were very thin or flat panels that had been shaped into long and thin rectangular strips. By passing an electric current through them they glowed green and could easily be seen in the dark. For my trial they were mounted around the flight deck edge and up each side of the hangar door. I then flew the Lynx by night to evaluate whether or not they assisted in making an approach and landing any easier. Normally, by night I would have had to rely on a glide path indicator (I had just evaluated and recommended approval for the GPI Mk3) which was calibrated on a nominal descent or glideslope profile. Too low, I would get a red light but when on the money, I would get a green. Too high and I would get an amber, but there was sometimes a risk, when being too high, that you would get a ghost image that looked green-ish. In order to fly to the ship I would be vectored by radar or visual circuit to pick up the GPI to be sure I could make an approach without becoming disorientated. The flight deck itself would normally be unlit apart from a series of 'jam jar' lights forming a horizon bar attached to the top of the hangar door. So landing on a small ship by night was an incredibly difficult task, especially if there was no discernible natural horizon. The horizon bar rolled with the ship and there was sometimes no

Author flying the Lynx HAS.3 from HMS *Marlborough*. *(DRA Bedford)*

alternative but to follow its guidance and then ascertain what your hands and feet were having to do to formate on this moving reference and then land when such control inputs indicated a quiet period.

This time around, I was assessing a horizon bar (part of the cruciform display) that was gyro stabilised, which helped. However, the ELPs were a game changer. I could immediately discern the outline of the back of the ship and despite the hideous sea states I was able to use almost a daytime control strategy as I could pick up all the visual cues I needed. On my final day I flew for nearly nine hours, over four by night, and clocked up a hundred deck landings which was a personal best. The last thirty I flew at night and I was achieving a complete cycle of take-off, reposition, land and engage the harpoon in around three minutes – which on a shitty dark stormy night, in a high sea state, was very impressive. But I'd had enough fun for one week and, having clocked up thirty-six hours of flying and 218 deck landings in total over seven days, it was time to call it a day. I loaded up with all the boffins and enough fuel to get home and set off from just east of Portland heading north east. The weather had started to improve, but although the wind had dropped slightly there was a low cloudbase with a low freezing level which forced me to fly at around 800ft agl. Before long I picked up the main Blandford to Salisbury road and at

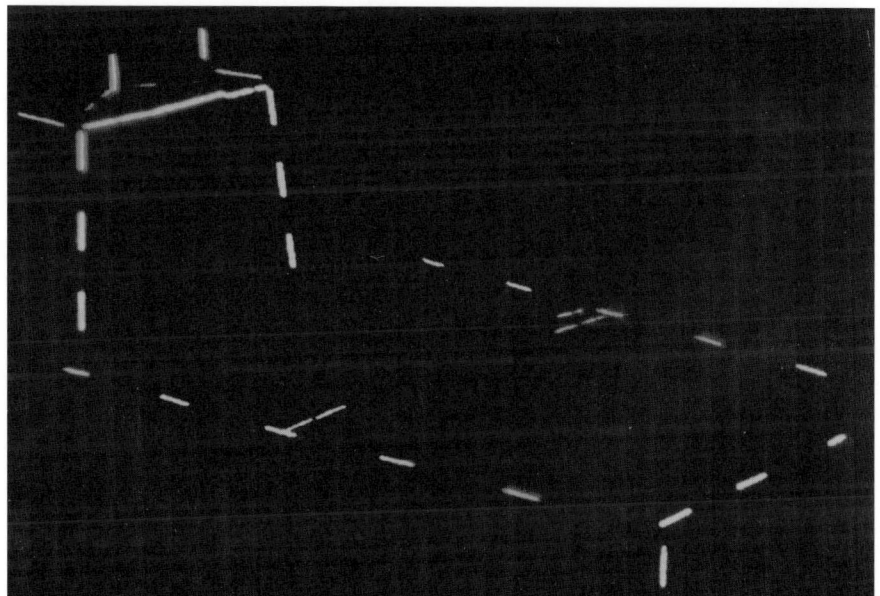

ELP Layout on HMS *Marlborough* for Trial Avalon. *(DRA Bedford)*

last, out of the gloom, spied the red obstruction light on the top of the cathedral which I felt I could almost reach out and touch, passing much closer than I would have liked, as the cloud had continued to lower. I was moments away from Boscombe Down, a pee and a beer, and started to relax slightly. Through a massive amount of hard work, and dedication to the task, I had achieved an amazing amount of trials flying in just seven days in the worst weather and sea states I had ever operated in and was feeling chuffed with myself. I had tuned into Boscombe's ATC approach frequency and, with nothing else flying, swapped promptly across to stud 3 to talk to the 'Tower'.

'Boscombe Tower. Good Evening. Gauntlet 70.'

'Good evening Gauntlet 70. You are clear to join downwind with Runway 23 active. QFE 996.'

'Roger QFE 996 set – will advise downwind.'

And it's then that I realised I was lost. Completely lost. I looked and looked and could not see any of the customary lights of the airfield. Nothing.

But how could this be? I had not mistaken Salisbury cathedral surely? And the airfield was only five miles or so further on. What was going on? My demeanour was not helped by having an aircraft full of passengers also all in need of a pee and a beer, ideally at the airfield where they had parked their cars.

'Tower – Gauntlet 70 – positioning to join downwind. Please confirm airfield lighting status.'

'Tower – Roger – you are clear to join downwind. Normal night lighting.'

Blige! I was in trouble. I still couldn't see the airfield.

'Tower, Gauntlet 70 – Please DEFINE "normal night lighting".'

'Affirm, all runway and obstruction lights OFF.'

'Say again!'

'All airfield lighting *OFF* for normal helicopter operations.'

'Gauntlet 70 – Roger – I need all the airfield lights ON – NOW please!'

It was a delightful moment when immediately in front of me a huge military airfield appeared from nowhere, out of the inky grey drizzle.

What had just occurred?

It turns out the Army Air Corps had decided to term flying using NVG as 'normal', and flying without NVG 'reversionary'. This meant they trained with the airfield lights all OFF. I was RN and not privy to this information but it became clear that Boscombe's internal communications had dropped a real bollock – thankfully with no serious consequences apart from two or three minutes end-of-the-evening stress to yours truly. I dropped the aircraft gently onto the dispersal. Slammed the two engine control levers back against the stops, sighed a big sigh, and shut this borrowed beauty down for the last time.

Phew! Knackered beyond, but I had survived another.

Having worked my socks off for days, I felt I had really earned my flying pay and had put all my experience as an RN Wasp/Lynx pilot and experimental test pilot into practice and achieved a very successful trial, getting the very most out of the expensive and time-limited resources we had.

Sadly, both Lynx ZD285 and ZD559 have ended up at the QinetiQ apprentice training school, although 559 was used for a time by ETPS. ZD560 is no longer resplendent in its raspberry ripple colour scheme but has been repainted green and sits outside Leonardo at Yeovil as a gate guardian and reminder of their development aircraft G-LYNX which won the helicopter speed record back in 1986.

Rest in peace ZD285, ZD559, ZD560.

Author (left) with Bedford scientists Trial Avalon. *(DRA Bedford)*

Chapter 9

Simulators and Aeroplanes

Just when I thought I was about to burst out of the roof of the building the opposite happened and I became light in my straps … never a good feeling in a simulator.

With a massive whoosh I felt myself being propelled earthwards until …

Grrrrrrrrr BANG!

I was thrown sideways and hit my helmeted head on the side of the cockpit. The lights went out. Everything stopped. There was no noise. I was about 30 degrees nose-down and 30 degrees rolled to the left. It was completely dark.

Bugger!

There were two aspects of being an experimental test pilot tasked with research and development flying on EFS that made it very different to the job of a 'release to service' regular TP on RWTS. The first was that we were involved across all the platforms operated by the squadron, and the second was our support of the Advanced Flight Simulator (AFS) at DRA Bedford and the other simulators at Farnborough.

As you will have already read, I had become something of an expert on simulators (sims) by the time I had joined EFS. Broadly speaking, sims fell into two categories, fixed base or full motion (FMS). Fixed base simulators were relatively cheap but usually proved very effective training aids. Two of my simulators at RNAS Portland were fixed base and they did a great job, especially of training observers how to operate the Sea Spray radar and Orange Crop Electronic Support Measures (ESM) equipment. For some aspects of flying, a pilot gains vital information from motion cues. These include angular cues such as pitch and roll, but also dynamic cues caused by acceleration. So simulators needing to be 'high fidelity' purport to generate the required cues. Such full motion simulators are normally mounted on a platform supported on hydraulic or electric jacks.

Simulators and Aeroplanes 143

The platform can be tilted in both the fore and aft and lateral axes, and the jacks can also stroke up and down to give some limited vertical acceleration, or heave cues. Such motion systems have been in use for decades for large transport aircraft which tend to have limited pitch and roll envelopes and rarely experience much more than 1.5G of acceleration/deceleration. Both helicopters and fast jets experience much greater attitude and acceleration cues making a standard six axis FMS rather limited. So in the early 1980s the Advanced Flight Simulator (AFS) was commissioned and built. It was housed in a unique, almost cube like, building on the south side of the airfield. The simulator had a bespoke motion platform. The cockpit module could be mounted such that it could be rotated 90 degrees. Thus the motion system was designed to produce only five axes of motion: pitch and roll, yaw and heave (vertical), and then surge or sway depending on the orientation of the cockpit. The cockpit could move a full 10 metres vertically at 3 metres per second and 8 metres laterally at 2.5 metres per second. In the vertical axis 10 m/s^2 could be achieved which created a 2G force for the pilot. All of these parameters may seem quite tame if you're sitting in your armchair reading this, but they far exceeded the capabilities of a regular training simulator. The only simulator more capable than the AFS was based at NASA (Ames) in the United States.

When the sad decision was taken to close the airfield at Bedford, eventually the penny dropped that the AFS was too large and costly to move, and therefore the scientists using the AFS continued to work at the airfield in an enclave of offices bolted onto the simulator complex until 2008 I believe. For me, this was frustrating. The boffins I worked with, needed me for a number of trials. To fly in the sim I had to commute from Boscombe to Bedford, which was a very tedious cross country drive of nearly three hours in each direction (given the rush hour traffic). The silver lining, however, was that the airfield retained a flying club until the airfield was sold off at the end of 1996. This meant light aircraft could be allowed to visit. Hurray! I had very promptly joined the Boscombe Down based Bustard Club, which initially operated a Beagle Pup aeroplane that could be rented for the day at quite reasonable rates. So I now had found a mode of transport that potentially would be more fun, less stressful, a good deal quicker and would allow me to gain some more fixed wing flying hours in my log book. There were downsides. It meant I was always under a good deal of time pressure to get to Bedford as early as I could and then dash home before Boscombe closed at 5.30 pm. Outbound, I was faced with another challenge. The Beagle Pup had limited payload. When I first flew it I was based at RAF Leeming learning how to fly the Bulldog which was effectively a Beagle Pup on steroids. I wanted to take my girlfriend flying, so joined a local club at Teesside. My check out was minimalist as the Pup was simpler and easier to fly than the Bulldog. When my girlfriend arrived I phoned the club before setting off …

'Please could you fill the fuel tanks in the Pup for me? I'm on my way to fly a passenger this afternoon.'

'Fill the tanks? Are you sure?'

I was a Navy pilot and had no intention of running out of fuel, so I confirmed my request and pulled up at the club an hour later. It was a very warm summer's day and as I taxied to the duty runway I was advised I would be departing with a tail wind.

'No bother,' I thought given the nearly 2,300m long runway. So I lined up when cleared, applied full throttle and very gently accelerated in a south westerly direction. I had driven down half of it when I began to get worried … very worried. In my sporty GTI Bulldog I would already be climbing through 500ft or more, but I was still glued to the tarmac. When I felt I could wait no longer I eased back on the joystick and, with the stall warner blaring, hauled this fine example of a British aeroplane off the ground. *Now* I know why my request to fill the tanks was queried. This was an example of a two seat trainer which could barely carry two people, even with minimal fuel. Thankfully my girlfriend was none the wiser to my mistake and, after surviving a gentle potter around the local countryside, I was able to 'sign the aircraft in' and scurry away before I was nobbled by a club instructor.

Phew! Survived another embarrassing moment.

But this characteristic was engrained by the time, as a much better educated and experienced experimental test pilot, I was trying to use the Pup as a taxi. In order for the timings for such days to work, I had to prepare the aircraft the previous day – which meant checking the oil and filling the fuel tanks to have enough for a return trip. This was in breach of the Bustard Club guidelines that encouraged only filling the tanks half full. All was normally well though when I rolled down the tarmac by 9 am and was in the AFS shortly after 10. But Bedford used to suffer dreadfully from early morning fog. Most of the time it would clear promptly but there were a couple of times when I had to abandon the Pup and leap into my car instead. Because I hadn't had chance to burn the fuel off I then had the problem of apologising to the Club for overfilling the aircraft.

Yikes!

I did many days in the AFS, gathering data for the ADS33 programme I've already mentioned, and a good deal of flying was to a Type 23 frigate as part of the work that culminated in Trial Avalon. Although I note in my log book I had two further complete weeks back at Bedford in my final month or so at EFS doing more work for the maritime deck interface projects.

Perhaps the most upsetting day occurred on a Friday. You will recollect from my Wessex chapter, I've always found flying on a Friday problematic. Boscombe tended to close by 4.30 pm on a Friday so I had to be airborne out of Bedford by 3.20 pm. All had gone well getting up to Bedford and I'd been cracking on with my simulator tasks. One of the unusual things about the AFS was that the 'box' effectively ran on rails. You could hear the hydraulics puffing and wheezing and hear the wheels running on their tracks, even over and above the simulated helicopter noise that was piped in to the box at high volume. I was running in to the Type 23 to fly yet another deck landing when suddenly all the cues were wrong. I could feel I was being accelerated up and I could hear a massive rumble as all the wheels lurched me higher.

Author about to get airborne in the Lynx – Trial Avalon. *(DRA Bedford)*

'Not good.' Just when I thought I was about to burst out of the roof of the building the opposite happened and I became light in my straps … never a good feeling in a simulator.

With a massive whoosh I felt myself being propelled earthwards until …

Grrrrrrrrr BANG!

I was thrown sideways and hit my helmeted head on the side of the cockpit. The lights went out. Everything stopped. There was no noise. I was about 30 degrees nose-down and 30 degrees rolled to the left. It was completely dark. It was 2.30 pm.

Bugger!

The AFS had crashed. Apparently this was not the first time that all the 'ones and noughts' in the software had become jumbled up, and all of a sudden the sim did its utmost to kill me. Thankfully, I had followed the brief to ensure I was strapped in, but being a helicopter pilot I confess my straps were looser than they should have been.

What now?

My immediate concern was to see if I was OK. I checked that all my limbs still functioned and that there was no blood pumping out from unseen wounds. Next, establish comms with the 'outside world'. This was potentially beyond my control as all the electrics had tripped. But eventually the intercom came live and I was being asked if I was alright.

'Yes, I'm fine – but I need to get out of here sharpish. I need to get back to Boscombe before the airfield shuts.

'Mmmmmmmm – we are working on it,' was the reply.

By 3 pm I had decided, being the task-orientated control freak you now realise I am, to take matters into my own hands. At the back of the 'cockpit' was a breakout panel. I decided to try it. Unstrapping briskly I swivelled in my seat until I was in a position to give this panel a thoroughly good kicking. I announced my intentions to the boffins who I feared might be in danger of getting the thing working again which might lead to me getting squished. Once out I was faced by a pitch black interior of the sim building – it felt like I had to do some night-time mountaineering, without moon or stars, but eventually I clambered my way over various bits of structure and found the emergency exit. I burst into the control room to see a bunch of concerned boffins pouring over a wiring diagram.

'I'd love to stop and chat,' I said 'but I really have to be going.'

With a nonchalant wave of my hand I rushed to my Pup, which I started without delay and seconds later was taking off along the taxiway to save time. I landed at 4.30 pm and had a beer in my hand by 5 pm.

Phew! I had survived nearly being really killed by a simulator. Another first!

The simulators at DRA Farnborough were less dangerous. And again they were well ahead of their time. Associated with the work I was doing in Lynx ZD285, which you will have read about earlier, I frequently found myself in a virtual reality (VR) simulator. Ironically I have just had to use such a simulator again, twenty-five years later, trying to evaluate the control laws for an eVTOL aircraft. Back in the middle '90s, VR sims were unheard of outside the R&D world. Invariably I would be placed into a Lynx cockpit and find myself wearing a relatively heavy Apache attack helicopter helmet with a projection device, bolted where the visor would normally fit, which added to the weight. I would be presented with a fantasy world in which to fly around. Invariably I was in an attack helicopter and was looking for suitable ground targets, much like my day out at GEC when I flew the Venom cockpit. By the end of a two-hour session the aircraft would be frozen and doors opened. I would find that my head was almost in my lap. Because I had no cockpit references to keep my torso upright I would slump, almost into a foetal position, to try and cope with the very heavy head I now had. Weird. But at least the Farnborough sims never tried to kill me.

Although flying the sims was interesting and invaluable for gathering research data, I think I would not be the only pilot who much preferred the real thing. And for me, one of the best aspects of being an experimental test pilot on EFS was the wide variety of platforms we were able to fly. I had briefly harboured a desire to be a Sea Harrier pilot; I'm not sure whether I would have made the grade or not but there were no slots available when I went through flying training. Thereafter I could have tried to do something called a SMAC 309. This was a brilliant course and with hindsight I should have applied for it anyway. The course was flown in the Fleet Air Arm Hunters at RNAS Yeovilton. They were operated by Fleet Requirements and Direction Unit FRADU and flown by very experienced, mostly ex-Navy pilots. Even if I'd failed selection, I would at least have enjoyed the Hunter flying.

One of the younger pilots on my Lynx conversion course did exactly that – after a tour or so on the Lynx he passed the SMAC 309 course and flew the Harrier. But soon bored with that he decided to move on and the RN placed him on Fixed Wing Standards Flight at RNAS Yeovilton. I had hoped to do more fixed wing flying on the ETPS course than I achieved so, finding myself with a few spare days on EFS, called Roger to see if he could help. I was up to date with my ejection seat drills and had all the correct flying kit for the Hawk, G suit, oxygen mask etc. Roger was delighted to hear from me and within minutes had, as I'd hoped, invited me to go flying with him. He seemed to have at his disposal two shiny black Hawk T.1s. In fairness, at the time, there was some ebb and flow of Hawks between the RN and the RAF so not all of the aircraft looked quite as nice. The Hawks were used for continuation training of the Fleet Air Arm's fixed wing pilots but were primarily tasked with supporting the Hunters on the FRADU task and eventually replaced them. This group went on to become 736 Naval Air Squadron in 2013. The role required them to take part in the RN's ship training in the Portland and Plymouth exercise areas.

For me it provided the most enjoyable flying of the year. I would pitch up to Yeovilton and after a quick brief, be taxiing in a Hawk. We would fly down to the South Coast and, when prompted, run in at a nominal 50ft towards whatever poor ships were due to be attacked that day. Sometimes we would pretend to be missiles dropped from a Falcon jet which itself was pretending to be a Soviet maritime attack aircraft. As a Navy pilot I spent a good deal of my career skimming the ocean waves for one reason or another, but doing it in a Hawk at nearly 500 KIAS was a real blast – I just loved every second of it. Job done, we would land at RNAS Culdrose for lunch and fuel before doing it all again in the afternoon. I guess for those employed to do it all the time it might have become boring, but for me, building my jet hours, it was an awesome day out of the office. I note the aircraft I flew were XX242, XX245 and XX315. The first two are now part of the Red Arrows team … so I have something in common with the Red Arrows. Now that is a boast that needs recording.

With some fast jet street cred under my belt I found myself flying the Hunter with the squadron boss as I've mentioned, but more fun was flying the Jaguar with my former course mate, Trevor. We flew in both XX835

Simulators and Aeroplanes 149

Experimental Flying Squadron 1995. *(MOD)*
Left to right: Christine, Chris, Paul, Tim, Dan, Tim, Jon, Trevor, Bill, Author, Tony, Cliff, Gary

and XX146. The first time we flew together in the Jag we briefed quite quickly and I found myself in the backseat of an unfamiliar aircraft still trying to get my head around everything as the lid closed, the engines were started and we began to taxi … and I couldn't breathe.

'Trevor … Trevor … I can't breathe.'

'Have you turned the oxygen ON?'

'Dunno.'

'There's a switch on the left side of your seat.'

Now he tells me.

Able to breathe we were soon hurtling up through layers of clouds with me doing my best to impress with my newly acquired fast jet expertise. But I blew it on the level off. Real fast jet pilots would have rolled inverted and pulled the stick back to stop the climb. But I did the helicopter pilot, 'gentle push forwards thing'. Not quite as impressive and apparently I surprised Trevor at the time. I guess if I'd achieved significant negative G we might have been in trouble. I went on to fly with Trevor in the Harvard and managed to drop my flying gloves once I'd completed strapping in. The floor of the Harvard is a long way down from where I was sitting and there was nothing for it but to completely unstrap and crawl to the bottom of the aircraft to retrieve them. Very embarrassing. But my embarrassments did not finish with the Harvard. Before long we were off to fly the Andover (XS646) together. I guess we were both slightly outside our comfort zone, as a Tornado pilot and Lynx pilot, but we were doing okay until I came in to land at the end of the sortie. Now, in mitigation, the Andover cockpit is a good deal higher off the ground than any other aeroplane I'd flown up until that point. I did all the right things. I was on centreline, bang on the approach speed, coming over the piano keys I was smoothly retarding both throttles, control column eased back to adopt the landing attitude – frankly perfect text book Andover landing technique – apart from I'd achieved it all about 3ft too high. Instead of the gentle touchdown I'd anticipated, we fell brick-like for what felt like forever and landed with a much more carrier-landing like finesse. Once we'd gathered up our dental fillings from the floor we realised all was still well and the undercarriage hadn't been pushed through the wings. The aircraft had been designed for ad hoc short field landing sites and it was going to take more than the amateur attempts of a Fleet Air Arm rote to ruin

Simulators and Aeroplanes 151

its day. Now an accomplished Andover pilot, I found myself invited to fly several more sorties on both the Andover and our HS748 (XW750) which was a similar aircraft. At least I could get my head around the 150 KIAS cruise speed which was more akin to a helicopter than a fast jet. Later on, when I joined ETPS, I found myself formally accepted as a co-pilot for the type which was to prove useful for when we used the aircraft instead of the BAC1-11 to get anywhere.

Phew! I had survived my fixed wing flying on Experimental Flying Squadron.

Sadly, the only aircraft still flying from those mentioned in this chapter are the two Red Arrows Hawks. The rest are in museums, training schools or scrap yards. Very sad.

ETPS Hawk XX342
(Andy Mogg MoD)

Chapter 10

Royal Navy Appointing – Fighting to stay an Experimental Test Pilot

I had been on EFS for only a few days when my office phone rang …

'Chris Taylor?'

'Speaking.'

'It's the appointer. I've got some good news. You're off to Canada!'

I should explain. Officers in the armed forces change jobs at regular intervals. In the Royal Navy it depended on the particular posting, but typically was around every two years. Based in London was a team of officers who had to ensure that all the possible 'jobs' were filled. They had to oversee the training pipelines to ensure that personnel were suitably trained for all the above jobs. They had to manage an officer's career, so that an individual would gain the required breadth of experience to allow him/her to be promoted from time to time, and then be suitably experienced to carry out increasingly senior managerial roles. Finally, they were supposed to take account of an individual officer's wishes. The Fleet Air Arm team comprised a Captain and a Commander and then a Lieutenant Commander for pilots and one for observers. My dealings then were normally with the Lieutenant Commander 'Pilot Appointer'. I was probably regarded as one of the more difficult characters on the appointer's books.

I had researched all three options, as flying helicopters for the Army had some attractions, however 'yomping' around Thetford pretending to be a soldier had rather deterred me from becoming a 'brown job'. So I was left dithering between the RAF and the RN. The RN did everything it could to encourage me to join and the RAF did the opposite. When I was 16, my careers teacher at school set out to find placements for us all, for the end of term period, after sitting our GCE 'O' Levels. As an aspiring pilot, I asked to visit the RAF. They declined, so I asked to visit the Fleet Air Arm – and what a good move that was. I spent two weeks at RNAS Culdrose, in Cornwall, where every day I was flown in a different type of aircraft and spent my evenings in the wardroom bar where I had a free mess bill and no one serving beer seemed to mind how old I was – now that got my attention in a very positive way. As a member of my school CCF, which was an Army contingent, early the following year I was allowed to apply to both services for a flying scholarship. This was a brilliant scheme whereby, after conducting aptitude tests at RAF Biggin Hill, successful applicants would be given thirty hours of flying at a civilian flying school – effectively providing the first thirty hours of the required thirty-five hours for the potential award of a private pilot's licence (PPL). After two days at what was left of the famous wartime base I was wheeled in to see an RAF officer.

'Taylor, I have some bad news and some good news.'

'OK … I'll take the bad news first.'

'You haven't reached the correct result in your aptitude tests to be awarded an RAF Flying Scholarship – BUT – you have been successful in being awarded a Royal Navy one – my colleague next door is waiting to chat to you.'

And sure enough I had received yet another early lesson in the RN and RAF doing things differently. The Fleet Air Arm pilot in the office next door explained that they weighted specific aspects of the test differently. Maybe my time at the wardroom bar in RNAS Culdrose had paid off!

'Hurrah!' I was off to Ipswich Flying School to learn how to fly the Cessna 150 over four weeks in my summer holidays. My parents very kindly paid for me to fly the extra hours and shortly after turning 17 I WAS A PILOT! I had achieved a PPL.

Now I had to turn my attention to my 'second year sixth' and getting my 'A' levels. But I was still dithering. I had reviewed the 'chop rate' for aspiring military pilots and it was bloody high. Already the pessimist, I decided I should get a degree so that I would be employable if I suddenly found myself chucked out. I reflect on this decision often. It had huge ramifications. By providing a safety net I had made my life difficult. As you will have already read, I was thinking about the possibility of being a test pilot and decided to read Electrical/Electronic Engineering. With that decision made I thought getting a cadetship to be paid through university would be a good idea. The RN only offered cadetships to 'career officers' who would predominantly aspire to be deck or warfare officers, so yet again I turned to the RAF. A recurring theme of my career! Back to RAF Biggin Hill for more aptitude tests and their officer selection programme, which included lots of leadership exercises in the gym. I did well.

'Well done Chris, you have passed the RAF officer selection process and we would like to offer you a university cadetship starting this September.'

I could hardly believe my ears – I'd done it. I was going to be paid by the RAF to get a degree and then be a fast jet pilot – great.

'Thank you sir, that's great news.'

'It would be as an Engineering Officer.'

'I'm sorry?'

'We are you offering you an RAF University Cadetship as an Engineering Officer.'

'But I want to be a pilot.'

'You will be studying electrical engineering and we really need good candidates to be engineering officers.'

'Errrr ... that's not what I expected.'

'Well, we could give you a cadetship as a navigator.'

'But I want to be a pilot.'

'In that case reapply as a graduate.'

Bugger!

So off I went to university and immediately ran out of money. In truth I still wanted to be a Wasp pilot in the Fleet Air Arm and presented myself at the Birmingham RN Careers Office accordingly. I was immediately seduced by the glamorous Second Officer WRNS who conducted my first interview. What was it about that uniform?

The problem with joining the RN back then was I had to choose between two crucial options. If I joined the RN as a pilot I would have joined on a short career commission as a Supplementary List Officer. I'd have gone to BRNC Dartmouth for a year and then straight on to flying – but again no safety net and no option for a university cadetship. OR, I could apply for a cadetship and join as a career or General List Officer. This meant I would have to train as a deck officer for a couple of years before commencing flying training, but it would pay me through another two years at university and it would give me options should I be facing the dreaded chop. I dithered. The siren with two blue rings on her sleeves seductively floated the suggestion that Sea Harrier pilots would all have to be General List officers to justify the training cost. It sounded plausible and, before I knew it, she had fluttered her very pretty eyelashes and I had applied to be a GL Royal Navy Officer. And it worked. Following a far more rigorous selection process than the RAF, which included swinging on ropes above tanks full of very smelly green water, I was offered a cadetship which started in the following September. I accepted. Tedious periods of training at BRNC Dartmouth were compensated for by my being taught how to fly the Fleet Air Arm Chipmunks based at Roborough, Plymouth Airport. Two Easter camps were each followed by summer camps at Perigeaux. As a PPL holder they gave me a Chipmunk. I flew one of half a dozen aircraft from Plymouth to the South of France and back and spent a good deal of time beating up French roads and railways pretending to be a 1944 Typhoon pilot.

So this was all good news. I graduated having done a good deal of my training in my vacations. One further term of polishing shoes, marching and running around and I was a proper Sub Lieutenant. The downside was that I now had to do all my RN deck officer training before I could go flying. Which I did. It included an awesome few months driving a Hong Kong Squadron patrol boat (HMS *Monkton*), some months in the Caribbean on HMS *Newcastle* (which is where I met the aforementioned CO of HMS *Marlborough*), then a few months at HMS *Dryad* (warfare training school near Portsmouth), learning stuff I promptly forgot. Eventually, after again working my socks off, I was unleashed upon the fleet. After a year as the Gunnery Officer on HMS *Alderney*, chasing dodgy French trawlers around, and another few months in the Caribbean navigating HMS *Londonderry*, I was finally allowed to go flying. Being GL was a mixed blessing time and time again. The big problem was that the RN saw me as a career officer and wanted to broaden my experience to fit me for a senior rank. Whereas I had always made it clear – I had joined aspiring to be a Wasp pilot and maybe a test pilot in the fullness of time. During my appointments to the various warships I served on, I was always being asked to drive the ship as a watchkeeper and was invariably more experienced and better qualified than those who were actually paid to be the watchkeepers. This led to a number of 'situations', including several rows with my seniors and my ramming a German frigate in the

Baltic. In 1940 I would have been given a medal, but not quite so much in 1984 …

As far as my aviation career was concerned, the appointer was always trying to get me to do 'fish-head' jobs, and I was always fighting hard to specialise in aviation. The ultimate specialisation was 'Experimental Test Pilot', but that didn't stop the appointer trying to mess me about.

As you will have gathered, I have a relatively short attention span and get bored quite easily. I like new and demanding challenges and during my time as a Wasp pilot I had asked to do an exchange tour as a pilot for the US Coast Guard flying the AS365 Dolphin out of Miami, Florida. It turns out that GL officers didn't have time for such exchange postings – apparently we needed to concentrate on our careers.

Bugger! I had signed the wrong form.

Instead I was offered my own ship. A Ton Class minesweeper – yep – all of my own. Now this would have been fun, but it wasn't flying, and it would have taken me away from home a good deal when I'd just got married, and besides, I wanted to crack on and learn to fly another type – the Lynx.

So – back to the beginning of my chapter. I had previously expressed an interest in an exchange posting and clearly the appointer thought he was on to a 'win-win' with his pitch.

'Canada?'

'Yes, Canada.'

'But I wasn't aware we had a test pilot exchange with Canada?'

'We don't. This isn't a test pilot job.'

'What?'

'You did a really great job running the Lynx simulator and specifying the requirements for the Lynx Mk.8 simulator. The contract has been awarded to CAE in Ottawa. We want you to go out to Ottawa for two or three years and supervise the building programme to make sure the sim is suitable for our needs.'

'Mmmmm – but I've just spent a very difficult year working flat out, sixteen hours a day, learning how to be an experimental test pilot. And surely EFS needs me?'

'Oh don't worry about that. Another RN TP is available to take your place, so EFS will still have an RN TP – just not you.'

'But what happens next? What happens to my test flying career?'

Royal Navy Appointing – Fighting to stay an Experimental Test Pilot

'Your what?'

'Well I'm only just qualified – I need to do some actual flight tests to consolidate what I've learnt – how will that happen if I go off to Canada?'

'Well it won't – but don't worry we will find something else for you to do.'

'But I want to be an Experimental Test Pilot – in fact, I am an Experimental Test Pilot.'

'Sorry – this is more important and there is no one else – so I'll send you a letter tonight and you'll be off in a few weeks.'

Bloody Hell!

I was completely devastated. I had spent the best part of two years preparing for ETPS and then had completed a year of gruelling training and now the Navy was about to throw it all away. I was literally dumbfounded. I rode my moped back to my married quarter and had a good rant with Ally accompanied by large quantities of Australian Shiraz. I wasn't at all happy – it was fair to say. In the morning I got myself organised and went to see my squadron boss. I explained what had happened the previous afternoon. In the RN I was used to both being a boss and serving under a number. Perhaps because of the divisional system, started in Nelson's day, in the RN we looked after our own. We fought tooth and nail to look after the guys under our command. I had assumed the same, but I hadn't worked with the RAF before. My boss, Jon, listened to all of the above and said …

'Well Chris, from my perspective, I'll be losing a newly qualified TP and gaining another, who is both qualified and more experienced so, frankly, it doesn't bother me whether you go to Canada or not.'

What?! Really?

Next stop was to see John, the Chief Test Pilot – the RAF Group Captain who ran the place and had an interest in the whole TP plot to ensure all the squadrons were properly manned.

I was invited to sit on his couch and pour out my story as I had just done to my boss.

'Well that's terrible,' he says. 'I remember when something similar happened to me. I was on a Hunter squadron having a great time and then …'

I confess, I can't really remember what happened to the CTP on his Hunter squadron. I was receiving sympathy at least, maybe even empathy, but more importantly I needed someone to give a shit and kick up a fuss. Off to see Bob. Bob was an RN Commander observer and the Senior

Naval Officer at Boscombe Down. Perhaps of equal significance was that he had been my boss previously on 702 NAS. We had been detached to a ship together when he had got the 'staff in confidence' signal that my wife was being rushed into hospital with a massive brain tumour. Bob got me off the ship the following morning and didn't expect to see me back at work for quite a while. When I did go back he agreed to me working 10 am – 3 pm so I could drop off my son and pick him up at nursery. I already owed Bob a huge debt and yet I found myself back in his office almost in tears – again.

He did get it. He did sympathise, he did empathise, and more importantly – he starting making phone calls. I went home that evening knowing that, at least, I had someone rooting for me and I was confident Bob would sort things out. I got on with my day job, which, as you will have already read, was incredibly hectic in those first few weeks. But Bob was a lowly Commander. To me that was a senior rank, but given the big guns we were up against he quickly ran into problems and called me into his office.

'I've tried, Chris. But the appointer doesn't understand how the TP plot works and because he can apparently source another RN TP, he can plug any gap your departure creates. The RN does not seem to appreciate the huge sacrifice you, and your family, have just made to put yourself through ETPS.'

Time to take matters into my own hands and I decided to see the appointer in person. Officers of my rank were entitled to a serious conversation about their promotion and career prospects. I wasn't bothered about promotion particularly, but they didn't know that. A day or two after sorting a meeting I was driving back from RAF Shawbury, where I was learning how to fly the Wessex, and on the train to London the following morning, bound for some splendid but decrepit Admiralty offices. The appointer spent over an hour going through my career to date. Wanting to be a helicopter instructor counted against me and wanting to be a TP counted against me, but I had really shot myself in both feet when I had turned down my 'own command'. Yep – chances of promotion in this man's Navy were about as likely as me winning the EuroMillions lottery when I had never bought a ticket. So it really didn't matter if I was sent off to Ottawa; my career prospects were already flatlining.

Bugger!

I returned home – despondent. But I have a character trait that is both a blessing and a curse. I am tenacious. Like a dog with a bone some would say. Like a terrier that never knows when to quit. That has caused a number

Royal Navy Appointing – Fighting to stay an Experimental Test Pilot

of people, namely my wife and those I've had to work with, some serious stress. In this case I was inflamed by the injustice of it. I was staggered by the waste of tax payer's money – the TP course was not cheap. And I was staggered by the lack of any thought given to my job prospects in the future – trained but never been a TP. What does that look like on a CV? Like trying to cover up a two year spell at HM government's pleasure. And I was incredibly disappointed and disillusioned by some of the more senior 'light blue' people around me who didn't seem to give a damn.

I made it home. Kissed my wife and put my children to bed with a good story narrated with tear-filled eyes. By the time I had driven back to RAF Shawbury I'd determined another strategy.

As you have already read, I was extremely chuffed to have won the Westland Trophy. I had been the best RW student on the course I'd finished only days earlier. At the dinner was a very charming RN Commodore who was the deputy to the Flag Officer for Naval Aviation (FONA). This chap was very pleased that the senior service had snatched this cup from the competition and he had enjoyed a liberal swig of Westland's champagne from the cup. He clearly had reported back favourably to his boss, as a few days later I received a delightful handwritten letter, in the customary green fountain pen ink, from FONA himself congratulating me personally and saying how impressed he was with my performance.

Now – normally the military etiquette is quite clear. If you have a problem you address it to your immediate superior. If he endorses the concern it is forwarded up the chain of command. Most things get sorted out within one or two iterations. I had tried that route – and I'd failed utterly and completely. Time for plan B as I started to bash away on my PC a reply to FONA's very nice letter. In fact I wrote similar letters to both FONA and his deputy. They were friendly and polite. I thanked them for their very kind words but went on to comment that they 'might be interested to learn' that their star student of ETPS was never going to do any more flight testing.

The letters were sent first class. Just two days later I gather the appointer was asked to meet with FONA's chief of staff. I confess I am not quite sure what happened next, but my career was suddenly being seriously discussed. And then, all of a sudden, I learnt that the other RN TP was needed to fill another post back in the Junglie community and would no longer be able to take-over from me.

'Really?'

So with him out of the picture I could no longer be spared from EFS.

'Really?'

I literally jumped for joy as I put the phone down!

The RN had approached my deputy on the Lynx sim – Jon. Jon was a very 'switched on' Observer and very nice guy to boot. He had enjoyed commanding his own patrol boat on exchange in Darwin, Australia. When offered the possibility of a couple of years or more in Ottawa he and his wife Carole were delighted. And they had a really great time out there.

Phew! Good result – smiles all round. Thank goodness for my tenacious nature.

Subsequently the RN decided it needed some expert assistance in evaluating the completed Mk 8 simulator and contacted DRA Bedford. You have probably already guessed that the Bedford expert on simulators and Navy helicopters was well – me!

Now as an experienced experimental test pilot I was invited to evaluate the CAE FMS and organised a good number of changes which made the sim a much better device. Changes I would not have had the authority or temerity to suggest had I not been an experienced experimental test pilot.

Good outcome. For everyone. All round. Phew!

The following year the phone rang again. Since the demise of EFS and our merger with RWTS I was sharing an office with my mate, Mike. Mike had gone straight to the Lynx from Gazelles and had been on the ETPS course a year before me. He was one of the course mates of the Ozzie, Dave who I had flown with in Lynx ZD285 the previous year.

I picked up the phone. It was the appointer again.

'I need to talk to both you and Mike but I've phoned you first.'

I glanced across the office to where Mike was sitting. Was this going to be embarrassing?

'Apparently the RAF can't find a suitable candidate to take over from your tutor, Kevin, at ETPS so they've asked us to help out and we've agreed to find someone.'

'OK?'

'And – Steve, your predecessor as the Bedford TP, now on exchange with USNTPS, Patuxent River needs replacing.'

'OK?'

Royal Navy Appointing – Fighting to stay an Experimental Test Pilot 161

Rotary Wing Test Squadron 1996. *(MOD)*
Front Row: Pete, Bob, Chris, Bob, Author, Tim, Mark
Back Row: Mike, Frank, Steve, Al, Rob, Crispin, Larry, Martin

'Well I don't mind which one of you does which job, but you two are both in the frame to cover both posts. I'm going to phone him now and then you can sort it out between you.'

I put the handset gently back on to the cradle, feeling somehow involved in a major conspiracy. Before the phone on Mike's desk had time to ring I'd already started to see myself in my RN 'whites' at some very pleasant cocktail party in Maryland.

'Pax would be great,' I thought. 'I'd get to fly the Bell 206, The OH-6, the Blackhawk and Seahawk and probably a number of the fixed wing aeroplanes such as the Otter, Beaver, King Air and maybe the jets …'

The phone rang. Mike picked up the handset and within seconds was staring at me. He clearly was receiving an identical brief. He eventually put the phone down. It was 5 pm.

'What do you think?' I asked.

'What do YOU think?'

'Hmmmmm – I think I need to go home and talk to Ally about it.'

'And I need to chat to Angie. – Let's discuss it in the morning.'

Blige! This was going to be very difficult. I guessed that Mike would want to go to Pax. So did I, but I had also decided that probably the best job in the world was working for ETPS or maybe the UK CAA, but I hadn't expected either as possibilities.

The following morning we grabbed a coffee and locked our office door – we did not want to be disturbed. I now had another problem. Ally was a solicitor and, although not doing much work at the time, pointed out with some clarity the previous evening that she wouldn't be able to practice in America. My son was 8 already. Three years in the States would mean he wouldn't be around to do the entrance examinations (11+) for secondary school so I was now weighing up my own enthusiasm versus the greater good for 'Team Taylor', and I'd arrived at the office with a new clarity of what I thought should be the best job for me to take for the family. But what if Angie didn't want to go to Maryland or what if Mike had received some form of epiphany in the night?

'So, Mike, what do you think?'

'What do you think, Chris?'

'Well – I think the Pax River job is outstanding but I have some family things going on – and the upshot is – it would quite suit me to stay in the UK – what about you?'

Royal Navy Appointing – Fighting to stay an Experimental Test Pilot

'Angie whooped with joy at the thought of going to the States – we will be well happy to go to Pax!'

'Phew!' We had, without resorting to duelling pistols at dawn, resolved the appointer's Hobson's choice and we both went home that evening very happy with the conversations we'd had earlier.

Mike and Angie had a fantastic time in the States. Mike extended his tour and was offered a further exchange with the US Army. They never came home and still live out there. One very happy bunny.

For me the security of another two or three years at Boscombe Down was just the catalyst I needed to start looking for a house. We moved out of our 'temporary' married quarter after three happy years there. The cul de sac was quiet and had proved brilliant for teaching both our children to ride bikes. It had a play area a few yards from the front door and the neighbours had become good friends. Even better – because the quarter had been declared sub-standard the rent had been reduced and we had now saved enough to put a deposit on a 'proper house' in Salisbury, which is where we will be enjoying Christmas yet again this year.

Thank goodness that all the hard work, late nights and lost weekends during ETPS resulted in me winning the Westland Trophy. If I had not, my story, and that of my family, might have turned out quite differently.

Chapter 11

Back to School – A Hell of a First Year

'Pan, Pan Pan, Tester 61 in the Basset with a single engine failure fifteen miles west of the field -requesting radar vectors for a visual rejoin.'

I had decided to get some help from ATC and allowing them to deal with the navigation gave me the chance to concentrate on nailing the required speed +/- 1 KIAS. But even with full power applied we continued to descend.

Yikes!

I arrived at the airfield boundary at around 1,500ft still descending despite my best efforts not to. There would be no chance of 'going around' from this approach. The aircraft, on a warm summer's day, with the fuel it had on board, was not going to climb. I had to get this right first time. My first ever flight in the Basset and I was dealing with a serious emergency.

'Well – Chris – you've had a hell-of-a first year.'
  Some of you will remember the line from Viper in *Top Gun* when he's balling out Tom Cruise's character, Maverick –
  'Well – Maverick – you've had a hell-of-a first day.'
  I had been looking forward to going back to ETPS. I had, by then, decided on what my two favourite jobs were likely to be. One was going to the UK Civil Aviation Authority as a civil certification test pilot, and the other was working at ETPS as a flying tutor. I had already determined the first one was never going to happen, as the guy in the RW job was only a bit older than me and was likely to be there for life. So I had set my hopes on ETPS and the phone call from the appointer a few weeks earlier had, on this occasion, been very welcome. I pitched up at the beginning of January 1997 to settle into

my new office. I would be working for Chris, the RN tutor (I was filling the RAF tutor post), and working alongside Peter from the AAC, and Eric, who had been the Principal Tutor for my year as a student. Again I was thankful to have won the Westland Trophy. It meant that at least some of the tutors that year didn't think I was a complete knob. Eric was now a civil servant and had been recruited by ETPS to provide long term course continuity and standardisation. What a great initiative. Additionally the QHI role had been civilianised and Bill remained in post, having retired from the RAF. So I was returning to some familiar faces but some new ones as well.

As always, we had to hit the ground running and I was invited to fly with Bill, Chris and Eric in the Gazelle, Lynx, Scout and Sea King without delay to ensure I was still current and competent. I had already flown with Bill a few times over the previous couple of years to revalidate my instrument rating and prove that I was 'Competent to Instruct' (C to I) on all the various types I flew. For only my second flight on my first day I was learning how to fly the AS355N Twin Squirrel. We needed a more modern helicopter to teach the students more current test techniques which included FADEC – or Full Authority Digital Engine Control. This concept was taking over from hydro mechanical governors and Wessex/Sea King style systems and effectively allowed a digital computer to control the helicopter engines and thus, rotors. This produced a much better controlled rotor rpm (Nr) and is the method of control for nearly all modern day twin-engine aircraft as I write this chapter. I was to fly with Nick. Nick was an ex-RN Wasp pilot among other things, and had trained at ETPS and served as a tutor at USNTPS, Pax River. He was now a civilian TP working for a highly regarded UK company that did a fair amount of flight testing on Aerospatiale/Eurocopter helicopters. I hadn't realised it at the time but we were to fly together often in the future. During this first flight we had been working our way through all the required training exercises and getting to the stage when we were almost finished when a 'caption' lit up on the aircraft's Central Warning Panel (CWP). It's always upsetting when these things happen, but thankfully we were already at Boscombe Down doing some hovering manoeuvres. Nick was confident we could taxi carefully back to the dispersal to get it investigated. I flew as attentively as I had ever done, alert for any further symptoms. He was very laid back, as became a man of his considerable experience, and suspected the warning was spurious. We shut down expeditiously and investigated further. The caption had been labelled 'Tail Gearbox Chip' and illuminated when bits of metal that had found their way into the tail rotor gearbox oil were attracted by a magnet to 'short' two electrical terminals. Nick pulled out the 'mag plug' and found it covered in gunge including metallic content. – (sometimes indicative of gears in the tail rotor gearbox starting to break up.)

Bugger! Good decision to abort our sortie promptly and head for home, but we were not going to do any more flying in this particular helicopter for a while.

Thank goodness the caption had illuminated when we were so close to the dispersal – otherwise we might have been obliged to land in some farmer's field or even worse, lost our tail rotor and crashed. This was not to be the only mechanical problem I would have with aircraft this year, but I didn't know it at the time.

I had been a good student two years earlier and thought I had learnt most of the subject matter thrown at me quite well. But now I was faced with the challenge of teaching it and I suddenly realised I knew diddly-squat. It is amazing, but a truth nonetheless, that you never really learn something until you have to teach it. Doctors have known this for years and use the expression, 'See one, do one, teach one,' and they are better medics for it. These days ETPS tutors need to be formally qualified as Flight Test Instructors but in my day it was all done by on the job training – and each topic was done just about a week or two before the students needed to be taught it.

Hells Bells! – nerve wracking or what?

Fortunately, all of the RW staff happened to be A2 QHIs, so had a wealth of airborne instructional experience to fall back on. The challenge was to relearn all the theory behind each of the exercises we had to deliver. This was accomplished through a couple of methods. Firstly the Principal Tutor Rotary Wing (PTRW), Chris, divided up all the various exercises between the four TP tutors – and thankfully gave the new boy the easier ones. All the tutors would join the students and sit in on each of their colleagues' exercise briefs. Then Chris organised for us to fly all of the required demo or tutorial flights with each other so that we could then deliver them to our students a few days later. I was literally just one step ahead of those I was teaching and I think I was on a steeper learning curve. Some exercises were more demanding than others. You will have read of my experience of learning all the engine-off stuff as a student. Now I had to teach it!

Blige!

Some of the sorties were only mildly dangerous. But teaching the 'avoid curve' was on a whole new level of instructional responsibility. For all of these sorties the tutor was the aircraft captain and had 'signed' for the aircraft. Although a student might well make a genuine mistake and be forgiven, the tutor was supposed to use their skill, experience and judgement to either prevent the mistake, or redeem the situation if not. Easier said than done. My appointed mentor was to be Pete, the AAC tutor. We were scheduled to fly together. It was very hot and there was zero wind – both of which make engine-off landings difficult – so he cancelled. The following day the conditions were the same. He cancelled. The third day there was no change. He cancelled. Chris told us to get it done by the end of the week. We cancelled on Thursday. On Friday the same conditions prevailed. We went flying. I was scared. I knew Pete was equally anxious …

Oh blimey!

But we survived. And I am very grateful to Pete. These conditions would be replicated years later when I was to test a Polish helicopter in Lublin, an episode covered in *Test Pilot*.

My appointed student had what we used to describe as 'golden gloves'. He was a very natural, instinctive pilot and quite sharp to boot. I was relieved I would fly with him for my first ever avoid curve instructional flight. Knowing Chris, with hindsight, I have no doubt he ensured my first ever avoid curve student was specially selected. A good deal of the sortie had gone well and I was beginning to relax slightly. It was still hot but there was now a 2–3 knot wind favouring the grass strip alongside Runway 23. We had flown a number of EOLs so far and we now needed to set up for the higher speed run. This was a very challenging test point and on what we described as the 'knee' of the avoid curve. For the recovery from an engine failure on the knee, lots of different stuff had to happen. We would be at 60 KIAS. We would have to lower the collective, to preserve rotor rpm, but we could not flare too soon as we were going too slowly. So we had to allow the aircraft to sink and then everything would happen in a rush. It was more art than science. We re-briefed.

'Are you ready?

'Ready'

'OK – commence your run in.'

'Tester 77 – Final – low level engine-off to 23 Grass,' we advised ATC.

We started running in towards the strip at 100ft above the ground. Closer … closer … not yet. I was ready to operate the throttle in the cockpit roof and was waiting for the imperative command of 'Now'. My student started the countdown …

'Three … two … one … Nnnnn … …'

I closed the throttle as I heard him shout …

'No!'

Bugger!

My right hand was on the throttle in the cockpit roof. My left hand was monitoring the collective and it seemed to be moving in the correct sense. I had no idea why he had called no. We were descending through around 50ft as my right hand flashed from the roof to the cyclic and I commenced a flare. I shouted –

'I have control.'

We fought for the controls as I flared like a bandit to try and stop us sinking. With an aggressive push forward on the cyclic I managed to level the aircraft just before our tail hit the ground. A firm hoik on the collective to cushion our descent and we had landed in a snotty heap. Not pretty but nothing damaged.

'What the hell?'

'Sorry – I noticed we were just below 100ft as we were due to commence – I thought that might be bad?'

Perhaps as a result of this lesson, learnt the hard way, I now always brief that the words 'stop-stop-stop' should be used in such circumstances. No and now are just too similar. Phew! I had survived my first instructional avoid curve sortie. Time to head to the crewroom so that we could wave our hands around in an animated manner along with all the other crews that came through the day unscathed.

Just as on my course of 1994, ETPS continued to visit a number of external aviation locations. One of the more exciting and enduring relationships was started in my first year at the school. We had used the VSS Basset on the course but it was important to try and give the students access to a variable stability helicopter. The DLR Bolkow 105 was no longer available so we jetted off to the National Research Council (NRC) in Ottawa, Canada, to fly their VSS Bell 205 (Huey). It was to prove a

Empire Test Pilots' School – Staff and Students 1997. *(MOD)*
Author is seated on the front row between Chris(RN) and Peter. *(AAC)*

memorable trip for a number of reasons. The VSS aircraft was an awesome research and training aid. It had already been used extensively, helping to develop the ADS33 MTEs that I had been greatly involved with during my time on EFS. Like the Basset, it was modified, to allow a subject pilot to fly the aircraft via a rather elderly analogue computer system, so the stability and control characteristics could be changed among other things. It also had some innovative 'inceptors', or control sticks, so it could be flown with an Airbus style sidestick which could include the functionality of both the collective and yaw pedals in addition to a conventional cyclic functionality. The two NRC TPs were very friendly and helpful and it was a good visit apart from two significant episodes …

Air Canada lost my luggage and Eric was nearly killed.

Probably Eric's near appointment with the grim reaper was the more significant event, but arriving late at the airport and looking at an empty carousel without my bag on it was depressing, especially when accompanied by a Tannoy announcement …

'All those on the London flight still awaiting their bags make your way to the Air Canada service desk – your bags are lost!'

Pants! Or rather lack thereof!

We had wanted to turn up for our first visit to NRC dressed smartly – not in the previous day's clothing crumpled by several hours of transatlantic flight. A mad dash to a local department store at least allowed us to purchase clean underwear and toothpaste etc. Eventually our bags turned up and we stayed a few days, which included a weekend, so Alistair, Eric and I rented mountain bikes to tour the local park. We had a few scary moments, hurtling down some rugged tracks, but I wasn't expecting the flirt with mortality we were about to experience. Bikes returned to the rental shop we walked back to our hotel. All we had to do to get safely home was cross a busy A road. We stood on the sidewalk and starting looking left and right and left and right again. I was looking left towards the nearest lane of oncoming traffic when out of the corner of my eye I caught a glimpse of some movement. I'm not sure quite what allowed me to process the event as quickly as I did, but before I knew it my right hand had instinctively flashed out to my right and just managed to catch the coat collar of Eric (whose body was already accelerating forwards following his outstretched leg), and hauled him to safety as a Canadian juggernaut truck rumbled past within inches. We were speechless. He had looked right (as per UK) and instantly stepped out as Alastair and I were looking left. He was a millisecond away from being jam on the tarmac.

Phew! And I thought the flying was going to be the dangerous part. Eric has never forgotten and counts his blessings that I was sharper than usual that afternoon.

Every year we would visit the Farnborough or Paris Air shows which were then, and are still now, the major shop window for new aircraft designs. ETPS would use its network of contacts and friends to blag invitations to the numerous hospitality chalets. It was, then, quite right and proper that we didn't waste such precious invitations and we would make the most of the beverages on offer. This particular year my invite was to the Eurocopter heliport facility. This was a bit of a B team invite, on the face of it, as the chalet was situated at the heliport, well away from the main runway which meant it was harder to see the flying display, but the food and wine were exceptional and I was thoroughly enjoying a bit of personal time away from the rest of the staff and students, when I suddenly heard my name announced on the PA system. I made my way to the desk to find I'd now been invited to the adjacent Bell Helicopter chalet. Foolish not to accept I thought, and said my au revoirs and staggered next door for a Californian Chardonnay. I'd barely had my second glass before I was being escorted outside and bundled into the front seat of a brand new and shiny Bell 430. Sitting was better than standing, I had decided, and, before I knew it, the nice chap next to me was explaining how to start up this FADEC equipped twin.

Merde!

Without delay I was invited to lift off and depart the airfield. I liked the Bell 430. It was the most modern helicopter I'd flown. It had an innovative addition. On ETPS we constantly lectured our students about 'attention getters' and 'tactile cueing'. Our fixed wing colleagues would often encounter aeroplanes where the joystick or control column would physically shake as the stall speed was being approached (Stick-Shaker). In the helicopter world we had hitherto had few examples of the employment of such devices. But the Bell 430 sorted that. As I approached the maximum available power/torque, the collective in my left hand suddenly commenced a high frequency vibration. A tactile cue discouraging over-torque. I liked it. It was almost humorous after several glasses of vino. It has not proved popular and I'm not sure if it has been used on other helicopters since. Meanwhile, I was working hard to stay composed under pressure, and try and ask appropriate questions without slurring my words. I reckon I had flown previously when still under the influence from the night before, but I had never flown immediately after one of the best piss-ups I'd ever been to. Ironically I flew rather well! Or at least I thought I did. Even better – I convinced this rather nice Bell helicopter pilot that a lift into downtown Paris would be really helpful. I summoned my fellow tutors and moments later we were landing in the centre of Paris, yards from our hotel for the night. It would have been a waste not to use all that saved time by heading to the nicest nearby restaurant for more red wine, steak frites and haricots vert.

The year was a challenge for a number of other reasons. Perhaps the most unexpected was that I was invited to become a BAC 1-11 co-pilot. The ETPS 1-11 was used ostensibly to teach the FW students about the handling of big commercial aeroplanes but, as I've already mentioned, it was also used as the 'company jet'. It was, without doubt, the best way to get staff and students around the world for our various visits and training commitments. The aircraft had originally been a civil certified aircraft and the crew had been defined as needing two pilots. We always manned the aircraft with our own Flight Engineer, Dave. Dave was the best thing about the 1-11, mainly because he knew the systems so well. So, in reality, flying the ETPS 1-11 was easy. Dave did all the hard work. We pilots just pitched up and drove. For visits where the RW staff/students would travel without our FW brethren it made sense to train one of us up to fly the jet as first officer. My trusty CPL(A) finally came into its own and I was selected from a cast of thousands to be that man. I loved it. I loved flying it because it was easy and different. But I also loved being an airline pilot at 30,000ft talking to air traffic agencies across Europe as we navigated back from yet another adventure. Although I loved it for variety and a bit of a change from grubbing around in a helicopter, it also served to convince me that I would soon get bored of working for the likes of BA.

On a roll from learning how to be an airline pilot, I found my name in the frame to be converted onto the Beagle Basset. Hurray!

I had really enjoyed my lessons as a student in the Basset and I was now being asked to convert onto the type. I was thrilled. Ironically, my FW colleagues were rather dismissive of the lovely Basset but if your main job was flying around in a Hawk a couple of times a day I entirely understood why. Now the ETPS Qualified Flying Instructor (QFI) was Brian, who I had a huge amount of respect for. It was he who had trained me how to fly the 1-11. In his former life he had been an F4 Phantom instructor and he told me this hairy story about landing with a student very fast at night. The aircraft was going too fast and the student didn't brake hard enough. Apparently there were no brake pedals in the rear seat of an RAF F4 and all Brian could do was keep swearing at his student as they rolled briskly off the end of the runway. I determined to be a better student in the Basset and after a comprehensive briefing, off we set. Brian was in the right-hand 'student seat', so he was without controls and even worse off than he had been in the F4. But he coached me through an exemplary take-off and climb through the clouds so that we could do the customary general handling, steep turns and stalling. He then elected to teach me how to fly the aircraft on one engine. Thankfully, I had already done a fair amount of training in twin-engine piston aircraft and had done some asymmetric flying for my fixed wing instrument rating – more of that in a later chapter. All went well initially. We closed the fuel cock and operated the feathering lever and, next thing you know, we were flying on one engine. We pottered around for a few minutes gradually descending as one engine wasn't quite powerful enough to keep us aloft and then we set about restarting the 'donk'. Out came the flight reference cards (FRCs) as we worked our way through the drill, ensuring the fuel was turned on and the feather lever moved forward. When prompted, I operated the starter motor as we descended another couple of hundred feet. I cranked the starter and looked expectantly at the engine – and then I looked expectantly at Brian.

'What am I doing wrong?'

'Nothing – have another go.'

I cranked again … and again … and again.

'Shouldn't we head for home?' I suggest, as we lose another couple of hundred feet.

'Why not!'

'A Pan call?' I offer.

'Why not.' As we lose another couple of hundred feet.

We were west of Boscombe and had been messing around at about 5,000ft. My working engine was 'firewalled' and I was flying at the blue-line 'best rate of climb' speed for One Engine Inoperative (OEI) flight and we were drifting down. In theory, the performance would improve slightly at lower altitude but right now neither Brain nor I could be sure that would be the case.

Bugger!

'Pan, Pan, Pan, Tester 61 in the Basset with a single engine failure fifteen miles west of the field – requesting radar vectors for a visual rejoin.'

I had decided to get some help from ATC and allowing them to deal with the navigation gave me the chance to concentrate on nailing the required speed +/- 1 KIAS. And we continued to descend.

Yikes!

I arrived at the airfield boundary at around 1,500ft, still descending. There would be no chance of 'going around' from this approach. The aircraft, on a warm summer's day, with the fuel it had on board, was not going to climb. I had to get this right first time. My first ever flight in the Basset and I was dealing with a serious emergency. Brian was unable to do much but I noticed he had placed his hands on the control column in front of him and was starting to make small control inputs.

Blimey! Maybe I'd got it wrong? I had thought the RHS controls were not connected but Brian seemed to be flying the aircraft OK as I continued a gentle descent on the downwind leg. Normally I would have already lowered the undercarriage, but I knew that the extra drag would markedly increase my rate of descent, and I wasn't prepared to accept that until I was sure of making the runway. Being a rote, I was more than used to employing guile and 'fudges' to avoid embarrassment and, instead of aiming for the runway threshold or piano keys, I aimed about a third of the way into the tarmac strip as if I was doing a forced landing. Once I was absolutely sure of making the runway I dropped the gear.

Phew! Three Greens.

A notch of flap and power back slightly on the good engine. As I floated over the piano keys I continued to monitor Brian's inputs on the controls. I followed his every move. In fact, our control columns moved like two synchronous swimmers competing at the Olympics. Holding it off the ground between us we kept it straight – powered back to idle and both main wheels kissed the tarmac. The nosewheel followed and, with the inertia and speed that I had, I was able to turn off the main runway before bringing the aircraft to a graceful halt. We needed a pickup for us, a tow for the aircraft and a beer – in that order. While we waited I chatted to Brian …

'Is that what they call an incremental conversion syllabus then? My first sortie I land on one engine and on the second I get to land on two?'

He laughed.

'But,' I continue, 'I didn't know the right-hand seat controls were connected at all?'

'They're not.'

'But YOU were flying the aircraft all the way around the final approach.'

'Was I?'

'Yes.'

'Well the controls are definitely not connected – and I didn't know I was doing it. Nervous reaction maybe?'

It is funny how people act in a crisis. Although Brian was the aircraft captain, and had signed for the aircraft, he was actually powerless to help but his hands couldn't help but try. And, in fairness, every time I saw Brian's controls move, I moved mine in sympathy. Madness not to make the most of all the help I could get. Thankfully, my second conversion sortie was without drama and I was added to the strength of ETPS Basset pilots – a role I absolutely cherished. Now a qualified VSS pilot I became

Author with his beloved Basset shortly before leaving ETPS. *(MOD)*

increasingly curious about the other VSS asset – the Astra Hawk. Hawk T.1 XX341 was the first of three Hawks built and delivered specifically for ETPS. Delivered in 1982 it did sterling work before being sent to Cranfield Institute of Technology. It was returned to ETPS in 1988 modified with a VSS system known as Advanced Stability Training Aircraft (ASTRA). In a similar fashion to the Basset, the front seat cockpit was extensively modified such that the subject pilot flew the aircraft through a computer. The P1 station became the rear cockpit and was modified to ensure the aircraft could be flown safely from that seat. The project pilot for the aircraft during my time was Rick who, before joining ETPS, had enjoyed a period as an airline pilot, having left the RAF some years earlier. I expressed my keen interest in learning more about the aircraft, the Basset lessons were the pre-cursor to flying the Astra Hawk for the FW students. As good fortune would have it, I didn't have to wait long before Rick called me up to invite me to fly with him. The aircraft had just completed some fairly major maintenance, including the fitting of a new engine, and so required a quite extensive post-maintenance check flight. The idea was that we would complete all the requirements of the check flight and then use the remaining hour's worth of fuel to fully explore the aircraft's VSS capabilities. We briefed for a couple of hours or so on the VSS system and, as time was starting to ebb away, we agreed to brief-as-we-walked for the check flight aspects. It was the last day of summer term at the end of July (alarm bells ringing?). As I reached the flying clothing lockers I was in for a disappointment. My G trousers were absent.

'What on earth?'

Turns out our friendly neighbourhood safety equipment specialist, Tony, had decided they needed a service and hadn't thought to tell me. Great.

'No worries,' says Rick 'I'll meet you at the jet.'

So, while Rick did the walk-round, I was busy getting fixed up with another pair of inflating pants. This would normally have been okay, but it meant we didn't have time to chat through the air test. Minutes later I was strapping in to the unfamiliar cockpit and Rick was starting up the Adour engine and calling to taxi. The departure was straightforward and we headed west conducting a number of required tests as we gently climbed. We reached 44,000ft as we coasted out overhead RAF Chivenor, near Barnstaple. The next required item was to conduct 'slam checks'. In my

Back to School – A Hell of a First Year

Astra Hawk. Note the aircraft is being flown solo from the rear cockpit. *(Tony Osborne)*

later life as a civilian test pilot I had to conduct these fairly often on ex-military aircraft needing permit renewal, but at the time this was the first occasion I'd seen one, let alone done one. The concept was to accelerate the jet engine from idle to maximum power in a given duration – inevitably 2 or 3 seconds or so. Hence the term 'slam', as the pilot was required to slam the throttle to the full power stop. This Rick did, just as required. There were some loud popping noises before it all went quiet – just like my recent trip in a glider at Netheravon. The penny dropped as I reminisced about being in a proper glider and I heard …

'Mayday, Mayday, Mayday. Tester 65, Hawk overhead Chivenor, engine flameout.'

Bugger!

'Roger Tester 65, this is Distress and Diversion on Guard. Vector 230 for St Mawgan.'

There is something we call Cockpit Resource Management (CRM) these days, which is all about how a crew should work together to sort out issues. It largely came about after a Boeing 737 had an engine problem and diverted into East Midlands Airport near Kegworth, only for the pilots to become confused and shut down the good rather than the failed engine. They crash-landed on the M1 motorway. The start of any good response to an emergency is to warn the crew. My warning came as Rick switched immediately to 243 MHz (Guard frequency) and called for help. In fairness, there was absolutely nothing I could do to assist. Conventionally, I could have flown the aircraft while the other party worked through the emergency drills and tried to restart the engine. But given that I had no controls physically connected to the aircraft, I was effectively a passenger. It was the beginning of the school holidays and the roads to and from Devon and Cornwall were already gridlocked with traffic as I contemplated the best possible outcome of now ending up at St Mawgan, near Newquay, rather than Boscombe, near my home. Since this incident, I have always adopted a philosophy which has served me very well to date. That is: at the very first sign of trouble, point to where you've parked your car.

On the day there was a strong westerly wind. Instead of gliding downwind to our home base we were now pointing into wind to try and make an unfamiliar airfield with no technical support – and of direct concern, I knew we could be facing a four-hour plus drive back to Wiltshire. We gracefully descended very quietly for what seemed like an eternity. After a few minutes our mental maths started to give us more peace of mind as it looked like our gliding angle was capable of getting us to our new destination. We couldn't try to relight or restart the engine until we were below 20,000ft, which suddenly felt quite low when compared with the 44,000ft we had started with. The relight drills in the Hawk were straightforward and didn't require too much workload, which is just as well, as there was still nothing I could do to help Rick apart from look out of the window for conflicting traffic and, in due course, the relatively large runway of St Mawgan – or Cornwall Airport as it is known these days. Eventually the Adour restarted but, given that we had no understanding of why it had failed, and given we were set up in a forced landing pattern, the wisest course of action was to continue our glide descent. Rick did a good job of flying the pattern and we floated over the runway threshold to be met by numerous fire trucks and an ambulance or two.

Phew! I had survived my first Mayday and first proper glide approach in a fast jet.

Thankfully the RAF had sprung into action and helped us park the jet somewhere safe while I got on the phone to ETPS. Although now late in the day, Chris had volunteered to come and pick us up in a Gazelle. We

KF183 was originally one of four Harvards used for photo chase trials activities. By the time I graduated from ETPS the aircraft was mainly flown for pilot continuation training and ETPS used it for a single sortie entitled 'Lat Dir 4'. I flew the aircraft a few times including a flight with Trevor on EFS. *(Chris Merkin)*

I flew this Twin Pioneer G-APRS a couple of times during my time as a tutor at ETPS. Now in civilian hands it had been a part of the ETPS fleet previously. It had an incredibly short take-off and landing capability. *(Scott Rathbone)*

Air Atlantic brought a DC-3 into Boscombe Down every year during my time there and I flew it numerous times. It felt liking stepping back in time seventy years. *(Michael Bajcar)*

I flew the Cranfield Jetstream extensively at Boscombe Down when running all the flight test short courses. The intent was to be able to have a much closer relationship between ETPS and Cranfield, but for no understandable reason the ETPS management pulled the plug on the initiative. *(Colin Work)*

I flew this DLR operated aircraft annually at Oberpfaffenhofen in Bavaria during my time as PTSC in support of the graduate FTE courses. *(DLR)*

I flew T-324 as an ETPS student on a visit to Switzerland in 1994. The crew transfer took place on the side of a mountain. *(Sven Zimmerman)*

I flew the Bo105 during our visit to Sweden. The instructor alongside me closed both engine throttles without warning and I had to autorotate into a clearing in the woods below. *(Jan Jorgensen)*

I flew the B204 (UH-1B) aircraft during my visit to Sweden as a student. It had very impressive engine-off landing capabilities. *(Rob Schleiffert)*

This AB212 was allocated to Jeff and me to complete our Preview exercise at Practica de Mare. As tested was remarkably capable for an elderly aircraft. *(Brendon Attard)*

I flew this Oryx 1229 which was the Preview aircraft tested in Bredasdorp South Africa in my first year as an ETPS tutor. *(Public Domain)*

I flew a similar Alouette III at Bredasdorp during my visit in 1997. It was memorable for nearly having a bird strike with an Ostrich. I was flying very low and fast along a sunken track. *(Gary Shepherd)*

I also flew this Puma 175 during my visit to South Africa in 1997. Unlike many of my aircraft which have been scrapped already this aircraft has been preserved in a flying condition by the SAAF museum. *(Public Domain)*

I ran the Preview team assessment of the CH53G out of Manching near Munich and flew this aircraft in 1998. A very impressive support helicopter with lots of power. *(Trevor Thornton)*

I ran the Preview Assessment team of the AH-1W Cobra out of Patuxent River 1999. This was the most awesome helicopter I managed to fly. *(Public Domain USN)*

During my time at Patuxent River in 1999 I visited the other team at Willow Creek and test flew the USN Sea Sprite. This aircraft was perhaps the hardest helicopter to ground taxi I have ever flown. *(Public Domain USN)*

In 2001 I ran the AG-64D Preview assessment out in Gilze-Rijen Airforce Base Holland. Aircraft flew like a Sea King but had a good weapon system including a monocular HMD. *(Mark Broekhans)*

I test flew the A129 by day and night out of Viterbo, North of Rome. *(Ennio Verani)*

I test flew this EH101 out of Westland helicopters, Yeovil during an ETPS visit August 2000. *(Public Domain)*

I flew the TH-6B during a visit to USNTPS and flew with Barbara who was the first female TP I had flown with. *(Public Domain USN)*

I flew the OH-58C a visit to USNTPS with my friend Mike. The aircraft was fitted with floats. *(Simon Bullimore)*

I flew the Blackhawk with Mike to transit between USNTPS and Willow Grove Naval Air Station in 1999. *(Jason Grant)*

I flew this Beaver during my visit to USNTPS in 1998. *(Richard A Cooper)*

This is the Otter I flew in 1999 but in a more recent colour scheme. *(DHC-3archive.com)*

The P-3 was used by USNTPS as an airborne classroom particularly for assessing various systems. I flew the aircraft when it visited Boscombe Down in July 2000. *(Norman Hibberd)*

Me flying Wessex XR503 as part of Trial Shark. *(MOD)*

Me flying Sea King XV371 over RWTS dispersal, Boscombe Down, in the final minutes of her last ever flight in March 1995. NB: My Wessex XR503 on the ground and the Airship I flew by the hangar. *(MOD)*

The crew of XV371 after completing her final flight. Al is on the left of the picture standing on my right. *(MOD)*

Me flying Lynx ZD559 to the rolling platform for some PR photos. *(MOD)*

Me landing the Sea King on RFA *Fort Victoria*. *(DRA Bedford)*

Author (on the left) about to man up the borrowed Lynx HAS.3 on HMS *Marlborough* – Trial Avalon. *(DRA Bedford)*

HMS *Marlborough* making way. Rough seas by any standard. *(DRA Bedford)*

Dad I've crashed the car! Standing by the ETPS Scout at Netheravon after I crashed it. *(MoD)*

flew home in stony silence as the summer sun began to set; I could tell he wasn't impressed. There was an element of déjà vu here. If this was the way my term was ending, it had started even less well.

On the first day of term, after a well-earned Easter break, we tutors would go flying in order to blow the cobwebs away, and get ourselves up to speed again, in order to safely fly with our students. I was allocated the Scout and was tasked to fly some engine-off landing training without anyone else alongside me. It had been unusually dry for some weeks and it was blowing a very strong and gusty wind from the north-west. Normally we would fly our circuit training to one of the grass strips alongside Runway 23 or 35, but on this day the wind was from around 290 which would have created a 60 degree crosswind component on either runway. So I elected to fly a few miles north to operate out of the Army Air Corps grass airfield of Netheravon. The airfield had a couple of grass runways on some very undulating ground, but also had an area known as North Field where helicopters could practise their manoeuvres.

I'd been here a couple of times before with our QHI, Bill, but never on such a windy day. I flew all the usual required exercises including a simulated hydraulics failure. I then moved on to fly some autorotative approaches gearing up to practise an engine-off landing. The gusty wind was not making life easy. I mulled over whether I should fly an engine-off landing or not. These were the worse conditions I'd flown the Scout in. So I practised another couple of autos first to ensure I had perfected the entry point and the required profile. I flew another 1,000ft circuit, lined up into wind, advising ATC of my intentions, and then closed the throttle as I lowered the collective lever smartly. Immediately the engine-out warning horn kicked off. Thankfully this only lasted a few seconds, but it was good to get it over and done with before I had to concentrate on my landing. More wind meant more lift and potentially a lower run on speed so I was feeling relatively confident as I passed 200ft or so. I was trying to nail 60 KIAS airspeed but the gusty wind was making this difficult and after one gust the rotor rpm had risen towards the upper limit, so I had been forced to raise the collective slightly to 'contain' the Nr. This was unusual in a Scout and with hindsight was a warning sign. At around 80ft I commenced a gentle flare as normal. Initially all went well as the rate of descent and airspeed both reduced as advertised. But then … without further warning I simply fell out of the sky. Almost certainly the gusty wind which had been blowing very strongly had, milliseconds later, decided to hardly blow at all. I suddenly lost my vital lift. I attempted to level the aircraft by pushing the cyclic forward and, as the blades of grass rushed up to meet me, I pulled the collective up to its top stop.

Bang!

I hit the unusually dry ground much harder than I had hoped. I bounced. Not much, but just a little. I have spoken to scores of proper Army Scout pilots since and they all swear – 'you can't bounce a Scout.'

Well I did. The aircraft landed again and trundled just a few yards more before coming to a halt. The main rotor blades had by now slowed considerably and were flapping and sailing in the breeze. There was no time to consider what to do. I could shut down immediately to check the aircraft, or wind up the throttle to get the rotors up to speed again while I thought about it. I did the latter. Now what? Just how hard had I landed? The Scout was built like the proverbial 'brick shithouse' and I thought it unlikely I'd done any damage to the undercarriage, but discretion being the better part of valour, I decided I would taxi in to dispersal where I could shut down without embarrassment and go for a pee in the nearby squadron building and have a good inspection of the vital parts before getting airborne again. I gingerly raised the collective lever to add more power to become light on the skids. I started to apply left pedal, ready to counter the torque reaction of the main rotors. All good so far. I raised the lever just a tad further and the aircraft started to yaw to the right. I obviously hadn't anticipated enough. I added more left pedal until my pedal had reached the end stop and I was still yawing to the right. This had all happened in less than a second and I hadn't yet accelerated to a normal spot turn yaw rate, so I gently closed the throttle (to stop the yaw) and allowed the aircraft to settle gently back onto the ground. I pulled the HP cock to turn off the fuel to the motor and completed a normal shut down as I advised ATC I had a problem and was likely to be stuck there for a while.

Seconds later, a face I really hadn't expected or wanted to see, hove into view. My fellow EFS helicopter colleague, Tim, had also left RWTS when I did and, for a few months, had been appointed as the airfield manager of Netheravon. As I clambered out he climbed off his indecently large motor bike as we inspected my aircraft together. It didn't take an engineering expert to spot the damage.

'Oh, you didn't want to go and do that!' says Tim in a voice that made me want to punch his lights out. But he was right, I didn't. It appeared that, as my mini-bounce occurred, one of the rotor blades had flexed down a good deal further than normal and had struck my tail rotor drive shaft with such force so as to shear it through. So although my pedals were applying pitch correctly – my tail rotor was no longer turning. There was no connection between the tail rotor and the main gearbox anymore.

Bugger! I had crashed a perfectly serviceable ETPS helicopter.

Bugger, Bugger, Bugger!

I walked the hundred yards or so to Tim's office where I could get on the phone. I wasn't sure of the protocol and knew the shit would be hitting the fan very shortly so I did what I had done many years earlier as a university student ... 'Dad, I've crashed the car!'

The phone was answered in the ETPS Ops room by Laurie, the Commanding Officer.

Author immediately after the Scout accident at Netheravon. *(MOD)*

Yikes! 'Please could I talk to Chris? I've just got a minor snag with the Scout I need to discuss.'

Chris was my immediate boss, and I have to say he was an absolutely great 'dad' in this context. After gathering the bare bones of the story he leapt into a Gazelle to come and pick me up. I don't remember him once bollocking me or chastising me in any way. Hence the déjà vu when Chris had to pick me up from St Mawgan. To have to be picked once in a year would have been bad, but twice in the same term might have been a local record.

I was sent home. I didn't sleep a wink. I relived every millisecond of the day leading up to the fateful impact with the ground. The following morning dawned. It was a Friday. It was my birthday and perhaps the shittiest one ever. I was 39 years old and had just experienced the worst aviation episode of my career to date. I felt dreadful. I drove into work in a daze and discovered I had been summoned to see the Chief Test Pilot later that morning.

Oh Shit!

I knocked on his door and was invited to enter. Nigel had recently taken over from John who I had seen about my possible posting to Canada. He offered me a comfy chair. There was a plate of biscuits on the table in front of me. He poured me a cup of tea. Was this going to be interrogation by charm?

'So Chris, how are you?'

'Okay sir, Thank you.'

'And are you able to tell me what happened? No rush ... take your time ...'

'I cocked up sir.'

This response seemed to catch Nigel out slightly and he looked puzzled. So I went on ...

'All my fault. No one else involved. The conditions yesterday were the worst I'd flown a Scout engine-off landing in. I did my best to practise by flying numerous autorotations, but when I went to fly the actual engine-off I was caught out by the gusty wind – lost lift – landed heavily and I believe a rotor blade cut through the drive shaft.'

'So you're admitting the accident was your fault?'

'Yes sir – entirely.'

Nigel looked at his watch. It was four minutes past eleven. We had another fifty-six minutes left set aside for this 'conversation'. He explained that pilots he'd interviewed in the past would either claim amnesia or blame the accident on every man and his dog, including the terrible parents they'd had as a youngster. The last thing he had expected was such a clear confession.

And so we ended up having a very nice chat. He told me that the engineers had already assessed the aircraft as repairable locally, and not many years later it was in civilian ownership being flown regularly. However, it was due a major service at the time and also deemed no longer relevant to ETPS training requirements given the antiquated design. So the aircraft was not to be fixed. I had killed the Scout. That was upsetting. But, while I was absorbing the information, Nigel was telling me all about his astronaut training. He had trained with NASA as a shuttle astronaut on an exchange programme. He was due to go into space in 1986 but, on the mission immediately before his, the shuttle Challenger blew up on launch killing all on board. Nigel's mission was cancelled and he never had chance for a second attempt. I found his story both fascinating and humbling and I had listened with rapt attention as I munched his biscuits and finished my tea.

In the afternoon Chris took me flying … in a Gazelle … to Netheravon. Chris had been a QHI on 705 NAS at RNAS Culdrose teaching ab initio helicopter pilots and had incidentally been a member of the Sharks helicopter display team. I was flying as handling pilot as we approached Netheravon airfield when without warning Chris reached up to the roof and promptly closed the throttle.

Holy Shit!

I reacted instinctively. I slammed the collective down and gently flared with aft cyclic to reduce speed slightly and increase my Nr. I knew it was now impossible to reinstate the engine. I stopped my deceleration and pointed at the airfield. It was all grass. I held my nerve and floated over the airfield boundary. A brisk 45 degrees angle of bank turn as I flared had me lined up with the prevailing wind over a flat bit of grass. Flare … check … level and bam – run on.

Phew!

'Well done!' says Chris. 'I was sure you would make it.'

Bloody Hell!

We spent the next hour flying around Netheravon with Chris giving me more and more challenging 'throttle chops'. By the end of the session, I reckoned I could survive an engine failure in a Gazelle from pretty much anywhere within half a mile of the airfield. This had been, dare I say it, a very Fleet Air Arm attitude. I'd had a similar experience many years earlier when I'd had a genuine engine failure in a Wasp. I ditched. The following day the CO of the squadron flew me out to the ship where I was learning to do deck landings. I landed on and he got out – simply telling me to complete the sortie I'd failed to complete the previous day.

Thank you Chris – to this day, I will always remember your kindness over those forty-eight hours in particular.

It was the weekend. I went home. I didn't sleep again. By Tuesday I was still feeling quite low, although all my colleagues were being as nice as anything to me. Chris took me flying again, this time in the Basset. We were in the ops room signing the aircraft back in when all manner of klaxons and alarms went off. Another accident. We all looked out of the ops room windows to witness the most alarming of sights. A pall of smoke and two people swinging their way to earth on ejection seat parachutes.

Blige!

This was really serious – and suddenly no one at Boscombe Down cared a jot about a heavy landing in an aircraft due to be scrapped. Something much worse had just happened.

I had flown Hawk XX343 just a couple of weeks earlier with Dave, the Principal Tutor Fixed Wing. We had flown together with XX342 doing some mock combat and some formation aerobatics which I thought were just a delightful way to spend ninety minutes or so. So much more pleasant than the rough and tumble of aeros in a light piston-engine aeroplane. Anyway, a fixed wing tutor was taking one of our RW students for a famil flight in XX343. They set off along the north easterly 05 runway. Allegedly the student couldn't keep the aircraft straight on take-off. Somehow the aircraft tried to get airborne too soon and possibly stalled. The consequent roll caused a wingtip to hit the ground. The tutor ejected both of them as the Hawk, at full throttle, careered off the runway, thankfully before reaching a queue of traffic awaiting a chance to cross the runway, and managed to plant itself in the only uncluttered earth bank on the north side of the airfield.

Phew! Aircrew ejected safely and the jet didn't hit anything important. But the possible consequences were eye watering. My misdemeanour was instantly forgotten and ironically, for the first time in days, I slept well that night. The RW student hurt his back and spent a few days in Odstock Hospital, which had become a spinal treatment unit during the Second World War. This RAF helicopter pilot had never been a fan of being a test pilot and, for him, this incident was the last straw. We didn't see him back at ETPS ever again.

While I was busy learning how to be a test pilot in 1994, more important things were happening around the world, including Nelson Mandela becoming President of South Africa having finally been released from the prison on Robben Island. This event was to have a direct impact on my first year as a tutor at ETPS as, with the apartheid system dismantled, the UK could now work again with the country's armed forces. We had received a South African helicopter pilot on the TP course immediately after mine and we had made an approach to the Test Flight and Development Centre of the South African Airforce (SAAF) based at the air force base of Overberg, located at Bredasdorp on the south-east coast. The centre had been formed and run by graduates from ETPS for a number of years and ETPS had approached the test centre with a view to finding another interesting aircraft for an end of course preview assessment. They had offered up the Atlas Oryx helicopter. Due to the UN arms embargo in the '80s the SAAF had not been able to purchase new aircraft. The Oryx, developed by Atlas, was a souped-up Puma similar to the Super Puma. Very powerful Turbomeca Makila IA1 turboshaft engines (1,900 hp) were fitted, giving the aircraft outstanding 'hot and high' and OEI performance. The airframe was improved with composite material such that the aircraft weighed less than an original Puma. This was likely to be a very interesting aircraft for a preview assessment.

As October 1997 approached, the SAAF confirmed availability of the Oryx. Now with only four RW students we only required two preview teams. I was allocated the two RN students, which I was very pleased about. They were not much younger than me and I knew we would be on the same hymn sheet throughout. Chris, as PTRW, did not need to run a preview team and elected to come along with me, as did the Commanding Officer of the School, Laurie, who was desperate to get a few more interesting types in his log book. He was especially keen to fly the Atlas Cheetah, which was a fighter aircraft derived from the French Mirage.

So by mid-October we were able to make plans. I travelled with Laurie and Chris as we planned to stay for only one week. My students would be there for two. We stayed at a to-die-for hotel in Arniston Bay and when we arrived at the test centre we were all very warmly welcomed. I remember us having a barbeque where the SAAF CO was very keen to make a long speech but reluctant to admit to having once flown a helicopter. I seem to recollect one of my students telling him his helicopter hours in his log book were a bit like VD – you might not want to admit it, but you had fun getting it.

As with all such detachments my priority was to ensure my team were getting the resources they needed to achieve the task. I also had to fly the subject aircraft to ensure I knew enough about it to supervise events and understand the subsequent report, which I thoroughly enjoyed doing. Most UK Puma pilots were fans of their aircraft. It was relatively manoeuvrable and fun to fly. The Oryx managed to 'fix' most of the inherent deficiencies and produced a very capable support helicopter. Our assessment directly led to the UK MOD becoming interested in the Oryx being a potential replacement for the RAF Puma. This procurement requirement led to the Puma Mk2 which bore an uncanny resemblance to the Oryx. With my formal flying completed, I was offered a flight in a regular Puma and an Alouette III. The Alouette III had evolved from the Alouette II, which was similar in many ways to the Gazelle I was now very familiar with. However, the Alouette III had a much larger cabin size and had been used as a gunship by both Rhodesia and South Africa in their recent 'bush war' conflicts. I flew with Andy, previously an operational Alouette III pilot and a SAAF TP. I was to meet him again many years later when I was working for a South Africa-based test pilot training school. We did a number of engine-off landings which were slightly weird due to the 'shopping trolley' tricycle undercarriage. The best part of the flight was flying around the local sand dunes and up some dirt tracks that were slightly sunken. It was possible for my eye position to be almost the same level as the surrounding country side.

I was blatting along at around 80 KIAS approaching a blind bend. Right cyclic and a bootfull of right pedal and …

'OSTRICH!' we both yelled.

As I hurtled around the bend, right in front of me was a stationary Ostrich. I had just enough time to consider the implications of having to fill in the paperwork for a bird-strike on a non–flying bird when the startled creature leapt to one side in the nick of time. What a hoot!

Meanwhile Laurie, after much pestering, got his wish and was invited to fly the Cheetah. He was as chuffed as punch and after appropriate briefing rushed out to the aircraft standing in the hot African sunshine.

Back to School – A Hell of a First Year   187

Sadly, in his enthusiasm to clamber on board, he didn't see the large tin of hydraulic fluid left there by the mechanic preparing the aircraft for flight; Laurie's Sunday best flying overalls, with all his squadron badges, were now covered in inflammable red oil. Sadly, it turned out the aircraft was unserviceable and instead Laurie went off to fly (in some borrowed overalls) in a very unusual aircraft – a DC-3 Dakota fitted with two PT6 Turboprops. I bet that was exciting.

Once we had run out of things to do and fly, I bade my students farewell and clambered into the back of the brand-new Avis 3 Series BMW with Laurie at the helm. Our driver made some interesting decisions on the way back to Cape Town to catch our flight home. Firstly, he thought it would be interesting to pull off the main motorway to see what a township looked like. Less than a hundred yards from the main thoroughfare the road had turned to a muddy track and we were rapidly being surrounded by a crowd of very large men that maybe thought a brand-new 3 Series was worth fighting for.

'Turn around Laurie!'

'Turn around NOW!'

We made it back to the motorway unscathed but with our 'roughy-toughy' egos in tatters, so Laurie decided to stop at a roadside diner for beer and food. We were in the high spirits of those that had just survived a near death experience or two and, despite my better judgement, sampled some local goat stew.

Mistake!

Laurie was already feeling rough by the time we got to the airport. My delayed reaction coincided with the Boeing 747 rotating to depart for London Heathrow. We were flying with South African Airways and they still permitted smoking on flights – horrible! I was in the middle seat of three. Shortly after take-off, the passengers either side of me bedded down for the night. Meanwhile I had decided the best seat on the aeroplane was the nearby loo. When I dared brave it back to my proper seat surrounded by cigarette smoke I lasted only minutes before dashing to the loo again.

Apart from the food poisoning, visiting Bredasdorp had been a fascinating experience and another career high. Although, whether it made up for the Tail Gearbox Chip Caption, two engine failures and killing the Scout is debateable.

It had definitely been a hell-of-a first year.

Chapter 12

ETPS Principal Tutor Rotary Wing

I was invited by the French Test Pilot school's CO to fly with him in an AS350 single-engine Squirrel. It was another déjà vu experience as I was bundled into the P1 seat with no briefing. My schoolboy almost-failed-French-GCSE 'O' Level offered me no help or consolation as we whizzed around the countryside. As we returned to the airfield the CO muttered something. I looked across for clarification … as he closed the throttle.

Merde!

The memory is a strange thing. I remember a good deal about my first year as a tutor at ETPS because it was all new, exciting and challenging. Of the next period I remember less about the routine instructional flying because, I guess, it had become routine … that is, if teaching flight test can ever become routine.

I should explain the normal rhythm of the school. Traditionally, for some years, there had been three rotary wing tutors and three British fixed wing (FW) tutors with a US Navy fast jet exchange pilot. The three Brits of each discipline would generally serve a three-year tour and one would be replaced every year. So we expected an initial year where we had to learn our stuff, a middle year to consolidate, and then in our final year we would suddenly find ourselves as the Principal Tutor and be seen as the expert, as well as having to plan and deliver the course for that year. When I returned to the school from EFS there had been a decision taken to recruit an additional (civilian) tutor of each discipline so that they could provide long-term stability, continuity, standardisation and course development, thus allowing the PTRW and PTFW to concentrate on running their course. In my case things had become rather out of whack. I joined, filling the RAF tutor post. In my second year the staff didn't change but Pete (Army) took over as the PTRW. In my third year Pete and Chris left to be replaced by another Army and another RN TP – which meant Eric and I had to train and standardise two new tutors at the same time. During this year I again started to quiz my appointer on what my next posting might be. I was now 'passed over', so no longer had a chance of being promoted and so no longer was likely to be pushed into career-type jobs. So what would the RN offer a reasonably competent aviator with six years flight test experience? Any ideas?

To put you out of your misery, they lined me up to become the CO of the Lynx Simulator – Yes – the job I had left six years earlier to become a TP. Was I likely to be able to use any of my flight test skills again? Well apparently not – so I quit. The term was that I requested 'Premature Voluntary Release' – known as PVRing. My request was accepted and so my extremely busy and stressful year of running the course, and training up two new tutors, was now made even more challenging as I now needed to start looking for a job and getting my civilian qualifications sorted. Ironically, with days to go, I was phoned up by the appointer again. It turns out the RAF still couldn't find a tutor to fill my slot and so I was asked if I would like to extend my commission by a further year. I do wonder, with hindsight, whether I made the correct decision, but I agreed to stay on. This immediately bought my wife and two children further stability at a crucial time when my son was about to start secondary school/grammar school. By then the new RN tutor was champing at the bit to take over as PTRW and so I handed over the reins to him at Christmas and returned to being a 'junior joe'.

During my four years at the school as a military tutor the pervading memories relate to the Preview Exercises I led, the additional aircraft we rented-in to fly from time to time, my initiative to replace the Scout, and the people issues I faced during my year as PTRW. You will forgive me, I hope, if I deliver my recollections in the way my memories are stored rather than purely chronologically.

I have already talked about my trip to South Africa to lead the Atlas Oryx evaluation. The following year, 1998, I flew the team to Germany in the 1-11 to fly a Bundeswehr transport helicopter – the Sikorsky CH53G, which was a German version of the CH53D already serving the USA (the USMC used it extensively in the Vietnam War) and Israel very well. In *Test Pilot*, I spent a good few paragraphs talking about the history of Sikorsky helicopters. By this stage I had yet to fly the civilian models

I would become very familiar with, but I'd flown the Wessex and Sea King which were both originally Sikorsky designs. We convened at the German Flight Test Centre – Wehrtechnische Dienststelle 61 (WTD 61), Manching near Munich in October. The astute among you will have realised that October and Munich can mean only one thing – Oktoberfest! I fear I was a bad influence on my RN student and his team mate. I have vivid recollections of drinking lots of lager and then, on rented bikes, cycling through Munich like maniacs dodging trams and red traffic lights by the slimmest of margins.

The aircraft itself was an absolute privilege to fly. It had already served the German Army well since its introduction into service in 1971 some twenty-six years previously. As I write this chapter the type remains in service with upgraded avionics and more powerful engines. My flight evaluation had to be done in poor weather as I had to depart Manching fairly promptly to fly on to America, but it was still an outstanding flight. If memory serves, the aircraft was started by a massive lever in the cockpit roof. I believe this operated an accumulator which flashed up an auxiliary power unit (APU) which then ran the electrics and hydraulics. I remember that it seemed really odd that we couldn't speak to each other (due to there being no battery to power the intercom) until all of a sudden everything was starting to happen. I guess it was designed this way to need minimal ground equipment in the field when operating away from engineering support. Once burning and turning I found it surprisingly easy to taxi, easy to hover and easy to fly. At the weight I flew at there was a massive margin of excess power and I found the aircraft surprisingly agile … time to fly my air display routine again. I'm not sure what the angle of bank limit was meant to be but I was able to fly my Lynx manoeuvres without any bother. My single flight was over just as I was really beginning to enjoy myself and I had to bid farewell to my students knowing they were going to have a lot of fun over the next few days. But so was I.

I was off to the United States Navy Test Pilot School (USNTPS) at Patuxent River, Maryland, USA – our sister test pilot school. USNTPS was the first school to follow the ETPS model. It was followed by the USAF TP School at Edwards Airforce base in California. (The USAF school does not cater for RW students). Finally EPNER in France was formed making up the four recognised TP schools at the time.

The visit was made better still because we were hosted by my former office buddy and Lynx mate, Mike. It was really good to see that he had enjoyed his time to date there immensely – I would have been embarrassed if that wasn't the case. Without delay he took me flying for an unforgettable trip in an OH-58C, the military version of the Bell 206 JetRanger which I'd already flown a few times and later was to become formally qualified on. The novel thing about this aircraft was that its front doors were removed and it was fitted with large floats to allow water landings. Once airborne I was allowed by Mike to evaluate the aircraft's handling qualities. Despite the large floats it still flew like a JetRanger – so on to the fun stuff. Landing in the bay. After a couple of regular touchdowns we practised water taxiing – a huge amount of fun as this predated my fixed wing float training. With all of that safely achieved, off we went to do some engine-off landings. What a hoot! The profile was exactly the same as usual but the aim was to touch down without any significant forward speed. So, at the normal height, I flared the aircraft to wash off speed, then partially levelled the aircraft but retained a slightly nose-up attitude as I raised the collective lever. This reduced my rate of descent further and also started to kill off my remaining forward speed. At the very last moment I levelled and flopped onto the water. Inside my head the crowd went wild again … right up until the moment I was 'goffered' by the large splash of water that then entered through my open doorway.

Uggh!

This was a whole new challenge. How to do an engine-off-landing (EOL) to water without getting wet? Time for another go. But now the next challenge presented itself. As I started to wind open the throttle to speed up the rotors, the aircraft started yawing to the right. I instinctively fed in full left yaw pedal – but we were still turning to the right – rather fast. As the tail rotor was driven directly from the main rotor gearbox it was still turning very slowly, and even with full pitch applied could not yet generate enough thrust to oppose the torque reaction of the main rotors. Normally, being in contact with the ground would be enough to prevent the aircraft spinning but, on the flat water of Chesapeake Bay there was no resistance and we began to yaw to the right faster and faster. Now this was very new indeed and rather unsettling. Mike was sitting with his hands folded, chuckling. Clearly he had seen this look of astonishment on numerous other pilots' faces. Eventually, as he knew from previous experience, the increasing speed of the main rotors allowed the tail rotor to spin faster and eventually the blades started to bite into the warm autumn air and our yaw rate started to decrease.

Phew!

All of a sudden I was back in control and stopped the spinning. I wound the throttle fully open and lifted into the hover with water dripping off our floats. Round again for another, I think. The second and third EOLs were 'creamers'. We flopped gently onto the water with no more cold water denting my pride.

Hurrah! Another skill achieved.

Time to head home for a pee and a cup of tea. The following day Mike handed me over to a couple of his colleagues. In the morning I was introduced to the delights of the de Havilland DHC-2 Beaver aeroplane. This is, by any standards, an iconic aeroplane and I was chuffed to be given the chance to fly it. Used by the UK Army Air Corps for many years it had seen operational service in numerous theatres including the conflict in Aden. It was used extensively in the States and Canada, often with floats fitted, for commercial operations around some fairly inhospitable parts of the country. The biggest challenge was climbing in. With the aircraft on the ground its tail dragger undercarriage left it sitting very nose-high, with

OH58 on floats similar to the aircraft flown with Mike at USNTPS. *(Wolodymir Nelowkin)*

a cockpit a long way off the ground. Once airborne though it was a very gentlemanly aircraft to potter around in. (The following year I was able to fly the de Havilland DHC-3 Otter which was like a scaled up Beaver. There were none in the UK but I had chance later to fly a twin-engine version used by the British Antarctic Survey team). In the afternoon I flew with Barbara in the TH-6B (OH-6) which was the military version of the Hughes 500. I guess, at the time, flying with a female test pilot was more unusual than flying the aircraft which I'd flown before. Both proved to be a lot of fun.

This visit to Pax paved the way for my return the following year. I had ended up running the Preview exercise for two Australian Army students and we had therefore sought out a suitable attack helicopter for them to evaluate. We were offered a USMC Bell AH-1W – known as the Whisky Cobra, or Super Cobra. I jumped at the chance and my students were grateful for the opportunity to grow their experience of such types. The pilot had predominantly flown OH-58 Kiowa helicopters to date. Revisiting Pax was a joy as Mike looked after us well once again. The Whisky Cobra was an awesome helicopter to fly and completed the journey I had begun five years earlier when I'd been able to fly the simulator at the Bell Fort Worth facility. The real thing was better. A bit like the Wessex, this aircraft had started out as a very successful single-engine aircraft and was based on the UH-1 Huey. It came into service in the '60s and was used extensively in the Vietnam War (I strongly recommend you read *Snake Pilot* by Randy R. Zahn). The USMC liked the aircraft but wanted two engines for safer over-water operations. So the twin version, initially known as the AH-1J, was developed by shoehorning in two engines. Further development and more powerful engines later, the aircraft became the AH-1W, which I was fortunate enough to fly.

The aircraft had a tandem seat cockpit with the gunner sitting in the front seat. I flew from the rear (pilot's) seat which felt a bit like being in the back seat of a Hawk. The rear seat was raised compared to the front seat and with a Hawk-like canopy I had a very good field of view over the gunner's head. This beast flew like a Huey on steroids and the Huey, as you will have already read, was no slack performer. Like a Huey or a JetRanger it was a naturally stable helicopter with its very large two-bladed teetering rotor system. It was fitted with a flight control system which, unusually, used 'control quickening'. Most flight control systems were there to damp down control response so as to make a helicopter easier to fly. In this case the aircraft was already easy to fly but needed as much agility as possible. So, as I applied an input in the cyclic the FCS was already driving the actuator to accelerate my input. I have to say it worked very well. It was extremely fast, with the excess of power and minimal drag airframe and we were cruising at 150 KIAS moments after take-off. I practised my strafe runs and rocket attacks and got up to 190 KIAS without bother. In the final few minutes we turned off one of the engines and, without masses of ordnance on the sides, I couldn't tell the difference. This really was an aircraft that carried its spare engine with it. When I was a Wasp pilot, invariably we were always working with colleagues flying twin-engine machines. As a joke we described the Wasp as a twin-engine helicopter – one engine on the aircraft and one in the hangar.

With the excitement of being an attack helicopter pilot behind me for a while, as the Principal Tutor I thought it would be useful to go and visit the other Preview team based nearby at Naval Air Station Willow Grove which was just 'up the road' North of Philadelphia. Mike was somehow able to whistle up a UH60 Blackhawk for me to fly myself up there. Not content with making the journey an opportunity to fly something new, Mike insisted we route via downtown Washington DC. Awesome. Just like flying over London for the first time, it took my breath away to be allowed to whizz low level past numerous iconic buildings that grace our TV screens frequently. The Blackhawk was easy to fly and cruised quickly enough, but it shook like an aircraft that had been abused a few times too often.

At Willow Grove I was invited to fly the Kaman SH2G Sea Sprite which had been allocated to the Navy students on the course. Again, I was looking forward to flying this legendary USN aircraft that had been the predecessor to the Seahawk LAMPS (Light Airborne Multi-Purpose System) aircraft which I'd first flown as a Wasp pilot. The Sea Sprite had an unusual main rotor system. Cyclic inputs moved the main rotor blades by moving servo tabs on the back of each blade. Given that the Royal New Zealand Navy had just replaced its Wasps with the Sea Sprite, rather than the Lynx, I was expecting something very special. Well that was not my experience. The Sea Sprite flew a bit like a Wessex but with all the crisp controllability completely removed. It had very poor control response to cyclic inputs. No doubt there was a fair amount of lag as a trim tab was moved which then had to interact with the airflow to drive the blade to a new position. No – it was not fun to fly. And worse than that, it was almost impossible to taxi in a straight line. It had a wide track mainwheel undercarriage and a swivelling tailwheel. As I tried to move forward it would yaw slightly one way or the other. Correcting this yaw with yaw pedal invariably caused it to yaw in the opposite sense. I found myself 'waddling' along the taxiway like a drunkard with water filled wellies. It is interesting the Australians ordered the Sea Sprite around the same time and eventually decided some years later it was not fit for purpose. The USN retired the aircraft only a couple of years after my flight. I was glad to be looking after the Whisky team instead.

Now an attack helicopter expert (!), the following year, I was invited to look after the Preview team testing the Boeing Apache AH-64D. Although the UK AAC operated this aircraft, we flew an example owned by the Dutch 301 Squadron at the RNLAF Airbase of Gilze-Rijen. For me this felt like a fitting conclusion to the work I had been involved with for the DRA several years earlier. I was finally able to fly using the Apache Integrated Helmet and Display Sighting System (IHADS) which used symbology very similar to the symbology we had been developing. The symbology was displayed on a monocular display that flipped down from the helmet and gave some operational problems with 'eye dominance' issues. Following the Whisky Cobra I had been expecting an exciting helicopter to fly, but actually it flew rather like a Sea King, which you will already know doesn't feature high on my fun-to-fly list. But like the 'mighty King', this aircraft was very stable in the hover and thus an ideal weapons release platform. I was delighted to have flown it and similarly delighted that *it endorsed my decision, of nearly two decades earlier, to join the RN and not the AAC.*

I did lead another Preview assessment. This was a rather sad tale in that I was programmed to go to Israel to continue my run on attack helicopters and fly the Bell AH-1F, which was the very latest version of the single-engine Cobra. I was excited, not just to fly the newest Cobra, but visiting Israel for such an assessment was going to be groundbreaking, and I was going to get a few days off to visit some Holy Land sites including Jerusalem. At the very last minute the Foreign Office decided that being on a flypro (flying programme), with other aircraft from the squadron strafing the Gaza strip, might not be a good idea and so they pulled the plug.

Bugger!

So instead of heading to a very exciting venue, and flying an exciting aircraft, I found myself piloting the 1-11 down to EPNER, Istres, South of France to Preview the AS365N Dauphin. The aircraft was a sad replacement with the only upside for the students being that it was fully instrumented so they were able to gather a massive amount of data easily. Having flown the Dauphin I was invited by the school's CO to fly with him in an AS350 single-engine Squirrel. It was another déjà vu experience as I was bundled into the P1 seat with no briefing. My schoolboy almost-failed-French-GCSE 'O' Level offered me no help or consolation as we whizzed around the countryside. As we returned to the airfield the CO muttered something. I looked across for clarification … as he closed the throttle.

Merde!

This is just what happened in the Swedish Bolkow 105, but on this occasion I was 100 per cent sure the throttle was not going to be reopened. Back into saving-my-own-skin as I flared back to 65 KIAS. Nailed the Nr in the middle of the green band, and looked for somewhere to land. There was no suitable flat grass strip like at Boscombe, but it became clear that I was expected to land within an area of loose greyish stones.

Yikes!

I flew another exemplary EOL. I was now becoming quite good at them, but landing on loose stones was a novel experience for sure. I was very glad that, having proved I could nail it on the first attempt, the reputation of UK experimental test pilots was still intact and we could retire to the café for some red wine, without having to do a second.

Phew! Survived another.

In addition to the Previews, at ETPS we rented-in numerous aeroplanes and helicopters to broaden the experience of our students. We would try to ensure there was enough money in the budget to allow the staff to fly these aircraft as well. Quite often we would use single-engine helicopters for the 'Pilot's assessment' exercise. You will remember, as a student I flew the MD520N Notar aircraft. During my time on the staff we flew the Robinson R44 and the Bell 47 piston engine aircraft which I had originally flown in the States. We flew the Enstrom 480, the Bell 206 JetRanger, the Bell 407 and the very modern Eurocopter EC120. This aircraft was, in many ways, the successor to the trusty Gazelle. It was of a similar size and was also equipped with a fenestron, or shrouded tail

Sea King ZF115 – Used for radio and navigation trials and for teaching on ETPS. *(Al Henderson)*

rotor. What was then quite unusual was that it was equipped with glass screens, rather than regular analogue gauges, and it used a system called 'First Limit Indicator', or FLI. Up until then, the helicopters I had flown would power limit on one of three parameters. Usually they would limit on torque at sea level. That was the amount of twisting applied to the main rotor gearbox. This was normally indicated to the pilot by a torque gauge. However sometimes the engine reached a limit before the gearbox. This would be a temperature or compressor speed limit. This was especially likely on hot days and at high altitudes, so we helicopter pilots became very used to scanning all the dials to make sure we were always fully aware of the limits that were affecting us so as not to exceed them. Instead, the FLI system monitored all the above parameters and converted them into a single power display with ten units being the maximum for take-off. As long as we stayed below the ten we were OK. There were also continuous limits once we had completed the take-off which were displayed in a similar fashion. So this should be a great system. It reduces pilot workload as only one needle needs to be monitored.

Sadly, on the EC120 there was some computational delay in the system and when applying 'max chat' the pilot had to be very careful to ensure any collective inputs did not exceed the rate at which the system could respond.

We also rented in numerous twins including the AS355N Twin Squirrel and the Agusta A109P, both of which we used to teach our students about FADEC. If we had any surplus money in the budget we would rent in a helicopter in January when our own fleet was usually still undergoing its annual end of course maintenance programme. So I finally had chance to fly a civilian Sikorsky, namely an elderly S76A. Our instructor for the aircraft was none other than Paul (nickname 'Steady Dim'), who had been my instructor and course officer when I was doing my ab initio Wings training on the Gazelle in 705 NAS at RNAS Culdrose. I'm not sure whether Paul thought I had learnt anything in the intervening twenty-seven years or not. At least he was happy enough to sign me off as competent to fly the aircraft. I ended up being the EASA project pilot for the very latest version – the S76D some fourteen years later.

Although the wide variety of helicopters was fun, we also rented-in some aeroplanes for the fixed wing students which we rotes sometimes were able to fly. Thus, I was able to sample the aerobatic delights of the CAP10. But perhaps more fun was flying the ex-ETPS Twin Pioneer that arrived resplendent in its original raspberry ripple colour scheme. This was a twin-engine transport aeroplane with a pretty good payload which could be landed on a postage stamp and was used extensively in our Borneo operations. Without much breeze I landed it in the length of the piano keys on the main runway – now that really is STOL (short take-off and landing).

The other classic that I managed to fly frequently was the Air Atlantique DC-3 Dakota. At the time, the company operated a number of such wartime vintage aircraft, mainly in order to spray dispersant onto slicks of spilt oil at sea. They also flew a couple for passenger flights and classic sightseeing trips. I loved flying that aircraft. It was an aeroplane that was both benign, but a handful at the same time. Our safety pilot for these flights was often Kath, a very experienced instructor. Getting in was the first challenge. The rear passenger door provided access but, just like the Beaver, it seemed to sit at a very nose-high angle. Climbing up the floor-way to the front seats felt like ascending a gentle mountain slope. Once strapped in, starting the machine was the next challenge. The blades had to be cranked and the magnetos turned on at just the right moment. With enough fuel and a bit of good fortune each engine would cough and splutter into life. The next challenge was taxiing. It was not as bad as the Sea Sprite – nothing has been. But if the tail wheel was unlocked, a lot of attention was required. A swing of the tail took a lot of stopping with differential brakes and asymmetric engine power. The trick, I discovered early on, was to get the tail wheel lock back in for every straight section of taxiway. Once on the runway, though, it all got a lot easier. Having spooled up both engines, with modest forward pressure on the control column, the rear end could be raised and the aircraft kept straight with its relatively powerful rudder. It wasn't a spectacular climber but it eventually would get to height and I would always do some stalling. This was before my time at the CAA, when I became very used to aeroplanes with challenging stall characteristics. And this charming lady definitely had challenges. The first time I flew I had Laurie, the CO, seated in a passenger seat – he was getting on quietly with some paperwork for some reason. As I brought both throttles back to idle, the aircraft slowed with the engines popping in protest. With little or no warning the stall was arrived at and the wing dropped nearly 90 degrees.

Bloody hell! I looked back to see Laurie's paperwork spread all over the inside of the cabin!

At the time I was still on a steep learning curve for testing aeroplanes and, given that the DC-3 was known for its short field landing capabilities, I thought its slow speed handling would be benign. Wrong. You will notice DC-3s often land on their mainwheels rather than in a three-point attitude and now you know why. One of the best aspects of flying our evaluations of these aircraft was the opportunity to fly simulated oil dispersant spray runs along the main runway at Boscombe. I flew a normal downwind leg but kept the undercarriage up. I commenced a gentle dive on base leg and was over the piano keys at 30ft and 90 KIAS. Just like beating up ships in the Hawk, the aircraft was now flying in ground effect which acted as a cushion under the aircraft. This worked in the safe sense, in that it helped prevent inadvertent further descent. So, as a rote used to flying low level, this had me firmly back in my element. Once we had achieved a couple it was home in time for tea and medals.

The most memorable fixed wing flight I had in this period by far was actually in a former EFS aircraft – the Bedford (VAAC) Harrier. Had Bedford remained open I would, almost certainly, have flown this aircraft previously, but with the fleet ending up at Boscombe Down it was hogged by the fast jet fraternity. The Harrier had been extensively modified like the Basset and Astra Hawk. In this case it had ended up being the primary

DC-3 Dakota flown at Boscombe Down for Qualevals. *(Michael Bajcar)*

research vehicle for the flight control laws that would eventually find their way into the F35 Lightning fighter. I would have been happy to fly in any Harrier, but to fly this unique asset was a logbook entry to die for. We flew a typical evaluation sortie with a rolling take-off and some high speed general handling in order to burn off fuel and get down to a weight where we could do the interesting hover work. For me the most exhilarating event came when I had managed to establish a hover. I was then invited to rotate a knurled knob on the left-hand inceptor. As I rotated the knob forwards the aircraft, without any additional control inputs, began a level acceleration at about 50ft agl. I was used to accelerating into level flight in all manner of helicopters, but this would always end up with lots of control inputs and the nose of the aircraft being pitched nose-down. But this Harrier just set off. The kick in my back literally took my breath away. By the airfield boundary we were doing around 300 KIAS.

Bloody Hell! What a fairground ride. Where do I slot in my pound coin for another go?

The next time around I was invited to fly the hover using the new 'unified control laws'. These I didn't like, which is probably the most I have in common with regular Harrier pilots. A Harrier joystick operated puffer jets to tilt the aircraft or the nozzles and effectively gave a similar effect as a helicopter cyclic in the hover. Pushing the stick forwards I went forwards – moving it left I rolled and then moved left and so on. However, some bright chaps at Bedford had determined that, for a fast jet pilot, this was counter intuitive. A fast jet pilot flying in formation, like a member of the Red Arrows, would use the joystick to go up and down relative to the other aircraft. If a pilot was too high he would ease the joystick forward a tad and the elevator input would pitch the nose-down slightly and the aircraft would descend. The throttle, although controlling thrust, would control acceleration; in formation it would be used to move forwards or backwards when compared to the other aircraft. So, for a regular fast jet pilot, he was used to moving forwards and backwards with the throttle in his left hand and up/down with the joystick in his right. The clever VAAC (Vectored Thrust Aircraft Advance Control) Harrier was modified so that the inceptors could fly a variety of control laws but were able to replicate this unified method. I have to say, as a helicopter pilot, moving one control to move forwards and a different one to move laterally felt quite wrong. The trials were supposed to use pilots from a wide range of backgrounds but tended to use nearly all fast jet people. In fairness, it was likely that all pilots converting onto the F35 would have exclusively a fast jet background, but some of you will remember earlier in the book when I discussed the throttle arrangement fitted to the V22 Osprey. As I write, a good number of battery powered vertical take-off and landing aircraft are being designed. A number of them have been influenced by the F35 control strategy. But these aircraft will not be flown by fast jet pilots, they will be flown by both aeroplane and helicopter pilots. I do wonder how sensible it is to use the unified control laws outside of the F35 cockpit.

In addition to bringing aircraft in to the school, during my time the rotary wing staff conducted helicopter evaluations overseas. Eric, Alastair and I were despatched off to The Centro Cavalleria dell'Aria at Viterbo in the mountains just North of Rome. I'm not sure how we organised it but we visited 1 Gr Sqd who operated the A-129 Mangusta attack helicopter. This was powered by Gem engines as fitted to the Lynx and was rather underpowered for its role. By now I was becoming quite an expert on attack helicopters. We were each offered an enjoyable daytime flight and then were foolish enough to fly again at night, in unfamiliar terrain, wearing NVGs. Although we each had experienced instructors in the 'other seat', their English wasn't good and my memories of the Bolkow 105 sortie in Sweden and the AS350 flight at Istres were hard to set aside.

But we all survived and, given that it was November, we had started and finished in good time – early enough to wander down the very steep street by our hotel to find an amazing pizzeria. It had low ceilings and a massive roaring open fire over which the pizzas were cooked, as we watched on in amazement quaffing large amounts of red wine from Tuscia. We set off back to the airport at Rome the following day with just enough time to be able to sample a further glass or two in the lounge, grateful that we had survived our challenging night flying. Just as morale was ramping up we ventured out onto one of the major cobblestone roundabouts in downtown Rome. The rumbling of the cobbles seemed particularly bad and I thought the car would shake itself to bits. We ground to a halt, and with care stepped outside among manic scooters and Fiat 500s only to find we had a flat tyre. What is it about rental cars in Italy?

The next few minutes put our night flying into perspective as we struggled to get this Kia heap to the side of the road. Thankfully Eric had been a Royal Marine and would, just like in *Ice Cold in Alex*, have lifted the rear of the car single-handed if we hadn't forced him to use the puny jack. Another officer selection leadership type exercise ensued and we quickly formed a team to change the wheel and get the heck out of there before being flattened by a juggernaut or two.

Phew! Survived another knackered tyre in Italy.

In my final few weeks at ETPS we were invited to visit PZL, in Swidnik near Lublin, Poland, to fly their helicopters. I flew the Sokol SW3 and then the SW4, which was still within its experimental flight test programme. I was asked whether I wanted to fly an engine-off landing or look at high speed flight. Apparently they needed to fit different rotor blades depending on what test flying they were doing. I didn't know then but I was to become very familiar with PZL, and the SW4 in particular. That evening was my first taste of PZL's hospitality as we were wined and dined before the ice cold bottles of Polish vodka appeared. Our hosts were generous and several glasses followed numerous toasts. As more than enough had been consumed, one of our team, who shall remain nameless, discovered how cheap the vodka was and promptly ordered several more bottles. By the time we finally ran out we had toasted everything we could think of that was Polish, or about our wading into the Second World War to help. I was glad we were not flying the following day and equally delighted that we survived the journey home given what I was to learn about Polish driving standards some years later.

One of the initiatives that I am proudest of from my four years as a military tutor was the acquisition of a replacement for the Scout helicopter – only fair since I was the one that killed it. On taking over as the Principal Tutor I was a worried that the Scout would never be replaced and yet we had possessed four different helicopter types on the fleet for many years, and even more types previously. Collectively, we tutors thought we should draw the line at a minimum of four (although ETPS has only three RW types these days). The biggest problem was the lack of alternative relatively small helicopter types then being operated by the military. The Gazelle was the only single engine helicopter still in military

Author starting Twin Squirrel ZJ 635 on ETPS dispersal. *(QinetiQ)*

service. Fortunately, the MOD had recently developed another method of acquiring helicopters, known as Civil Operated, Military Registered (COMR); or Military Registered, Civil Owned Aircraft (MRCOA). Basic helicopter training had traditionally been done by each of the three armed services independently, but they had all ended up using the Gazelle to fly fairly similar syllabi. A private contract was awarded to run a tri-service Defence Helicopter School at RAF Shawbury. The school used the AS350 single-engine Squirrel but had it modified slightly for service use.

Meanwhile the RAF had a dedicated VIP transport squadron (32 Squadron) and they had acquired three 'off the shelf' AS355F1 Twin Squirrels. This aircraft was almost the same as the AS355N we had previously used for teaching our students all about FADEC. So, I proposed: could we lease a bog-standard AS355F1 from our friends up the road at Kidlington, slap a military registration on the side and be good to go in weeks? You would have thought so. In the end it took twelve months – but in December that year, like a teenager buying his first car, I collected our very shiny, freshly painted aircraft ZJ635. Its new paint job, carefully produced by a professional designer, belied its rather well used pedigree. It had previously been G-NEXT and used by the CEO of that organisation as his personal runabout. While I would like to take all the credit for this new helicopter, the credit is equally shared with our business manager Dick. Dick was another ex-Royal Marine and won a Distinguished Service Cross for some very heroic flying of a Sea King Mk4 as a member of 846 NAS (covered in his book *Special Forces Pilot*). Dick spent a huge amount of time and energy overcoming the financial challenges and the MOD's concerns about adding a fourth AS355F1 to the military register. I have to say this new type really added a buzz to the team. We all had to learn how to fly it, teach on it and then use it for some of the flight test training. One of the benefits of this aircraft was it had a relatively modern cockpit with the required instruments and equipment to fly in cloud. This was to prove helpful twelve months later.

My year as Principal Tutor was busy with more than just running the course and acquiring new helicopters. The Test Squadrons were now becoming more autonomous in terms of their budgets and manpower. RWTS had realised it had no work coming up suitable for an ASW Sea King Pilot, so one of my Royal Navy students was about to be stitched up. Since he was now surplus to requirements, it turns out that the appointer

Author and Dick receiving the 'new' ETPS helicopter. *(QinetiQ)*

was intending to send him back to a Sea King ASW squadron after graduation, without giving him chance to do any test flying. It took a good deal of effort and some very long and heated phone calls before we managed to change his posting to the new Merlin Mk1 Operation Evaluation Unit (OEU), where a good deal of what he had learnt on the course could be put to some use.

Early on in the year, before we had really got going, the Principal Tutor for the FTEs, Brian, dropped by to 'have a word'. Although the course was very definitely split such that I managed the RW aspects, there was also a Principal Tutor FTE who oversaw the training of both FW and RW FTEs. It turns out that one of the RW students was struggling to understand the academic material. Ironically, in my experience, the FTEs used to have a more academic head than the pilots. They were nearly always university graduates, usually in engineering, and some would have MSc or PhD qualifications. Also they were younger, not having had to spend many years learning how to be a pilot and then gaining a couple of tours flying operationally. So it was a surprise to learn that one of the RW FTEs was not coping. Meanwhile I was also having pilot problems. Our RAF student was starting to attract the attention of his tutors. Sometimes he would fly okay but sometimes he would not. This was a worrying trait in a potential test pilot. He had already come to my attention for treating our Ford Galaxy pool car as if it was his own. So I had already had to be Mr Nasty. Now I faced another challenge but I needed to find out what was going on first, so I invited him to fly a consolidation training flight in our Lynx one Friday afternoon. I clambered in alongside him and suggested we head out to the west of Boscombe where we could revisit a number of the exercises we had already flown in the Gazelle, to see if he had grasped the subject matter, whether he could fly the required test techniques, and whether he could operate the aircraft safely.

Initially things went OK. Nothing special, but he was able to fly the longitudinal stability tests. He knew that stick position/displacement could be measured and the stability determined. Great. So, onto longitudinal dynamic stability. This is referred to as 'stick force per G' by FW TPs, but the same principles apply. We need to fly the aircraft at different amounts of G. Ideally, we expect to need to pull the stick further back/aft as we pull more G. We would like the relationship between stick force and G to be linear, or with a tendency to require increasingly more stick force for each G increment. Some aeroplanes and helicopters are 'manoeuvre unstable' and the G will tend to build with less and less stick force required. The Scout would need the cyclic stick pushed forward as G was increased, as would the Lynx if the FCS was disengaged. The principal test technique for helicopters and aeroplanes is to roll on angle of bank (AOB) and enter increasingly tighter turns. A sixty degree AOB turn generates 2G. So I invited this student to fly some turns, as he had done earlier in the week in a Gazelle. And he really started to struggle. He couldn't maintain height, or airspeed, or the angle of bank for that matter. I took control and gave him another demonstration of what was required.

'OK, there we are – have another go. It is moderately difficult I know, but I'm sure you'll get the hang of it.'

'No thanks.'

'Sorry?'

'Can we go back now? I'm not feeling well.'

So I zipped us back to Boscombe Down wondering why my woes so often occurred on a Friday afternoon. Back in my office, with large mugs of tea in hand, it was time to really bottom out what was going on.

'I get airsick,' he opens.

'Sure, we all can find pulling G difficult – it can upset our stomachs.'

'I just get really tired, I then can't be bothered to fly anymore.'

'What?'

'Yep, it happens to me in a car. I used to find driving my Mini difficult and sometimes I'd just have to pull up on the side of the road and go to sleep.'

'But you're a front line RAF pilot and instructor.'

'Yeah. The RAF has already sent me on its Institute of Aviation Medicine (IAM) course in the Hawk to try and sort me out.'

'And?'

'Well you'd better read my docs.'

Bloody hell! I thought. What on earth was this about? Something very new. It was already late in the day and Happy Hour was kicking off in the bar. I told him I would get back to him on Monday and dashed upstairs to find his confidential documents folder. I had never had to do this before. We didn't have the documents of our foreign students and the UK students had already, in theory, only been selected from a pool of 'above average' pilots. But, sure enough, I saw course reports of two visits to the IAM. This was pretty rare in itself. When I read through his confidential flying and professional reports it became obvious that this issue was not new and was not flight test specific. And yet this man had managed to survive posting after posting with average grades. First thing on Monday morning I chatted to Dave, the new school CO, before dashing across to see the RAF doctor for advice. I was, personally, very relieved when he decided this was clearly a medical rather than a 'flying ability issue'. It meant I would not have to formally chop a pilot student while we were in the middle of chopping an FTE.

Why me?

I can't remember saying much to this pilot apart from 'goodbye', and as he left I wondered about what the future might hold for him.

Meanwhile, I slept soundly knowing the right outcome had been achieved. But my troubles were not yet over. Having started the year with six students I was already down to four and we hadn't got as far as the mid-year formal course photo yet. So when the next problem child was identified I was, I confess, now a tortured soul. But I monitored his progress and chatted extensively to the other tutors. This was a character that would tend to pass a sortie – just. By the third term the traditional expectation was students would complete the course. With a third of my initial students already having gone I was reluctant to lose another. As you will now know, the final student exercise is the Preview assessment. Ten hours of, hopefully intensive, flying would lead to a full flight test report (usually a couple of inches thick at least). This was then marked and assessed by the exercise tutor, and then the students would prepare a formal thirty minute presentation using photos, diagrams, graphs and so on. Eventually this pilot's report was delivered. Although teamed up with a competent FTE, the FTR was not great.

Holy Moses!

I passed the report around the other tutors, as it was important that we marked such reports fairly and consistently. The outcome was, we all agreed, not as hoped for. This wasn't usual. By the time students arrived at this stage in the course they had already written all the various parts of such a report and demonstrated at least a minimal competence. Time for a very difficult discussion. I remember we spent most of the morning going through what they had done, what they thought about the aircraft, the data they had gathered, the analysis they had achieved and then how they had documented it all. Needless to say I was facing two very unhappy bunnies. If there was any good news, it was that the overall exercise grade was based on both the written report and their formal presentation. On previous occasions, there had been students who had written glowing reports and then produced a very lacklustre performance on the stage. What I now had to ensure was that this team would achieve the opposite. They needed an outstanding presentation to haul themselves out of the mire.

The next few days felt just like the anticipation of one of my children playing in a school concert or taking part in a nativity play. (You will have already read about my proud parenthood including the sewing on of sequins for my daughter's dance costume.) So I dropped into 'dad mode' and started to spend a fair amount of time discussing what they wanted to say and how they were going to say it. I then sat through numerous practice sessions trying to help them polish their performance. When the big day came I think I was the most nervous guy in the room. This team was the product of the training I had delivered. I had led their Preview exercise and mentored their preparation. If they didn't perform well it would clearly confirm that I was a useless instructor and mentor. No pressure then. The thirty minutes passed excruciatingly slowly. I held my breath as every new PowerPoint slide appeared, which they took turns to speak about, and slide by slide we crawled to the finish line.

Hurrah! Made it. All we had to do now was get through another thirty minutes of questions.

Traditionally, the exercise tutor would ask the first such question. I wanted them to start this session confidently. So, be a smart arse and ask about something really obscure? Nope! I can't remember what I asked, but it was a straight ball. And with that they were off and managed to hang on until the end. And actually, it wasn't such a bad presentation in the scheme of things. Again we convened the 'murder board' and we all had been reasonably assured that the minimal standard had been met.

Phew! No need to change the seating plan for the McKenna Dinner.

So after four years as a military RW Tutor I'd killed the Scout but acquired the Squirrel, chopped two students but saved one, worked my socks off to stay ahead of the game but flown more types and had more fun than I ever would have thought possible four years earlier.

Happy Times!

My final few weeks as an RW Tutor on ETPS were impacted by my need to find another job. My PVR application to the RN had been accepted and my final day in 'the mob' was to be the day before my birthday, 3 April 2001. My time on ETPS was due to complete at the end of the course, though I dare say they might have found me something to do for a while. But ETPS was continuing to expand its civilian staff. There was initially a proposal to recruit another civilian RW Tutor. I threw my hat into the ring but the job didn't immediately materialise. However, Dave, the boss, came to see me with a proposition. The school was trying to expand its involvement with flight test short courses, both for internal training of Boscombe Down Trials Officers and for numerous external customers in both the military and in industry. Dave had decided the embryonic team he was establishing needed a full-time dedicated test pilot. I was offered the job and I accepted … time to tell the family we wouldn't need to move house just yet.

Phew!

On 2 April 2001 I climbed aboard (my) Twin Squirrel and flew to HMS *Heron*, RNAS Yeovilton. I walked to the main provost building to see the Fleet Master at Arms. I handed in my military ID card and removed my Lieutenant Commander rank tabs and replaced them with four silver bars. I filled in a couple of forms and apologised for losing my S10 Anti Gas Respirator – goodness knows which house loft I'd left it in.

With the paperwork complete I walked back to my Squirrel and flew myself 'home' to Boscombe Down. Surely this must have been the most painless way ever to have left the Royal Navy. The downside was, that after twenty-two years of service, I didn't get chance to have the customary 'dining out', where copious amounts of alcohol are used to remove any twinges of regret.

Although my time with the RN was complete my time with ETPS was far from over.

Chapter 13

Licences

Holy Moses! This was a rifle range in the middle of conducting live firing. We saw the flag at the same time. I can't remember the expletive from the rear seat but it was accompanied by …

'Go around Taylor, full power.' I complied. I whacked the throttle fully open, put the carburettor heat back to cold air, raised the nose to the climbing attitude and applied left rudder to counter the torque and prop wash effects.

As we flew over the astonished 'pongos', the aircraft suddenly started to shake violently.

'Oh my God, Taylor, we've been hit, we've been hit!'

As I approach retirement, one of the constant dilemmas I face is whether or not to renew or revalidate my many different piloting qualifications, which I have worked so hard to gain over the last forty-six years. My guess is that many of the readers of this book will be pilots or have connections with aviation and may well be acquainted with many of the issues I refer to. I write this chapter mainly to try and explain some of the challenges and opportunities I faced during my time at Boscombe Down and how, ultimately, this period led on to the next phase of my life as a civil certification test pilot working for the UK Civil Aviation Authority.

Many would be forgiven for assuming that qualifying as a military pilot automatically qualifies an individual as a civilian pilot also. This is certainly true in a number of other countries, with France being among them. In France, every aspect of a military pilot's training is accredited and the appropriate licence, type rating or additional qualification issued. During my military aviation career that was, sadly, never the case, although some limited exemptions were up for grabs which I did my best to make the most of. There are very few military pilots who are able to remain flying in the military all their lives. So for me, I always knew that, at some stage,

I would have to leave the Navy (sooner rather than later, my then fiancée Ally had stated, as a part of our marriage planning).

As you will have read, my career as a pilot commenced with a Royal Navy Flying Scholarship and I found myself in the summer of 1975 learning how to fly the Cessna 150 at Ipswich. I was allowed to sit all the required exams during my spare time at the British School of Flying, and with a bit of financial help from my parents I achieved enough flying to be able to gain my private pilot's licence (PPL). Immediately I was walking the treadmill of currency, revalidations and medicals that haunt all of us who fly. To keep my PPL current (legal) I had to fly five hours in every thirteen months. That doesn't sound too onerous, but for a schoolboy, and then university student, it was a very big ask. I got through a couple of years by renting a Cessna C172 from a club at Blackpool and splitting the rental cost with mates. I chose Blackpool because it was clear of any 'difficult' airspace, and a combination of the distinct coastline and the massive Blackpool Tower meant it was unlikely I would ever get lost – although I did manage to join a left-hand circuit at Squires Gate airfield, only to find out when I landed that the circuit was in fact right-hand. That would explain why I couldn't see the rest of the circuit traffic.

On arriving at university I applied to join the RAF University Air Squadron, convinced that my enthusiasm to be a military pilot, albeit most likely in the Fleet Air Arm, would be a clear vote winning strategy. Who knew that there was so much rivalry between the senior and junior service? Although I wasn't to spend my weekends flying Bulldogs, as you have read, I joined the RN during my first year and was promptly invited to fly in their de Havilland Chipmunks at their 'Grading Flight' based at Plymouth Airport (Roborough). So I flew out of there each Easter vacation and, each summer holiday, a few of us were invited to fly a 'squadron' of aircraft down to Perigeaux, in the South of France. This activity kept my PPL current and on joining BRNC Dartmouth for my initial training I was welcomed back at Roborough to keep my hand in. Thereafter I would join flying clubs wherever I was posted, rented C150s and C172s and ensured I flew enough hours each year to get the magic stamp in my logbook. I even wised up to the fact that the American FAA would validate my UK PPL and, when visiting the USA on a number of ships, I was able to rent aeroplanes at a fraction of their UK equivalent cost.

I finally was allowed to commence my flying training in the Fleet Air Arm. After passing my medical (just) I was returned to Roborough to fly the Chipmunk again in order to prove, to the very experienced grading staff, that I would be able to cope with the onerous flying training I was about to commence. At the time the RAF didn't have such a system, which I think is maybe why there was such as disparity between their aptitude tests and those of the RN. We were given just twelve hours training followed by a Final Handling Test. This FHT would determine whether or not I had wasted the last five years of my life aspiring to be a Navy pilot. If I failed this I was really up poo creek without a paddle; not least because the RN would expect me to carry on serving as a deck officer for another few years and I had already had more than enough of that.

No pressure then!

As usual, with such flight tests, I failed to get any sleep the night before. I drove to Plymouth already in a state of maximum stress. The news on arrival made matters worse. Instead of flying with the Grading Officer, a nice RN Lieutenant Commander, I was to fly with the Chief Flying Instructor (CFI), Stu.

Bugger!

We briefed without delay and, before I knew it, we were snaking across the grass to get airborne. I was meticulous with all my checks and drills. In my head I had done nothing but rehearse this flight for over twenty-four hours. With suitable height gained I was asked to fly steep turns and with the required (HASEL) checks completed went on to conduct stalls every which way. I was then invited to fly a series of aerobatic manoeuvres. These were not my forte but the Chipmunk was such a delightful aircraft to loop and roll I had a few minutes when everything seemed to be going well. And then the CFI closed the throttle on me.

Cripes!

I immediately rolled upright and pattered the required diagnosis to be informed …

'Taylor, your engine has failed. Show me a forced landing.'

As I continued to mutter my engine shutdown drill, and put out my 'pretend mayday call', I was desperately searching for a field. Ideally a flat field, orientated into wind with a smooth surface. Just when I was getting desperate I spied an almost ideal forced-landing site. It was about 800 metres long, straight into wind. It looked smooth enough and flat.

Hurrah! All was not lost. I commenced my glide landing pattern – abeam the strip at 3,000ft, letting the site disappear under my low wing. Turning through almost 90 degrees when I could see it again to end up on a curved downwind leg, or 'low key' as the military call it. I was 'bricking it'. I had to get this right. I was hoping the CFI would ask me to go around early. He didn't. I checked the engine hadn't really stopped and warmed it slightly and still we descended. Nicely lined up. I was going to float majestically over the hedge with the red flag flying by it.

Red Flag? *Red Flag?*

Holy Moses! This was a rifle range in the middle of conducting live firing. We saw the flag at the same time. I can't remember the expletive from the rear seat but it was accompanied by …

'Go around Taylor, full power.' I complied. I whacked the throttle fully open, put the carburettor heat back to cold air, raised the nose to the climbing attitude and applied left rudder to counter the torque and prop wash effects and it was then my nerves finally got the better of me.

As we flew over the astonished 'pongos' the aircraft suddenly started to shake violently.

'Oh my God, Taylor, we've been hit, we've been hit!'

'No sir, it's my leg.'

'What?'

'My leg has gone into spasm and I can't stop it shaking.'

I've never had the issue before or since but with no sleep, massive stress and more adrenalin than sensible, my left leg had started to shake uncontrollably, transmitting high frequency oscillations to the rudder.

I throttled back, lifted my left foot briefly from the rudder bar and the shaking thankfully stopped. After my leg resumed its composure I was directed to return to Roborough to demonstrate my prowess at landing – which went well. Thankfully, the forced landing debacle was almost forgotten and allowed us both to laugh about it once we had calmed ourselves down with large mugs of tea.

Phew! I had passed and enjoyed more than a few beers that evening!

I went on to fly the Bulldog and then the Gazelle and then the Wasp. So I was now a qualified service pilot (QSP) and had a couple of challenges. I wanted to keep my fixed wing licence alive and I wanted to ensure that, in the fullness of time, I could fly helicopters as a civilian pilot. When it comes to gaining licencing qualifications the main criteria then, as it is

Fleet Air Arm DeHavilland Chipmunk T.10 WK608. *(Alan Wilson)*

now, is 'flying hours'. Each qualification will have an associated minima. Frustratingly, the cross credit for helicopter hours versus a fixed wing licence was poor. I could've been the best helicopter pilot in the world, but unless I logged five fixed wing hours a year I wasn't competent to fly a Cessna 150 – *apparently*. This challenge continued and still does to this day. At least as a QSP I was able to blag some free flying. I managed to convince the guys at Roborough I needed some more Chipmunk time and, bless them, they gave me a couple of periods of refresher flying, where I was mostly sent off solo to practise my aerobatics. You would think I would be better at it than I am.

All this Chipmunk flying was to prove helpful. By 1989 I was established as an Instructor on 702 NAS at RNAS Portland. I was still struggling to keep my fixed wing PPL current and to start trying to work towards a fixed wing commercial licence. Again, frustratingly, I needed to build more FW hours in my logbook. I'm not sure who alerted me to the existence of the RAF Air Experience Flights (AEF) dotted around the country, but in March of 1989 I found myself flying again with Dennis. Dennis had been one of my helicopter instructors on 705 NAS and was a very nice chap. I was still feeling guilty about scaring him with my extremely shoddy flying, the morning after a drunken mess dinner, when the forecast weather was supposed to be thick fog all day, but had dawned sunny with stronger wind than expected. He was now the boss of No2 AEF based at Hurn, Bournemouth Airport. He had been issued with three Chipmunk T.10 aircraft and was tasked with, five days a week, flying air cadets for air experience flights. Being RAF he couldn't accept my RN Chipmunk qualification, which was fine by me, as he gave me another four hours of training and more solo flying to qualify me on type. I was now a member of 2 AEF. I would try to fly cadets every other Saturday. Even better, the AEF would organise summer camps when we would get to fly a Chipmunk all day, every day, for up to two weeks. I organised to fly out of St Athan, as Ally's sister and her family lived just up the road. Parts of my summer holidays were spent building hours, mostly upside down in loops and rolls, while my wife and children had an equally fun time, paddling in the sea and building sandcastles. I managed a similar holiday (again with my sister-in-law's family) at RAF Brawdy which had been an RNAS station flying Hunters until relatively recently. In addition to building Chipmunk hours I would tap into the University Air Squadrons who flew the Bulldog that I had previously trained on. Their instructors needed to stay current to fly at night and I discovered they would often fly with an empty spare seat. I would blag as many such flights as I could to build up my night hours.

During this time I needed to study for, and pass, a whole bunch of CAA examinations, despite all the military aviation training I had done. It turned out that the same set of exams required to get a helicopter airline pilot's licence (ATPL.H) was virtually the same as required for a fixed wing commercial licence (CPL.A). So to some extent there was some overlap. Studying for the exams was miserable. This was 1989 and I was working hard at being an instructor, flying Chipmunks at weekends and trying to be a good husband, and father to our baby son. By 1990 I had completed the basic exams. The next challenge was to fly what was then called an 1179 flight test with a CAA examiner. Although the RN got very few exemptions, the RAF had managed to wangle some. It turns out that the CAA allowed QSPs to fly such 1179s on military aircraft (on which they were already qualified) with a CFS Instructor, as long as they paid a fee. Back then the Flag Officer Naval Aviation (FONA) had his own Chipmunk and his own Gazelle and I asked to borrow them. I talked nicely to Fergus, who was part of RN FW Standards, and with Pete, who was RW Standards. Getting hold of the examiners and the aircraft and the weather all on the same day was never going to be easy but somehow I managed it.

The Chipmunk flight was the easier. I was current on the type and it was a joy to fly with Fergus, who was very friendly throughout. In fact, I followed him into the CAA some years later. Ironically the Gazelle sortie was more problematic. Although qualified on the type I hadn't flown a Gazelle for nearly eighteen months. This was before my TP days, so I hadn't yet become used to leaping in and out of different types. The other challenge was that my examiner was also the RN Lynx examiner. In a few weeks' time I would be flying with him in a Lynx in order to demonstrate my 'above average' instructional ability in order to qualify as an A2 grade QHI. Even though this trip in a Gazelle was not formally part of the recat, I knew Pete would be using the sortie to form an opinion of me and my flying ability. Ironically, it was not the engine-off landings that fazed me, but conducting an approach into a confined area. The Lynx had two engines and a powerful tail rotor, so the overriding criteria were the size and shape of the area itself – a hole in a small wood. But the Gazelle, with only one engine, had to be flown with an expectation of engine failure and the possible requirement to fly a forced landing which would pretty much have to be done into wind.

Blige!

I confess, my reconnaissance of the chosen area was a good deal more long winded than expected as I had to balance the various priorities. But I seemed to manage okay and Pete was happy enough to sign the CAA form. Even more importantly, he awarded me my A2 QHI category on the Lynx three months later.

Phew!

All that I needed to do now was pass the performance examination for the Chipmunk. There were various groups of aeroplane, Group A being the big commercial transport aeroplanes, Group C being the light twins and Group E being the single-engine aircraft such as the Cessna 150. An exam had to be passed in each required group. I had elected to 'open' my CPL with the Chipmunk – needless to say this was an unusual choice as I wasn't aware of any commercial Chipmunk operations anywhere in the world. The Chipmunk and the DC3 Dakota didn't fall into a particular performance group. I was invited to Gatwick to sit the 'Performance Unclassified' paper, for which there was no training course or any notes.

Yikes!

But thankfully I blagged my way through this random test and – hurrah! – was awarded an ATPL.HG (Helicopters and Gyros) and a CPL.A (Aeroplanes).

Bloody marvellous! I now had the basic qualifications to get a job. But as any professional pilots will realise – neither of these qualifications would be good enough in themselves. More was required. On the helicopter side I was already an instructor and was allowed to become a civvy Flying Instructor based on my Gazelle training. But in those days, if I was to be allowed to instruct on piston-engine helicopters, I was required to log thirty hours of piston helicopter time. At today's prices that would cost me around £9,000 if I simply rented a Robinson R22 or similar. Additionally, as a fixed wing pilot, I would need an instrument rating. All such instrument flying logged in a helicopter counted for next to nothing so I would need to qualify on a twin-engine aeroplane and then learn how to fly it around the various navigation aids – at Bournemouth in my case. So I devised a cunning plan.

I elected to take my four weeks' resettlement leave as early as I could, before it was expected my wife would need a further neuro operation, and took myself off to the USA again. I had found a company based in Atlanta, Georgia, who operated the Bell 206 JetRanger and, more importantly, the Schweizer 300 piston-engine machine. They had a contract to fly these Schweizer aircraft around the State inspecting the routes of underground fibre optic cables. These cables, and the data they allowed to flow, were so important that the telephone companies became paranoid about the risk from road works and JCBs turning up unannounced. So every day they would fly from dawn to dusk along set routes looking for any potential roadworks. It turns out that if I paid them … yep you heard that right … if I paid them, they would let me fly these sorties for only $50 per hour. This company was laughing all the way to the bank, but it allowed me to clock up the hours I needed in record time for less than £1,000 – quite a saving. Also out in Georgia I was able to get someone to teach me how to fly the R22, the Bell 47, and the twin-engine Seneca aeroplane which I knew I would be flying at Bournemouth when I returned home, in order to gain my instrument rating.

I learnt a heck of a lot during three weeks in Georgia. My qualification flight was conducted by a very experienced Vietnam veteran Huey pilot. After most of the flight had been completed he gave me an emergency that no one had ever given me in a real helicopter previously. While sitting in the hover, without warning, he whacked in full right yaw pedal to simulate a tail rotor failure. We were instantly spinning clockwise with the outside world a blur!

Blimey!

'Close the throttle,' he shouted.

I did – I rolled the twist grip throttle in my left hand smartly closed. Almost instantly, with the engine torque reaction removed, the aircraft stopped spinning. All I had to do was manage the decaying rotor rpm to allow me to land on the concrete without damage.

Phew! It was probably this training that allowed me to cope with the outcome of my Scout accident some years later.

The following week, at the end of one very long day, I was landing my Schweizer at an unfamiliar airfield in order to get some fuel and sleep before a dawn departure the following day. My co-pilot, who was a 'proper employee', stopped me as I was about to shut down.

'You're pointing the wrong way,' he drawled.

'I've landed into wind, that's the right thing to do,' I responded

'Nope it's the wrong way. Turn it around. Trust me.'

Despite the Schweizer alongside us having landed in the correct orientation, I lifted back into the hover and landed in a bit of a snotty heap downwind. Neither of us had any money to squander so we ate all of the free popcorn, drank the free black coffee and slept on the sofas of the FBO (Fixed Base Operator) who provided ground services such as fuel and rest rooms. At the first glimmer of a pink sky in the east I dusted myself off to clean my teeth and the like, and pre-flight the helicopter. Although parked downwind it was now pointed directly into the dawn's rising sun. The other aircraft cockpit was covered in an inch of ice. My windscreen had already melted clear. Genius! I also learnt a good deal from my co-pilot about the avoid curve. I had been taught to fly helicopters by the Royal Navy. Surely this training was the best in the world? It turns out that the approach I was taught to fly took my helicopter right through the avoid curve. This was long before ETPS and my understanding of such things. In fairness, the RN was predominantly teaching Wessex, Sea King and Lynx pilots of the future, and a nice steady approach made a lot of sense. Instead, my co-pilot, when flying an approach in the Schweizer, maintained at least 60 KIAS until the last possible moment – and, of course, I now totally understand why.

Once I'd clocked up enough hours on the Schweizer I decided to part with more significant amounts of money and learn how to fly the Robinson R22. My training was typically minimalist and I was signed off after forty minutes dual flying. I immediately went off on my own to consolidate my bare-bones training course. Having flown a couple of circuits I set myself up for another autorotation. Just as on my dual sortie earlier that morning, I lined myself up with the chosen piece of grass and rolled the throttle closed as I progressively lowered the collective lever.

Baaaaaarp!

What the heck?

Before I could blink the low rotor rpm horn was blaring. The collective was fully down. What could I do?

'Flare … Flare … *Flare,*' I shouted to myself. By washing off speed, with aft cyclic, I managed to raise the rpm sufficiently to turn the horn off.

Phew! I wound open the throttle as I caught my breath.

Next time around I set myself up for a 180 degree auto so that I could pull some G all the way through my descent to maintain my rotor rpm. Again, this was before my TP time and was my first experience of the R22. My instructor had been a big chap and we had burnt off an hour's fuel so the aircraft was now a good deal lighter than when I had flown dual. That said, it is not normal for a low rotor rpm horn to be blaring if everything is normal and, almost certainly, the rotor blades had been set up with slightly too much pitch applied.

I managed to achieve all I needed in three of the four weeks I'd set aside, and dashed home to be reunited with my children and my wife – who was not doing so well. She needed another operation to try and remove more of the brain tumour more urgently than we had hoped. In fact she needed it pretty much immediately.

I was now juggling a number of balls and spinning a lot of plates. In addition to my increasingly overwhelming domestic situation I needed to fly formal 1179 tests with CAA examiners in order to add the Schweizer and R22 to my ATPL.HG before I forgot how to fly them. And I had to crack on with my fixed wing instrument rating within the leave I had booked, and I had to get back to work at RNAS Portland. My 1179 for the R22 went well enough, given I'd only had forty minutes dual instruction. My Schweizer check ride nearly ended in disaster. I was flying out of Goodwood, which I didn't know well, with an examiner I had never met before. I started the aircraft from a checklist to make sure I didn't miss anything out. With the engine running and blades turning I made the radio call and lifted gently into the hover ... and immediately almost crashed. What? My brain cells were struggling. I had flown nearly thirty hours on this type and was far more confident of passing the test than with the R22. What was going on? I was really struggling to make small precise cyclic inputs. I hastily landed back onto the ground in a snotty heap. I finally realised what I thought was going on.

Helicopters such as this did not have hydraulic systems and the cyclic control was potentially free to move of its own accord, which could spell disaster on the ground. The Gazelle had a knurled knob at the base of the cyclic which would add friction if required, but it was never used in the RN or RAF versions I had flown. The Schweizer was fitted with two friction devices. One added friction to the cyclic fore and aft, the other laterally. In the States we had never used these friction devices and I had never had to check them before take-off. However, on this aircraft, one friction was fully applied and the other was not. So the stick was very easy to move in one axis and almost impossible in the other. This must be about the worst possible combination of controllability challenges. Because this was a check ride, I had another challenge. If I admitted my mistake I would have almost certainly failed the test before it had begun. So, as I was struggling not to crash, I was saying to my innocent examiner ...

'I think I might need to slightly adjust the cyclic friction ... landing back on.'

I then had to make a big fuss, like a safe cracker, of finely tuning each friction knob so that it appeared I was making very subtle changes rather than in fact winding all the friction off both!

Phew! Survived without embarrassment and passed.

With Ally surviving a further two major neuro operations I managed to get back to work to fit in another shedload of Lynx flying, before my Easter leave was spent at Bournemouth going round and round the various instrument approaches in a Seneca that was costing me a small fortune. I had been canny enough to use a Government Career Development Loan scheme to raise the funds but they would all have to be paid back. The instrument scan on all such flights should have centred on the Attitude Indicator (Artificial Horizon), but instead it centred on the standard clock as I watched my meagre funds dwindling as the minute hand clicked painfully around.

I would like to say I received good instruction … I would like to say that. Instead the staff at the school I went to seemed only able to rant at me whenever I wasn't precisely on the required numbers. I received no 'top tips' of how to actually fly procedural instrument approaches. But thankfully, I was by now becoming quite an experienced pilot and was able to work out how to do most things myself. After ten painful hours it was time to fly my test with a CAA employed examiner. The guy appointed was incredibly experienced and he had been at Bournemouth for years. The initial Instrument Rating test has to be, without any shadow of doubt, one of the highest workload and most stressful sorties devised by man. Not least because of the huge amounts of personal money involved. The cost of renting the aeroplane alone was eye watering, and the examination fee on top ensured it had a serious impact on where we might be able to go on holiday anytime soon. So I was doing my best not to fail the test, and by working my socks off had done OK up until the time we needed to head back to Bournemouth to fly an approach. I called up on the radio …

'Bournemouth Approach – Exam 20. I am fifteen miles south east. Request a hold followed by an NDB approach with an ILS to follow.'

'Roger Exam 20 – You are clear own navigation to the Beacon. Join the hold at Flight Level 50. Expect RW 08 however this may change to Runway 26 as we have the approach calibration taking place.'

Bugger!

In fact the runway in use changed every five minutes or so as an external agency was checking the approaches to each runway in turn. Doing this test when you know the runway in use is hard enough, but with flip-flopping criteria my brain was hurting. I say to my examiner …

'This is getting really silly. I don't think this is sensible.'

'I can't comment or advise you,' says my examiner.

'OK, I think I'm going to have to call it a day. I think we need to stop the test.'

'Good decision, couldn't agree more,' he says.

Phew! I rejoined the airfield visually and landed as quickly as I could to save rental time. I had made a sensible decision and was awarded a partial pass for what I had achieved so far – but I hadn't completed the test. It took another four weeks before I could set up the further test with a different examiner which needed to be fitted around an increasingly complex pattern of caring for my wife and two small children. I passed!

It was during this period that I had, as mentioned earlier, reluctantly decided to turn down the offer of a place with the RAF and instead accepted the Royal Navy's very kind offer of a job running the Lynx Simulator at RNAS Portland. So now, although I had been expecting to fly as a civilian relatively soon, I needed to start preparing for the ETPS selection as I've written about previously. I was mindful of this when I was approached by a flying school at Bournemouth. They could no longer afford a full time helicopter instructor, but had sold a huge number of 'Trial Lesson' vouchers which they needed to honour. I agreed to join their staff as a part-timer to work on Saturdays. During the week I was flying my socks off for 702 NAS, so trying to fit this in was stressful but it gave me some much needed R22 experience, which I thought would assist me in my desire to expand my aviation experience before the ETPS interviews, and assist in job finding if I had to leave the Navy any sooner than planned. In fairness, doing the trial lessons was fun. Invariably the voucher had been a present – so I was often part of the wish fulfilment of a finally realised dream. Where practical we would fly over the punter's house and take lots of photos etc. The challenge came when I was asked to fly with 'proper students', or guys with PPLs that wanted to be approved for self-fly hire. Instructing ab initio Lynx pilots I had the benefit of numerous sifting filters from aptitude tests, grading, Bulldog training and Gazelle training. So most (but not all) of the muppets had, by and large, been chopped already. Flying as a civilian is like learning to drive a car. You can keep taking lessons until the money runs out. And some of these characters had a heck of a lot of money.

I arrived at Boscombe Down with both helicopter and aeroplane licences. I was a helicopter flying instructor and had amassed enough experience on piston-engine helicopters to be employable at a flying school if I needed to be. As I explained earlier, towards the end of my tour as an RN Tutor at ETPS I was offered a lacklustre appointment (to return to the Lynx Simulator), so again took the decision it was time to leave. My helicopter qualifications were now reasonable but my fixed wing ones less so. Rather than an Airline Transport Pilot's Licence (ATPL) I had only a commercial licence (CPL). All I needed (hah!) to upgrade was to sit all my exams again at a higher standard and fly a hundred hours at night in an aeroplane. My 500 hours of low level night flying in Wasp and Lynx helicopters, in all manner of shitty weather, credited me with just fifty of the required hours. So, undaunted, I hatched a plan. And while busy as the clappers running the ETPS course, all my evenings were spent swotting for CAA exams. I failed the first attempt but passed the second, which was just as well as that was the last sitting of the exams I had worked for before the system changed.

Phew!

Exams achieved, and with some ten hours aeroplane night flying logged previously, all I needed now was a further forty hours. I gave up on the idea of blagging more Bulldog time as being just too difficult. Instead I decided I would have to part with some more hard-earned cash. Fortuitously, as you will have already read, I found myself out at Patuxent River from time to time. Some investigation led me to discover a flying school at St Mary's (just down the road from the USN base) where they rented Cessna 150s for just $16 per hour. At the time that was about £10 per hour. In the UK it would have been seven or eight times that amount. So I put together a cunning plan to achieve forty hours flying over eight nights – easy. At least I was able to do it late in the year when it went dark early.

This was to prove some of the scariest flying I've done to date. When I planned my proposed night-time adventure, in the summer months in the UK, my biggest concern was possible tiredness leading to a loss of concentration. So I planned some navigation exercises where I would fly over 200 miles and find somewhere to grab fuel, supper and coffee, and then fly back to St Mary's. On the first night I did just that. I had a one hour check-out flight with a local instructor, refuelled, had a pee and then set off west to Charlottesville via Fredericksburg. I landed in time for things still to be open and managed to get all that I needed and returned successfully. The problem was that for most of the journey, I was flying over inky blackness, swamps with alligators and the like. If my engine stopped, I decided, I would be very unlikely to find somewhere to land.

Yikes!

On the second night I flew north to Lancaster – this was even worse. I was over very swampy ground or on the edge of Chesapeake Bay. I decided that, on this route, if I lost the engine my chances of survival were bugger all. Time for a different strategy. The 'pukka factor' of flying around over hostile terrain, in a poorly maintained single-engine aircraft, was more than enough to keep me wide awake. So time for Plan B. In the States, at the time, there were numerous general aviation airfields and most of them were equipped with runway lights. Even the unmanned fields could be encouraged to turn their lights on by clicking the 'press to transmit' button repeatedly on their published VHF frequency. I managed to find a series of such airfields and worked out that if I flew high enough, if the engine stopped I would be able to get the lights on in time to do a safe forced landing. In addition, I planned much of my Plan B route to follow the I-95 interstate highway. The equivalent of a UK motorway, this road had a very helpful difference. Instead of a central reservation of a few feet wide, there was a strip of usually uncluttered grass at least as wide as most UK grass airfields. So my new route required me to climb steadily to 5,000ft towards a VOR navigation beacon which I could then overfly and track directly away from until I picked up the I-95, which took me down to Richmond International which, at night, was quiet enough for me to route through their overhead. Then, airfield to airfield, I hopped down to Norfolk, Virginia, which was an amazing sight at night. It was a massive base for the US Navy's East Coast Fleet. The place was lit up like a Christmas tree … hard not to find. So from the third night onwards this became my regular pee, fuel, food and coffee stop. Although this was long before I had any GPS navigation aids, I reckon I knew exactly where I was (to within a few metres) every second of the flights, and more importantly, I knew exactly where I was going to land should the engine stop. On the sixth night, as I taxied out from the FBO, suitably rested and refuelled, I had a meteorological experience that I had never had before. The bottom half of the aircraft was completely shrouded in mist or fog. But I could still see to taxi and I wasted no time in completing my checks and getting airborne. It was the end of October, it was cold and as I had realised, very humid. In the UK humidity tends to be associated with warmer maritime airflows, but not so in Virginia. As I climbed steadily to 1,000ft or so I noticed my rate of climb was degrading quite rapidly.

Bugger!

What's going on? With few other options I applied full heat to the carburettor. Initially this caused my engine to lose even more power and now I had stopped climbing. Time to head back to Norfolk? But eventually the carb heat did its job and cleared the build up of ice. Back to cold air and a gentle rate of climb returned for a couple of minutes before I stopped climbing again. So full carb heat … pause … two … three … ice cleared … back to cold air and climb some more. I needed to get to 5,000ft for my safe forced landing strategy to be valid. After about half an hour my intermittent use of carb heat worked and I reached my lofty cruise altitude.

Bloody hell! This was not fun.

I had consistently been achieving over five hours of flying every night and was starting to think my goal might indeed be achievable. On my penultimate night, I was given a different aircraft for some reason. This was a dog. I had become used to my regular machine and was becoming comfortable with the way the engine sounded in the quiet of the evening. Right from the word go this replacement didn't inspire confidence. On the way home from Norfolk it was not running at all smoothly. Carb heat made no positive difference so it was not icing on this occasion. Halfway home I was overhead Richmond International. I was by then an experienced military pilot and a risk averse flight test professional. Overhead Richmond at 5,000ft I was, for a while, safe. Whatever happened I could safely glide to one of many available runways. I asked to fly an orbit … and another … and another. The snag with night flying, I have realised over the years, is that your senses are heightened. You hear every noise, smell every hot or smoky smell and feel every vibration through the seat of your pants. Was I just becoming too soft/paranoid in my old age? I had flown a Wasp for hundreds of hours, low level over the sea at night in all kinds of shitty weather. I reached the moment when I was about to have insufficient fuel to continue – so, driven on by the wavering fuel gauges, I set off northbound along the I-95. I was aware of every stroke of each piston on the clapped out engine but on and on it roughly droned. At last I could see my destination … nearly there … keep going please! I joined high, as I always did. The surrounding dense woods would really ruin my evening if I had to land in them. Carb heat applied, throttle closed I descended in a gentle spiral dive to land successfully, taxi to the parking area and pull to halt.

Phew! – I had survived another.

The following morning the engine failed. I had left a comprehensive debrief in the technical log book and the aircraft was being flown by an experienced instructor who was, thankfully, able to glide to the runway and land without embarrassment. It could have been me.

Holy Moses!

My last night I only needed three more hours and I reckoned if I pottered gently I could achieve that on just one tankful of gas. Guess how far I travelled away from St Mary's that night? Less than ten miles. And what an awesome flight it was. It was Halloween. As I climbed through around 4,000ft I started to witness the most amazing moonrise I have ever seen. It was red. It was huge. It got bigger and bigger and then the colours changed. Was it now blue? Purple? Orange? I was stunned. If that wasn't enough, it turns out Americans set off fireworks on Halloween – who knew? I had the best seat in town for one of the most amazing shows I've ever witnessed. I was watching the clock. I needed forty hours of night flying in my log book. At 39 hours and 45 mins I tipped a wing, throttled back, with full carb heat applied, and descended back to the real world. It wasn't yet 9 pm and some very strong Bourbon had my name on it back at the Officers' Club. I had achieved exactly what I set out to do, and a few weeks later I was the recipient of a shiny green brand new ATPL.A. Frustratingly, when the UK merged its licensing standards with Europe, an ATPL could only be granted with a certain amount of 'multi-crew' time. I had this in spades in helicopters but not in aeroplanes. I now have four UK licences which include my very hard won UK ATPL.A which, every time I take it out of my bag, reminds of the risks I endured to obtain it. If only I had known I would never use it in anger I might have spent every night in the bar at Pax rather than just the last one.

Chapter 14

Principal Tutor Systems and Short Courses – The Last Straw

This is the final chapter of this book. My final chapter at Boscombe Down could well have marked the end of my time as an 'Experimental Test Pilot'. But it started so well …

As you will have read, I was approached by Dave, the CO (Commanding Officer) of ETPS in my last few months as an RW Tutor. Dave is an excellent pilot, very sharp, incredibly entrepreneurial and an excellent people manager. He had realised that a number of other test pilot schools were being established around the world and they were starting to grow their business by delivering a whole host of short courses in flight test; 'short' meaning anything less than the year it took to train a test pilot. Inevitably, organisations that liked a school's short courses would sooner or later consider sending their students to said training provider for the full (expensive) graduate TP course. Dave wanted to head off this commercial activity by ensuring ETPS stayed 'in the game'. Additionally, the school was becoming increasingly responsible for internal training of a whole bunch of people who would work within the flight test/trials area. He had appointed the school aerosystems tutor, Stan, as the man to oversee all such activity. Stan was not getting the support he needed from the school's test pilots and so I was duly recruited as a 'short course TP'. I was initially suspicious. On the face of it, the short course activity at the time was fairly minimalist and, frankly, the associated flying for the internal course was rather lacklustre. After a handful of conversations, a number of aspects of the proposed job were agreed and were attractive enough to grab my attention. I would teach both RW and FW flight test and would, therefore, be given instruction and standardised as a Fixed Wing Tutor. The Civil Certification eight-month course would come under the Short Courses umbrella and I would help deliver it. We would

Principal Tutor Systems and Short Courses – The Last Straw

plan to increase our links with Cranfield University and aim to become capable of operating their Jetstream twin turboprop flight test classroom, which would mean I would need to be qualified on the aircraft. We would investigate and grow the capability of using civil registered aircraft that I would fly for the school.

Ultimately, TPs are motivated not by money, but by what they get to fly. I very much liked the idea of teaching FW, operating the Jetstream and flying civvy types for flight test training. So before I knew it, I had signed on the dotted line and at the end of the year moved out of my RW office to a portacabin across the carpark, where I teamed up with Stan and Terry (both aerosystems tutors) and Matt who had an incredible CV as an FW FTE. I didn't know it then but Stan had decided to leave ETPS and within weeks I found I was not just the short course pilot, but the Principal Tutor as well. In fairness, this had the potential to be a dream job for me. I was working within ETPS, which I enjoyed, but I was also my own boss. I was going to get some new aviation challenges and would become much more commercially aware. But a number of things would change all that. In July we became part of QinetiQ (a new commercial organisation that took on all the assets at Boscombe among other places). Dave, the CO was posted away and, subsequently, QinetiQ signed a Long Term Partnering Agreement (LTPA) with the UK Ministry of Defence, potentially scuppering much of what I had been asked to do.

But back to January 2001. In my final few weeks as an RW tutor I had not wasted any time and had started to consider what I might need to do in order to be able to undertake the required mandate. During that period we yet again rented-in the Bell 47 and it was flown into us by a United Kingdom Civil Aviation Authority flight operations inspector. I wasted no time in picking his brains. This led to a meeting with Dave and a few of the other RW tutors. It had been mooted I should get a helicopter instrument rating. Our visitor explained that, as a QSP with a military instrument rating, I would not need to undertake any very expensive additional training; I could just book a test with a CAA examiner. My RW colleagues were not enthusiastic, but Dave suggested I couldn't afford not to seize the opportunity. At least I already had an FW IR so knew roughly what was expected. I planned to fly 'my personal AS355F1' for the test and promptly booked up an examiner as there was generally a three-month lead time and I was due to leave the

RN in … three months. I chatted to my mate Nick, at Kidlington, and he gave me some top tips about what the test would involve and then I flew a couple of practice flights on my own. For the test itself, things would be complicated. I would fly in the P1 (Captain's) seat, with screens (borrowed from Nick) covering my side of the windscreen, and a CAA examiner would monitor my conduct as I would demonstrate I could fly a public transport helicopter flight in cloud.

But this was a military registered aircraft and the rules stated I would have to have a safety pilot who could keep a good lookout while I flew 'heads-down' on instruments. I managed to convince Eric to be that man, as the other RW staff had beat a hasty retreat. We flew one practice flight together before the test day dawned. As usual I had not slept. The weather forecast wasn't good. I had hoped it would be better in the morning as I tossed and turned all night. In the morning I met my examiner, Tony, and we walked to my office braced against the gale force winds and heavy rain. These tests always follow a similar format. The student, that was me, started the process by giving a comprehensive brief about the aircraft, airfield and weather. I was then required to inform the examiner whether I thought the weather was suitable for the test itself. Trying to get the aircraft and an examiner together on the same day had been troublesome to say the least, as I did not really have much support from the rest of ETPS for this initiative. I knew that cancelling might jeopardise the whole project but I found myself saying …

'So with a low cloud base, low freezing level, gale force wind and heavy rain and poor visibility I do not think the weather is suitable for a helicopter public transport flight …' I was despondent.

'Before you continue,' says my examiner, 'let me show you my diary.' His next availability was twelve weeks away.

Knowing that would mean I would no longer be in the RN, and this cunning plan might fail, I responded promptly …

'What I meant to say was that, although the weather is marginal, I deem it entirely suitable for the flight to continue as planned.'

'Good decision,' he replied, clearly keen to get another task out of his inbox.

My real problems were only just beginning. I would be flying in accordance with civil rules. Eric had to captain the aircraft in accordance with military rules … and guess what? They were not the same. Because of the very cold temperatures, we were limited to flying not above about 2,500ft. The military rules required that we would normally fly above Flight Level 30, or 3,000ft.

Bugger!

So I now had to organise a special clearance from the RAF Air Traffic Controllers at Boscombe whereby they would let us fly at the minimum safe altitude of 2,200ft and hand me directly over to the controllers at Bournemouth. On a good day this was a very high workload flight. It was starting to become ridiculous. But we had briefed (several times over), the planning was done and we had a full tank of gas, so off we went with me using various crib lists supplied by Nick to make sure I did everything in the pukka civvy fashion. We spent most of the flight in heavy rain and cloud, so the screens and safety pilot notion were rather bonkers. There was so much water leaking in that Eric tried to protect the avionics by covering them with his flying gloves. As I bounced around the sky, somewhere near Bournemouth, I desperately tried to make sure the needles on the navigation instruments were always pointing in the correct direction, despite the wind blowing at 90 degrees to the runway. On my final approach I was being blown sideways so fast, that by compensating, I ended up looking for the runway lights out of my side window.

We struggled back to Boscombe flying a genuine instrument approach in order to find the airfield, and I threw my Squirrel onto the concrete dispersal with a sigh of relief. Before the rotors had stopped my examiner chirped …

'You were absolutely correct, really quite a shitty day and your initial decision not to fly was spot on. That said, you flew a good deal better than I could have done so you've passed.'

Bloody Brilliant! Thank you Tony.

One challenge down, many more to go. The next on the list was 'become a Jetstream pilot'. ETPS had rented in the services of the Cranfield Jetstream G-NFLC for some years. The aircraft was a flying classroom with a number of on-board workstations. It was an ideal training vehicle for a number of exercises and used particularly for FTE training. As soon as I knew about the potential for a closer relationship with the university I was excited. Cranfield was already underwriting degrees based predominantly on the twelve months of study our long course provided. If we could work together on short courses we would be a world class

Author in (his) Twin Squirrel ZJ635. *(QinetiQ)*

provider of such training. I arranged to fly with their Chief Test Pilot (CTP), Dodge, before I had even started my new job and continued to fly with him every time the aircraft visited, but I was not yet qualified on the type. Investigation revealed this was the only Mk1 version of the Handley Page Jetstream flying in the UK and, compared with all the other Jetstreams, was fitted with quite different engines (2 x Turbomeca Astazou XVIF) similar to those fitted in the Gazelle. There were no approved training schools for the Mk1 anywhere … but wait … the RAF multi-engine training school, 45 (Reserve) Squadron, based at RAF Cranwell, was still using a version of the Mk1 Jetstream. They would in due course transition to the Beech King Air and I would end up testing their aircraft frequently as a CAA TP.

Principal Tutor Systems and Short Courses – The Last Straw

The first step was to contact the CAA. I needed a letter. A letter from the CAA, in those days, gave the required authority for something outside of the 'norm' to happen. I found the right person to talk to and got my letter. The letter confirmed that, if I was to qualify on the RAF Jetstream, I could then, as previously, nominate a CFS examiner to conduct an 1179 flight and, after due payment of a fee, I could be awarded a type rating. Hurrah! Some more wheeling and dealing was now required to convince the RAF they needed to train a random rote from ETPS how to fly their aircraft. The CO of the unit threw me at his standards team – which actually was extremely good news. I was adopted by the very small cadre of multi-engine experts who, over three very intensive weeks, taught me everything they knew about the aircraft, military multi-engine operations and procedural instrument flying. After lots and lots of late nights swotting up the aircrew manual and some intensive sorties in the simulator and three on the real aircraft, my instructor David sent me solo. Unlike my shenanigans with the Wessex conversion, David was keen to ensure that it was crystal clear that I was fully qualified on the type and so I needed to log some solo time. This could have been daunting. But thankfully my time in the 1-11 and the Andover, along with lots of time in the Basset, had been an ideal lead-in. To some extent I was qualifying as a military multi-engine pilot *after* having done bucket loads of military multi-engine test flying. However, life, in my experience is never easy, and just as I was about to set up my 1179 test with Fred, the RAF's most experienced multi-engine A1 QFI, the CAA tried to throw a spanner in the works. Out of the blue they announced that military pilots gaining such type ratings needed to have logged at least a hundred hours on the type before taking the test. I'd logged a tenth of that. Back to phoning Gatwick. Thank goodness for my letter. That formed the authority for my cunning plan which the CAA honoured, despite the moving goal posts.

Hurrah! I had qualified as a Jetstream pilot in the nick of time.

Now I needed to become a fixed wing test pilot (FW TP). It normally takes a year. Yikes! Again I am grateful to Dave, the CO, for continuing to support this very unusual sidestep from one discipline to another. He got the ball rolling by commencing my conversion using the trusty Basset. I flew with him and all the other FW Tutors that were qualified on the aircraft, and a few days later I was teaching longitudinal static stability to a bunch of fast jet pilots – I loved it. It was great to see how a Harrier

Cranfield University Jetstream. *(Fred Seggie)*

pilot approached the aircraft when compared to, say, a Sea King pilot. The greatest fun was with an American F16 pilot who just had quite a different control input strategy to everyone else I flew with. I guess that is what comes of flying with an almost fixed inceptor for years.

In addition to now teaching FW flight test on the Basset, I chose to attend all the FW exercise (Phase) briefings while swotting up on the theory in the evenings. My fellow short course FTE Matt, was also incredibly knowledgeable and we could brainstorm topics frequently. I was now managing the Civil Certification Course and was keen to instruct on as many aspects as I could so did all the Basset flying and simulator instruction. We used to teach a couple of topics using commercial large aeroplane (Boeing 757) simulators at Burgess Hill. A couple of very high risk areas for testing commercial aeroplanes is testing the minimum 'unstick speed' (Vmu) (which requires conducting numerous take-offs with the tail of the aircraft in contact with the ground), and the minimum control speed on the ground (Vmcg) (which investigates control authority during a take-off roll following an outboard engine failure). I was lucky enough to have been part of a group of tutors that visited Airbus in Toulouse, and I had a long session in the simulator with Claude, the CTP who personally flew all such test flights on their aircraft for many years.

He explained how each of these high risk test programmes was manned and achieved. I was able to put together some lesson plans, initially for my own short course students, but I very quickly found myself teaching the subject matter to the long course as well. I loved the variety.

Because of my increasingly close working relationship with Brian and the FTE staff, a further great opportunity came my way. Every year the long course FTE students would have their own major exercise in addition to later being teamed up with pilots for the Preview. This FTE exercise was run in Braunschweig, Germany, using another unique aeroplane, the DLR VFW-Fokker 614. The aircraft was designed at the beginning of the 1970s as a replacement for the DC-3. It was an unusual design in that the two Rolls Royce turbofan engines were mounted in pylons on top rather than below the wing. This configuration was helpful for conducting operations to unprepared runways as the engines were less likely to get damaged by ingesting stones and the like.

Unfortunately, the marketing of the aircraft was not done well and major airlines were purchasing long-rather than short-haul aircraft. Less than twenty aircraft entered service and the programme was cancelled in 1977. DLR had acquired one of the aircraft and extensively modified it for the Advanced Technologies Testing Aircraft System (ATTAS) project. The aircraft design was useful for this modification in that the engine 'thrust line' was pretty much lined up with the centre of gravity and fuselage drag. So changes in engine power did not introduce the traditional

DLR ATTAS aircraft. *(DLR)*

pitch changes associated with podded engines fitted beneath the wings. The glass cockpit was effectively straight out of an Airbus and the flying qualities could be extensively modified via computers. This was a step beyond the Basset, Astra Hawk and NRC Bell 205. The exercise involved me acting as project experimental test pilot and discovering, on the first sortie, some serious handling qualities issues, especially with Dutch Roll. The student FTEs would then analyse the flight control laws and make changes which I would again be asked to evaluate, and help improve, over about seven flying hours. I thought it was an excellent exercise and I just loved acting as project TP surrounded by such enthusiastic FTEs.

So far so good. I had gained an RW IR, qualified as a multi-engine pilot, gained a Jetstream type rating and had demonstrated my competence to fly as an FW TP. The other major part of my new job was to introduce the use of civil aircraft to deliver flight test training. Ironically, ETPS has recently changed to an all civilian registered training fleet, but twenty years ago this was seen as a very radical concept. Thankfully I had the full support of Dave and went about researching the best way to achieve this, safely and legally. I spoke with a good number of people at the CAA and a number of training schools around the UK, but especially those relatively close to Boscombe Down. I elected to introduce the use of the Bell 206 JetRanger initially for a number of reasons. I was already qualified on the type. We always rented the type each year to demonstrate the characteristics of a teetering rotor system to our RW students. It was relatively cheap and would prove an ideal helicopter for delivering the internal QinetiQ trials officer training. There were two available for rental at the training school based at Thruxton just up the road.

My research had led me to believe there was only one satisfactory way to achieve what was needed. I would need to become a bona fide instructor of the Thruxton based flying school. So I would need to be checked out by their Chief Flying Instructor and added to their documentation and insurance policy. Shortly after my return from RAF Cranwell the time was right to put this to the test. Each morning I would drive to Thruxton, check out the aircraft and fly to Boscombe Down and land on the ETPS dispersal. I would then operate the aircraft for the day, just as I would have done a Gazelle, and then at the end of the day I flew it back to Thruxton, dragged it into the hangar and drove home. They were long but incredibly successful days.

Principal Tutor Systems and Short Courses – The Last Straw

Over the next four weeks, among other things, I flew over thirty, one-hour long sorties. I flew with all the RW staff and students and the new Chief Test Pilot, Laurie, who had previously been the boss of the school. I also used the aircraft to deliver a number of familiarisation sorties to my short course trials officer students. With an established methodology I now had one final problem to solve; that of doing something similar in an aeroplane. I needed to be an FW Flying Instructor. The course to become an FI is quite lengthy, but again I wrote to the CAA and pleaded my case. Given my extensive RW instructional background they agreed I could attempt to complete the training in half the regular number of flying hours. Time to talk to another David who was the CFI at Old Sarum airfield, Salisbury. David was previously an RAF Test Pilot and Boscombe Down Chief Test Pilot and was very highly regarded in the flying training world. He agreed to undertake delivery of the required training, which suited me as I lived just down the road from the airfield. I had only two weeks to achieve nearly twenty hours of flying in some really dreadful weather. I did the course in a tail dragger Cessna C152, G-DRAG, and had to land in limiting crosswinds most days. About halfway through, David called me into his office.

'Chris, are you doing all the homework I set you?'

'Yes, absolutely,' I replied, but the reality was most of my evenings were kept full enough trying to keep up to speed with all the emails and admin of my day job. More effort required clearly and, as always, I was trying not to short change my family in the busy period running up to Christmas. More juggling and plate spinning and I finally found myself flying with yet another highly experienced examiner, Chris. Thankfully, my now considerable instructional experience had stood me in good stead and David's very pedantic teaching style had equipped me well. I passed my FI test with flying colours and within days had my ATPL.A annotated with my aeroplane FI rating. Hurrah! But I had one last mission to perform in 2001, that of Santa's reindeer.

For many years RWTS had flown their circuits over a small village school nearby. As a quid pro quo, every year, they would fly a helicopter into the school with Father Christmas carrying a bag full of presents for the kids. This particular year all of their available helicopters were unserviceable.

Blige! They asked ETPS to cover it. Unfortunately most of the aircraft fleet was unserviceable and on the required day, 19 December, all of the ETPS RW staff were planning to be on leave already – it was effectively the very last day that Boscombe would permit flying before closing down for the seasonal break. I found myself being volunteered and was advised 'my Squirrel' would be made available. I dropped into the school on the way home the day before to do a reconnaissance. I would be landing in a small playing field area. It was big enough but there were lots of telephone wires and trees and power cables around so I would have to be quite cautious and do a steeper than ideal approach. I enquired about Father Christmas. He was the Chair of the school governors and I was told he was a very big bloke.

Yikes! As I was almost out of the door, I casually asked,

'I presume he's a fit chap … no heart problems or anything?'

'Actually, since you ask, he's just recovered from triple bypass surgery.'

'Oh great!'

This flight was being personally authorised by the Chief Test Pilot. I called him up to inform him of my latest bit of info and was given the green light to press on. I was due to land there at 1200. I briefed the ground crew and advised them that I only wanted a small amount of fuel so that the aircraft would not be too heavy and I would have more power margin available to make the steep approach I wanted to do.

'Too late, it's already full,' I was told, 'and it's got a starting problem. We managed to get it going yesterday but only just.'

Hells bells!

Santa arrived at 0930. He was indeed a natural for the role and could barely get into his polyester red and white suit. I had decided he should cover this up with a set of proper flying overalls but I couldn't find a suit big enough. At least 'my Squirrel' was really a civvy aircraft and this kind of task was bread and butter for most of the operators of the type. So we briefed. I had decided to get airborne around 1030 and burn off most of the fuel before attempting my confined area landing. With the paperwork done and the lousy weather assessed (low cloud, drizzle etc.) we clambered into the aircraft and I flashed through the checklist on an aircraft I was now becoming very comfortable in. In a timely fashion I pressed the 'tit' on the left-hand throttle to start the first engine. There was a noise but the engine failed to spin.

Principal Tutor Systems and Short Courses – The Last Straw

Drat! I had been advised that if this happened a mechanic would clamber up the side of the aircraft and spin the engine around a bit. It appeared to be a similar problem to one I'd had on an old Morris Minor where the starter motor engaged a cog to mesh with a starter ring which would then be spun up. For some reason I had a similar issue. I made the aircraft safe and a mechanic climbed up, did what was required and when he was clear I pressed the tit again. The same thing happened again … and again … and again … and again … and again. Time to give the starter motor a rest.

As I have already mentioned, I am advised that one of my character flaws is that I am too stubborn. Some would describe it as being tenacious, or say I was like a dog with a bone. In fairness, those descriptions came to define my three years in this particular job, to the frustration of both me and those around me. I continued to try to start the engine. After an hour I was beginning to assume my natural bad luck had spread to envelop even Father Christmas and the scores of young children who were about to be sorely disappointed. I got on the radio.

'Tower, Tester 77. My aircraft is still refusing to start. Please could you ask the firestation if they would consider picking up Santa in one of their fire trucks?'

'Errrrr Standby.'

The firestation started to warm a fire truck and I briefed my passenger to standby just in case.

It was 1152. One more try?

I pressed the tit. This poor starter motor finally found some teeth to bite on and slowly but surely the engine started to spin. *Very slowly*. Ideally I wanted the engine to be spinning quite fast before I introduced the fuel, but I realised I was already achieving all I was going to get and trickled in some gas. The engine temperature shot up … 500 … 600 … 700 … 800 degrees. The normal limit was 810 °C but I was allowed to go over this for up to ten seconds as long as I stayed below 927. I squeezed the throttle open a tad … a few more revs … 850 … a little more … 880 … 900 … (I was now counting; one thousand and one, one thousand and two, one thousand and three …) At last the engine started to accelerate and the main rotor blades started to turn. Within seconds it was burning and turning, and the engine temperature dropped below the critical number of 810.

Phew!

I wasted no further time in flashing up the second engine as I talked nicely to ATC. The place was empty apart from me and they cleared me to lift and cross the main runway immediately. It was 1158.

I pulled as much power as I dare, conscious of the thrashing one engine had just received at my hands and I accelerated rapidly to 120 KIAS. I was supposed to be on the ground at 1200, but I reckoned a low sporty flypast right on the dot would tick that box.

And the kids went wild!

A sporty wing-over, which was really required so I could look down over the school and ensure no changes to the previous day, and with no more dithering I promptly arrived in a very expeditious fashion. (Ironically if you are heavy, and thus power limited, flying a faster approach is required.) I was not willing to shut down but I'd organised some expertise on the ground to meet me and collect Father Christmas from his sleigh without risking life and limb. And with a cheery wave I lifted into the hover and climbed aggressively straight up into the cloud in order to disappear as if by magic, and it did give me chance to practise some more instrument flying before the much-needed large medicinal glass of white port was quaffed later that afternoon.

Phew! I had survived my first year in the job and got Santa to his gig on time.

In all it had been a very successful start to my time running ETPS short courses, but things were going to change in the New Year – and not for the better.

A number of significant changes had occurred in my first year as a civilian. QinetiQ was formed as a commercial organisation with a remit to be a profit-making business. I had become a QinetiQ employee instead of being a civil servant. A new building had been added onto the ETPS hangar and I'd moved office. Sadly, Dave, the ETPS CO moved on to another post.

In theory moving office to the new building should have been a good thing, but in practice it created divisions. All the flying pilot tutors remained in their offices on the south side of the building and I was located with nearly all the civilian and QinetiQ staff on the north side. Easy communication, when we all had offices on the same corridor, now became more difficult. The birth of QinetiQ should have been a good

Principal Tutor Systems and Short Courses – The Last Straw 241

thing. The organisation was now suddenly charged with being more entrepreneurial and making money. However, it was early days. Most employees were ex-civil servants. The process for doing business was not mature. In my context, the use of assets and resources was very poorly understood.

The new CO arrived against this confusing backdrop and apparently had a single focus: that of delivering the graduate course of TPs and FTEs predominantly for the Ministry of Defence as the 'customer'. Meanwhile the management structure became even more complicated. ETPS had been born as an RAF Squadron in 1943 and when I passed through as a student all the staff were military or civil service. There was a classic pyramid structure with a military Commanding Officer (the boss), who reported to the Chief Test Pilot, who reported to the Air Commodore. All the staff worked for 'the boss'. However, in this new brave world as a QinetiQ employee, I found myself being reported on and managed by a fellow QinetiQ aviator who was a flight engineer on the Heavy Aircraft Test Squadron. We never worked together and he had no knowledge of ETPS. I worked directly for a number of QinetiQ business managers who, in the main, had an accounting background and were principally there to balance the books, although this did improve as time went on and I ended up working for Bill, who had much more of a marketing mindset. All of this was complicated enough, but 'the boss' apparently seemed to think I still worked for him, which I didn't! Inevitably such confusion led to some crossed wires and some very heated email exchanges.

My second year commenced with my being contacted, almost covertly, to attend a meeting. A financial review had been taking place of the costs of running ETPS and now some more technical input was needed. In some ways I was ideally placed to offer advice as I knew a good deal about both the FW and RW activity, and yet was no longer directly embedded within the mainstream tutorial staff. However when I found myself in a much larger meeting some weeks later, with the CO and the senior staff, it was clear some were not impressed by my involvement. Following this uncomfortable meeting I was tasked to lead a technical review of the training we did. I was joined by Kevin who had been the RAF tutor when I was a student. He was now a QinetiQ employee and had taken over from Dick, who had been so helpful with the acquisition of my Squirrel. We held regular meetings with the Course Development Managers of both disciplines (John and Eric). Invariably these conversations were interesting and illuminating, but they were often extremely difficult as Kevin and I were seen as the enemy. We achieved a great deal but at a cost of increasingly frosty working relations.

During this period, other aspects of the job I signed on for were sliced away. QinetiQ had not yet built up an understanding of how to manage and conduct safe civil flying, and the embedded military had become increasingly risk averse. After eighteen months of working extremely hard to gain a Jetstream Type Rating and establish a good working relationship with Cranfield University, with a view to making more use of their facilities, receiving an email from 'the boss', out of the blue, telling me it was all to be cancelled, was far from heart-warming. Not only was I not to pursue any further Jetstream flying, but all the other initiatives I had started, in order to be able to use civil registered aircraft, were put on hold. I confess, with my morale at rock bottom and my nerves shredded, I made it through to summer leave by the skin of my teeth. As I reflect, I was poor company for my family on the holiday we took together. I had ended up becoming incredibly frustrated and cheesed off with the situation. I was close to resigning when we returned after the summer break but was talked into staying by a number of QinetiQ managers and 'the boss', who assured me all would be well. In fairness, I was to be so busy in the autumn term that I was, for a while, able to set aside my personal disappointments.

Earlier in the year I had received a call from Andy. He was a fellow member of SETP and the Chief Test Pilot for Eurocopter, Deutschland. Could I help him out with a training requirement?

'Almost certainly,' I responded optimistically. He had two ex-military employees who needed to gain flight test qualifications. In the UK at that time we did not issue specific licence qualifications to Test Pilots. The ETPS graduate certificate was effectively a military qualification. However, in both France and Germany TPs needed to have a formal qualification added to their licences – which they had already gained through their military training. A graduate TP was known as Classe A in France, and TB1 in Germany. However, a good deal of flight testing could also be done by Test Pilots and FTEs trained to TB2 or Classe B standard. (This qualification allowed full 'envelope expansion' flight testing of single-engine helicopters and more limited scope testing of multi-engine aircraft.) So I was asked if I could design, develop and deliver a TB2 course for two German students. Of course, I agreed I would try. Bill, my business manager was immediately on board and I set about determining the course syllabus requirements.

I realised I would get very little support from outside my short course team, which was me and my FW FTE, Gary. Gary had taken over when Matt had quit, having become more cheesed off than me a few months earlier. Gary could offer encouragement but no actual technical input as he had a purely FW background. I reckoned I would have to do this pretty much single-handed, but thought I could probably achieve it using the Gazelle, over a three month or so period. I wrote the syllabus, designed the programme and worked out the flying hours and other required resources. I costed everything quite tightly and precisely as I knew we might initially appear to be more expensive than the alternative options. Bill was delighted. As was Kevin. So far so good, right up until the point where I needed to be assured of access to the required aircraft. All the military registered aircraft were operated under military rules with a hierarchical authorisation structure down through the military chain of command. So any of the senior military pilots could 'red card' such activity without discussion. The new CO was not enthusiastic. From his perspective there was more risk of a flying accident and more risk of assets, vital to delivery of the graduate course, not being readily available. Eventually he agreed that I could run the course September–November, when the RW course had already completed all its formal exercise flights that needed the Gazelle. But my problems were not yet over. Days before the students arrived I was told they could not use, or be given, the ETPS training notes.

'What? Why not?'

'The current notes are only for long course students, you'll have to write your own.'

The notes ran into five volumes as thick as the old Yellow Pages directories. Had I started then, I would still be working on them now. Time for some lateral thinking. Fortunately, two of the RW staff, Eric and Alastair, had written a book, *Helicopter Test and Evaluation*, that contained more than enough info for my second-class flight testers. Could we buy them all a book? Thankfully that was allowed. And so the course commenced with four students. I had a German pilot and FTE as expected. We had also managed to interest the Dutch Navy. They had never sent a student to ETPS before and were using my course as a cost-effective 'dipping of a toe into the water'. And QinetiQ gave me one of their young trials officers, Dan, to see how it would all work. Just as in my first year as an RW tutor, I was now working eighteen-hour days to try and stay just one step ahead of the students. Although I could base some of the training material on historic documentation, a lot had to be rewritten or drafted from scratch. Every evening I was writing documents for use the following day. Adding to the fun my PA had her first baby and, quite rightly, was off work taking her maternity leave. Sally was a great asset and very supportive of all that I was trying to do. However, admin assistants were part of a large pool that could apparently be allocated on some whim or other. I had to work really hard to ensure Sally was reappointed to me on her return. Just part of the joy of being in charge of 'short courses'.

Halfway through the course and out of the blue, I got another metaphorical kick in the teeth. The boss (who was able to red card all my planned flying) had decided we should do some additional engine-off-landing currency flying. On the long course this was not an unusual practice. All of us were always considering ways to improve the quality or safety of the training all the time. But my short course had been costed to the minute. I didn't have any spare flying hours in my budget and my students were always going to fly their engine-off landings with me or another instructor. But, sadly, common sense did not prevail and in the end I had to fly dozens of fifty-five instead of sixty minute flights in order to 'save' an hour for this unplanned/unneeded sortie. Towards the end of the course, when I had very few days left to deliver the outstanding content, I completely blew a fuse when I was, without any notice, told I couldn't use the Gazelle the following day as some staff from USNTPS were visiting and it had been decided to offer them an 'experience flight' in the Gazelle.

I needed to fly it that day. Weather and other factors were already conspiring to make timely course completion difficult. I just could not afford to lose a complete day. After tearing my hair out – and throwing all of my teddies out of the cot – and banging my head against the nearest brick wall, I brokered a deal and found myself flying so early the following morning the rest of the school hadn't yet arrived at work.

Phew! Achieved another.

The course was completed on time, on budget, and I had four very happy students who had learnt most of the content of the graduate course

Principal Tutor Systems and Short Courses – The Last Straw

TB2 Short Course – Author with students. *(QinetiQ)*

in a fraction of the time and at minimalist cost. Andy, the Dutch Navy, and QinetiQ were all similarly impressed by my efforts. Hurrah! And with that I had safely and very successfully achieved my second year in the job.

Both the German students went on to have very successful flight test careers with Eurocopter – now Airbus Helicopters. The Dutch Navy pilot became head of their NH90 Helicopter Test Programme and paved the way for many of his colleagues to be sent on the full graduate TP course. The QinetiQ FTE was well received back into his team and the following year was sent on the full FTE course, sadly getting little credit for his three months with me. He now flies as a pilot for BA.

As my third year in post commenced, it appeared like my flying would be limited to guesting on the 'long course' and flying the air experience flights for the internal Foundation Course for QinetiQ trials officers. Events took another bizarre turn at the end of the first term when QinetiQ signed a contract with the Ministry of Defence known as the LTPA (Long Term Partnering Agreement). This had a huge impact on my activities. The agreement effectively ring-fenced all of the QinetiQ resources for the use of their prime customer, the MOD. In effect, we could only use spare capacity for non-core business. Short courses were non-core and the penny was quick to drop that trying to achieve anything using the military registered fleet of aircraft was going to be incredibly difficult. Ironically, that reopened the door to flying civil aircraft. In effect, I no longer had access to the ETPS fleet to deliver the Foundation Course, which was seen as an essential training package. Thankfully, I had maintained my links with Thruxton and in June 2003 was back delivering flight test training in a G reg aircraft. Hurrah! My previous hard work had saved the day.

I am particularly proud of the final two short courses I ran.

The University of the West of England had, for a number of years, been running the Aerospace Integrated Graduate Development Scheme (IGDS). The MSc included a number of modules which students could select to make up their degree. They had previously had a Flight Test Module, and this had been delivered via the International Test Pilot School who had recently vacated their Coventry base and moved to London, Canada, and are now doing very well. With their departure from Coventry, I contacted UWE and offered to put together an equivalent module which was to consist of lectures, tutorials, some flight test flights, and then a post-course, assessed, report-writing exercise. I had roped in Andy, our Principal Ground School Tutor, who was very supportive of what I had been trying to do. And Gary, my FTE sidekick was up for it. I designed the course, costed the course, produced the lectures and notes and then … I was told … I couldn't use any of the ETPS aircraft!

Fine!

I completely re-planned and re-costed the course and posted the joining instructions; and despite this being a QinetiQ course, being delivered by QinetiQ staff, with all profits heading straight into QinetiQ's account, I was then told … I couldn't use any of the QinetiQ (ETPS) Classrooms. *Seriously?*

F … Fine!

Instead I organised the use of a wonderful facility in Clifton, Bristol. This was basically a massive house overlooking the Avon gorge. It had conference centre facilities and good food. Andy, Gary and I decamped to Clifton for three days and had a blast! We delivered all our lectures in this lovely house and ate well in Clifton's wine bars in the evening. On the Thursday, those that were FW orientated were flown by my friend,

Dodge, in – yes you've guessed it, the Cranfield Jetstream – operating for the day out of Bristol Filton, which sadly is now closed. I took the rest of the gang to Thruxton and flew them in a JetRanger. In the evening we all gathered at the Officers' Mess at Boscombe Down, which was now entirely independent of the MOD/LTPA, and we had a mess dinner with a wonderful speech from Roger. Roger had been a very senior RAF TP and run the Bedford/Farnborough activity for some years. He was now working as a consultant for ETPS and assisting with marketing. Among his stories was his tale of testing the Jaguar for short field operations off the grass strips at Boscombe. The weather was terrible and the strips waterlogged. On his final sortie he forgot to take the brakes off but with the jet's stationary wheels aquaplaning managed to get airborne in a shorter distance than when they had been rotating. What a hoot! We had run the best ever IGDS flight test module and we had not used a single MOD/ETPS/Boscombe Down resource.

And the crowd went wild!

My final course of the year I am equally proud of. I had designed an FW Stability and Control course using the Basset. It took weeks of convincing the powers-that-be that this was safe, with reams of risk assessment paperwork needing to be approved and filed. And I was only permitted to run it when the Basset could not possibly be required for anything else. Hence it was delivered in November when the students were busy with Preview. My student, Charles, was a CAA employee who had worked for their Flight Test Department for some years but now was being asked to do more flying. The timing was spooky.

As you might have realised, I am perhaps too tenacious for my own good, and writing this chapter and reflecting on this particularly painful three-year period, I would now agree wholeheartedly. I really am a dog with a bone. I had been recruited by Dave to investigate and fulfil a number of potentially beneficial initiatives. I had literally poured my heart and soul into trying to make a number of possible opportunities real. But ultimately I was 'pushing peas uphill with a fork'. Most of the ETPS staff would have been happier if I'd gone to the pub every lunchtime (rather than just Fridays) and gone home immediately thereafter and thus cease working my socks off to try to do new stuff. I get that now, but I'm not wired that way. By the third term of my third year I had aged a good deal more than thirty-six months already and was running out of steam.

Then I saw a job advert in *Flight International*. I had ruled out working for the CAA as an RW TP some years ago, but right in front of my eyes was an advert for an FW TP. I called up Roger, who always seemed to know people who knew what was going on. Turns out the CAA needed somebody to take on the testing of light fixed wing aeroplanes. I would be the first to admit that I lacked street cred as a fast jet or heavy aircraft TP but, by then, I had a good deal more flying time in light aeroplanes and General Aviation aircraft than almost any military TP I knew. I applied.

Application submitted, I then found myself teaching Charles (who I was now hoping to work with) all I knew about flight test. No pressure then. The interview happened and I was called up that evening by Terry – CAA CTP. He offered me the job there and then. He was delighted to have such a well-qualified and experienced applicant, and I was delighted to have just pulled the 'yellow and black handle' marked 'rapid exit' from ETPS. I chatted to 'the boss' the following day out of courtesy and handed in my written one month's notice almost immediately thereafter. I elected to stay on a couple of extra weeks until the middle of January in order to hand over my job and finish off some administrative tasks. I should not have bothered. As I realised then and subsequently – as soon as you have been cast out, no one is interested in your opinion about anything. At the

Author with Charles from the CAA after flying the Basset. *(QinetiQ)*

Principal Tutor Systems and Short Courses – The Last Straw

McKenna Dinner – in the pee break – I was accosted by the new business manager at ETPS

'What will it take to get you to stay?' he asked

'What do you mean?'

'More money?'

By then it would have taken a team of wild horses just to slow down my departure, let alone prevent it. Fittingly, my last ETPS flight was in the Bell 206 JetRanger out of Thruxton with a civilian colleague. I had finished my decade at Boscombe Down very contented with all that I had personally achieved, in most cases despite, rather than because of, those around me. Time to move on.

ETPS Hawk XX342
(Andy Mogg MoD)

Postscript

I left ETPS in January 2004 and immediately started working as an FW TP for the UK CAA and subsequently EASA. However, this did not entirely conclude my flight test teaching. For another ten years I returned to the school each year to give a morning's lectures on civil certification. As a CAA TP, I became frustrated by the lack of an affordable, basic, flight test course for the scores of people I encountered trying to test light, fixed wing aeroplanes. After discussions with the Light Aircraft Association (LAA) I designed a one week 'short course', where all the basic stability and control requirements were covered with both theory and practical exercises in a whole variety of quirky aeroplanes sourced by the LAA. On leaving the CAA it wasn't long before I found myself supporting the Test Flying Academy of South Africa based at Oudtshoorn (known as the Ostrich capital of the world), and then more recently I was appointed as the Chief Flying Instructor (RW) for the International Test Pilot School based in London, Canada. At ITPS I found myself designing and delivering training courses in order to train experienced test pilots how to be Flight Test Instructors – a course which was sampled by an EASA audit team and which was a huge amount of fun to deliver. As I write this part of the book I am now delivering the flying aspects of a flight test course to students from Coventry and Birmingham universities.

Equally, my involvement with Boscombe Down has never ceased. As mentioned earlier, I joined the airfield's Bustard Flying Club – mainly in order to commute to Bedford, but have remained on the books ever since as a flying instructor, and for a good number of years I returned to fly with 2AEF; their Chipmunks had long since been replaced by Grob Tutor aeroplanes. No longer a serving officer, I had to join the RAF Reserves, rose to the dizzying rank of Flight Lieutenant and was awarded my only medal. I thoroughly enjoyed flying air cadets around the skies of Wiltshire, leaving most with big cheesy grins at the end of nearly thirty minutes of looping and rolling, and this more than satisfied the itch for the alternative career I might have had in a light blue uniform.

In 2016 I found myself working back at Boscombe on two separate contracts. I worked for ETPS for a day a week helping to rewrite their lesson plans into a format now dictated by the MOD. At that time I found little had changed in the school in the twelve years I had been away. Additionally I picked up a contract from Gama Aviation who were tasked with making some improvements to the Army Gazelle cockpits, specifically to give them the capability to be able make GPS approaches. In order to complete this testing on a military aircraft, owned by the Army but also being tested by QinetiQ, I found myself part of a joint test team with two serving Army TPs and a number of trials officers. I was based in exactly the same office I had occupied when in EFS some twenty-plus years earlier. I was back doing exactly what I had done two decades previously and inside my head I was 38 years old again. I received quite a shock when I looked at a photo of the team taken after a flight. There are three thirty-somethings and a knackered, grey-haired bloke standing on the end of the line-up. Life moves on.

Author with Joint Flight Test Team and Army Gazelle at Exeter Airport. *(Author)*

In 2019 I organised a twenty-five year reunion of my TP course. Ironically, to find examples of the aircraft we had flown, we spent a day at the Boscombe Down Aviation Collection, Old Sarum, which I wholeheartedly recommend for a visit. Irony of ironies, ETPS had by then adopted an entirely civilian registered fleet of training aircraft. It seems that I had been on the right track all along, but perhaps just ahead of my time.

As we gathered for the McKenna Dinner twenty-five years after we had done so for the first time, I think we were all excited to be reliving happy memories. I was particularly looking forward to the award of the Westland Trophy when I hoped to congratulate the winner and share in the champagne. But it wasn't awarded. I do not know why, but a good number of the trophies were no longer handed out. Sad. Definitely time to move on.

Conclusion

When I considered writing my first book *Test Pilot – An Extraordinary Career Testing Civil Aircraft*, I was keen to collect my recent flight test stories and anecdotes. I was hoping to make the book humorous and entertaining to a general readership. I discounted including my time at Boscombe Down as I felt it did not readily fit in with that premise. As you will have read in this book, that decade was marked by intense hard work, unwavering resolve and, ultimately, by untenable frustration. As a result, this book has ended up having a more traditional structure, with a beginning, a middle and a (sort of) end. The reality is, this book explains to the reader how I came to end up working for the CAA and how I came to acquire the necessary qualifications and experience to be able to cope with the various challenges I then faced.

Rather than chat about all aspects of my personal life, as some writers might, I have chosen to concentrate on narrating my professional story as an experimental test pilot. However, it has been a revelation to me, as I have endeavoured to recollect what my family was going through as I was recording each flight in my rather full logbook. We faced some very tough times along the way. I would not have been able to continue with the aviation career I have enjoyed had we not had a massive amount of support from family, church and friends. I do wonder, with hindsight, whether decisions I made along the way were the best, both for me and more importantly, my wife and two children. Teaching at ETPS had been an excellent professional period and provided an almost five-day week 'normal' existence. Leaving ETPS to join the CAA added a good deal more turbulence to family life, not least because I was on the road or overseas a considerable amount of time. Both my children are parents themselves now and I would like to think have turned out rather well. But I'm sure my sometimes absentee parenting example has been noted. I would like to think that the passion I have had for my flying has been more than outweighed, many times over, by the passion I have for the welfare of my family, but they will be the judge.

For those reading the book with a passing interest I hope you have gained some better level of understanding of the selection process, the course content, the employment of, and the ethos behind being a test pilot.

And for those who might one day aspire to become test pilots themselves, then I would quite simply urge you to do it. It is not an easy road. It is hard enough trying to gain even the most basic of flying qualifications. Achieving a PPL takes time and dedication and alarming amounts of money. It is normally beyond the resources of most individuals to become test pilots without financial support from the military or industry, but, with there now being more training options than ever before, there will be more possibilities and opportunities. Inevitably, the pilots who attend any of the test pilot schools will have needed to demonstrate above average flying ability. They will need to have enough academic background to absorb the massive amount of theoretical knowledge required. They will have to have a breadth of experience in their aviation career to date. Most importantly, they need to have the character, integrity and temperament to cope with all that will come their way following completion of training. It is fair to say that most graduate test pilots inevitably return to more conventional pilot roles after their first job or two. In Europe there are relatively few full-time posts for test pilots. I count myself fortunate that I am still working as an Experimental Test Pilot as my varied and roller coaster ride of a career is now nearer to its end than its beginning. It has not been the easiest of career paths to take and has taken up a good deal of my own time, energy and financial resources to achieve. But I like to think I have done the best anyone could with the cards I was dealt. Without doubt, the projects I have been involved with have resulted in aircraft being safer to fly and my numerous students have been better prepared to conduct their own evaluations and flight tests. I believe I can be confident that my chosen career has, to some extent, made the world a better place.

Additional Reading

As I have explained, this book has aimed to cover the ten-year period I spent at Boscombe Down. It is one of a trilogy of books. My first book

Conclusion

Test Pilot – An Extraordinary Career Testing Civil Aircraft was published by Pen and Sword in March 2022 and documents many of my more humorous and challenging incidents since I left Boscombe Down to join the United Kingdom Civil Aviation Authority in January 2004. My third book, *Naval Aviator*, should be published towards the end of 2023. This book tells the story of how I turned my childhood passion to be a pilot into reality with more than a few bumps along the road. I was involved in four different collisions at sea and had my engine fail on my Westland Wasp helicopter during my period of learning how to land on a ship. If you have enjoyed reading *Experimental Test Pilot*, I am confident you will enjoy my other two titles.

Glossary

A

AC	Alternating Current as opposed to DC Direct Current
ADS	Aeronautical Design Standard
AFCS	Automatic Flight Control System – designed to damp out the control response of the aircraft and include higher functions such as height and heading hold. Complicated systems include flying anti-submarine or search and rescue profiles
AFS	Advanced Flight Simulator at Bedford
agl	Above Ground Level
AH	Attack Helicopter as in Scout AH.1
Aileron	The control surface at the trailing edge of each wing – operated by moving the joystick laterally. Moving it left causes the left aileron to tilt up and the right aileron to tilt down which causes the aircraft to roll left.
ANR	Active Noise Reduction
ASE	Automatic Stability Equipment – a poor man's flight control system
ASI	Air Speed Indicator. Uses pressure measured by the pitot tube which is compared with static pressure around the aircraft – the difference is displayed, usually, by a needle on a gauge and indicates in KIAS or MPH or sometimes kilometres per hour etc.
ASW	Anti-Submarine Warfare
ATC	Air Traffic Control. Sometimes conducted from a control tower by looking out of the windows but also often using sophisticated radars and radios.
ATPL	Airline Transport Pilot's Licence

B

BA	British Airways.
BERP	British Experimental Rotor Programme – A BERP rotor blade had an extended paddle shape at the end and gave better performance at high speed and in hot/high environments
Blades	Shorthand for rotor blades.
BRNC	Britannia Royal Naval College (Dartmouth).

C

CAA	Civil Aviation Authority. The UK aviation Regulator based in London and Gatwick. Responsibilities include the airworthiness of UK registered aircraft although most of the aircraft on the UK register from 2003–2020 were the responsibility of EASA.
Can-do	Usually used in the phrase 'can-do attitude' associated with military or ex-military personnel who are keen to get the job done despite external pressures or regulations.
CEO	Chief Executive Officer
CFS	Central Flying School – tri-service organisation within the RAF that administers all military flying instructors
CG or cg	Centre of Gravity
Chop	As in 'chop the power' or conduct a 'throttle chop' means to rapidly or instantly fail an engine or throttle it back to idle. Also used to mean to 'wash out' a student. To chop a student because they were failing to meet the course standard.
Civvy	What military people call civilians – the rest of us!
Clutch in	To 'cotton on'. To 'get it'.
CO	Commanding Officer or Squadron Boss.
Cock	Used a good deal by aviators! Within this book it refers to an ON/OFF lever – e.g. the fuel cock turns the fuel on or off.

Collective lever	This lever, usually operated by a helicopter pilot's left hand, changes the pitch on the rotor blades – collectively – that is at the same time. More pitch creates more thrust or lift allowing the aircraft to go up. Lowering the lever fully removes most of the pitch from the blades allowing them to autorotate in a glide.
Condition (On Condition)	'On condition' means the aircraft is flying at a given height, speed, power etc. ready for the next test point.
Control (As in Stability and Control)	In order to fly an aircraft, a pilot has to be able to control it. The flying controls in the cockpit should allow the pilot to manoeuvre the aircraft as required. Certification requirements include specific tests to ensure required rates can be generated by control inputs.
Convergent	An oscillation that is well damped will have a decreasing amplitude with each cycle and is known as convergent.
CPL	Commercial Pilot's Licence – not as good as an ATPL
CTP	Chief Test Pilot
Cyclic	This is the stick, usually mounted between a helicopter pilot's knees, that controls the pitch on the rotor blades in a cyclical fashion. That means that pushing the stick forward causes the rotor blades to increase their pitch as they pass over the rear of the helicopter, which causes the rotor disc to be tilted forward, thus angling the rotor thrust or lift forward. This has the consequence of pitching the nose of the helicopter down and allowing the aircraft to accelerate in forward flight. It is the equivalent of the aeroplane's joystick.

D

Dead Stick	Meaning stationary propeller or stopped engine – as in 'dead stick landing'.
Directional Stability	Sometimes known as weather cocking – the tendency of an aircraft to point into the prevailing airflow. Aircraft are expected to have positive directional stability.

Disc	Created when helicopter rotor blades spin round. Externally, when spinning, individual blades cannot be seen but the blur of rotating blades form a disc, which can be seen to tilt as if a dinner plate. Tilting the disc changes the main vector of the provided lift.
Dit	Navy slang – short story, anecdote, often humorous.
Divergent	An oscillation that grows in amplitude is known as divergent as opposed to convergent.
DLR	Deutsches Zentrum für Luft- und Raumfahrt – DLR. A centre of excellence in Braunschweig, Germany
Donk	Navy expression, meaning engine or powerplant. Derived from the use of 'donkey engine' which was originally a small steam-driven engine often used in winches and cranes.
Donk Stop	Engine failure.
DRA	Defence Research Agency. Flew research and development aircraft from RAE Bedford and RAE Farnborough until 1994, before aircraft transferred to Boscombe Down and Bedford was closed – ultimately taken over by QinetiQ in 2001.
Dutch Roll	Named after Dutch bargees who apparently used to stagger home rather drunk after several lagers in the local tavern. An oscillatory motion of both roll and yaw which, if divergent, means each cycle gets bigger – very unpleasant.
Dynamic Stability	Often the consequence of an aircraft's static stability. Usually referring to an oscillatory response and will be damped/convergent or undamped/divergent. The period and amplitude of oscillations determines whether any dynamic instability is acceptable.

E

EASA	European Aviation Safety Agency. Formed in 2002 and provided the European Union's aviation regulation function from 2003 – which included the UK until the end of 2020.

EFS	Experimental Flying Squadron. The remnants of the aircraft used at Bedford and Farnborough
Elevator	The control surface at the rear of the aircraft's tail. It is connected to the joystick which, when pushed forwards, tilts the elevator down, causing the aircraft to pitch nose-down.
EPNER	École du personnel navigant d'essais et de reception = the French Test Pilot School similar to ETPS
ETPS	Empire Test Pilots' School. Formed in 1943 to teach military and industry pilots how to flight test aircraft. Based at Boscombe Down since 1968.
eVTOL	Electric Vertical Take-Off and Landing

F

FAA	Fleet Air Arm or Federal Aviation Authority – America's aviation regulator.
famil	Short for familiarisation – used to describe a certain type of flight to gain familiarisation about an aircraft or a geographical area
FCS	Flight Control System – a computer within an aircraft that helps the pilot fly it.
FCMC	Flight control mechanical characteristics
Fishhead	Slang for someone in the RN. Pongo = Army, Crab = RAF. Other definitions are to be found in the Urban Dictionary – much to my horror!
Flame Out	Literally – to put out the flame on a jet engine – 'Flamed out' means the jet engine stopped!
Flaps	Surfaces that can be lowered on the trailing edge of the wing to create more lift and reduce the stalling speed. Normally used for landing.
Flash Up	To get a jet engine started.
Fleet Air Arm	After the First World War the newly formed RAF was to provide aircraft to support the Royal Navy. The outdated aircraft they allocated to this task formed the Fleet Air Arm. By the 1930s pilots were required to

	hold commissions in both the Royal Navy and Royal Air Force. In 1939 the RAF returned the FAA to Royal Navy control and at the time of writing it has remained independent, operating numerous helicopters and fixed wing aircraft including the F35 Lightning.
FLIR	Forward Looking Infra-Red (camera or sensor)
Flyco	Flying Control – Like ATC Tower.
FMS	Full Motion Simulator.
FOV	Field of View – how much the pilot can see of the outside world from a normal seating position.
FRADU	Fleet Requirements and Direction Unit. Royal Navy Hunter aircraft based at RNAS Yeovilton.
FTE	Flight Test Engineers – the clever people who often team up with test pilots for flight test programmes.
FTR	Flight Test Report.
FW	Fixed Wing. Fixed wing aircraft = aeroplane.

G

G	G is the term relating to acceleration due to gravity. 1G is the normal acceleration we all feel due to gravity. 2G would be twice that acceleration – at 2G our bodies would appear to weigh twice as much as at 1G. 2G could easily be experienced by an aircraft, in a steep turn, for example. Aerobatic aeroplanes typically will pull to around 6G for certain display manoeuvres and military fast jets as much as 9G temporarily.
G- Reg or G – registered	UK Civilian registered aircraft are allocated a four letter code prefixed by G-
Gash	Navy expression for rubbish or trash. To 'be gash' is to be rubbish at something.
GCE	General Certificate of Education
Goffer	Naval expression meaning a wave that breaks over the ship. To be goffered meant to be hit by such a wave.
Goofers	RN speak for a bunch of spectators gathered on a ship to watch aircraft landing.

Gopping	Not very nice, grotty.
Gotcha	A test pilot expression for an aircraft's characteristic that's potentially going to catch you out and lead to an accident. An aircraft may have a number of 'gotchas'.
GPMG	General Purpose Machine Gun – standard Army infantry weapon when I was a cadet at school.
GPS	Global Positioning System – satellite based very accurate navigation system.
Grobble, Grobbled	To grobble is to fly low and slow below cloud and murk, trying to stay in contact with the ground and navigate as best one can – often using a series of line features.
Gyro	Can be short for Autogyro or gyrocopter – an aircraft using free-spinning rotors to provide the lift required for flight but in this book is used to refer to the gyros in attitude indicators – instruments.

H

Handling Qualities	This expression is used to describe what an aircraft feels like to fly. An aircraft with good handling qualities is likely to be stable and easy to fly with easy to use controls.
HAR	Helicopter air/sea rescue
HAS	Helicopter anti-submarine
HC	As in Wessex HC.2 Helicopter Cargo
HMA	As in Lynx HMA.8 Helicopter Maritime Attack
HMD	Helmet Mounted Display
HQR	Handling Qualities rating based on Cooper-Harper
HUD	Head up Display

I

Inceptor	Posh word for flying controls
IFR	Instrument Flight Rules – used by pilots when they have an instrument rating and a suitably equipped aircraft. Used when the weather is too bad to fly visually (IMC) or when flying in certain types of airspace or sometimes by choice for safety reasons. Jokingly used

	for 'I Follow Railways or Roads or Rivers' when a pilot may follow a line feature particularly in poor weather to assist with navigation.
ILS	Instrument Landing System. The normal way a non-military aircraft recovers to an airfield in poor weather.
IMC	Instrument Meteorological Conditions. Weather with visibility and/or cloud base worse than VMC.

J

joystick	A joystick is the control/inceptor, normally between a pilot's knees which is connected to both the elevator and ailerons which allows the aircraft to be controlled in pitch and roll.

K

KIAS	Knots Indicated Air Speed. This is the speed on the airspeed indicator on the aircraft's instrument panel and the instrument which is used to tell the pilot how fast he is going. For a whole bunch of reasons this indicated airspeed may not be true – but it is the speed the pilot flies to.
Knots	A speed terminology – originally derived from nautical use, when a rope with knots in it would be trailed behind the ship and the rate the knots passed through a sailor's hands would indicate speed. It equates to nautical miles per hour. A nautical mile is bigger than a statute (regular) mile so 100 knots = 115 mph for example.

L

LAA	Light Aircraft Association – has delegated authority from UK CAA to look after the airworthiness of home-built aircraft, gyros and some historic types.
LAMPS	Light Airborne Multi-Purpose System.
Lateral Stability	Sometimes known as dihedral stability. It is the tendency of an aircraft to roll away from sideslip. Aeroplanes are expected to be stable laterally.
Lat-Dir	Lateral and Directional Stability.

LHS	Left Hand Seat
Lift	The term associated with the characteristic that keeps an aircraft in the air and opposes the downward effects of weight. Can be created by a wing or a spinning rotor or other methods.
Longitudinal static stability	This is the tendency for aircraft to stay at a trimmed attitude, angle of attack – effectively airspeed. Aircraft are expected to have positive longitudinal stability – that is they should tend to remain at a trimmed airspeed. If they possess very strong stability the control stick and displacement required to change speed will be large – if stability is weak only small stick forces/displacements are required to change speed.
LPD	Landing Period Designator – A traffic light system assisting with confirming ship deck motion.
LSS	Longitudinal Static Stability.

M

Manoeuvre Stability	Also known as 'Stick Force per G'. When a pilot pulls back on the stick the aircraft will pitch nose-up and the aircraft will experience increasing 'G'. Ideally the G should build in a linear fashion with more force required to achieve more G. The force required to rip the wings off should be high enough for the pilot not to do this by accident! Some aircraft, helicopters among them, have a tendency to be manoeuvre unstable and can be pitching with increasing G while the pilot is having to push the stick forward to control it – this instability is not a good characteristic.
Mayday	Urgency radio call – something serious.
MFD	Multi-Function Display. Used in conjunction with a PFD as a part of a glass cockpit to show ancillary information.
Mob	The mob – slang for the Royal Navy.
MOD or MoD	Ministry of Defence.
mother	RN expression meaning the ship we are embarked upon.

MTE	Mission Task Element – Part of ADS33.

N

NAS	Naval Air Squadron.
NASA	National Aeronautics and Space Administration.
NDB	Non-Directional Beacon. A beacon on the ground that a cockpit instrument would detect. A needle on the gauge would point at the beacon which could be used as a landing aid.
NPAS	National Police Aviation Service.
Nr	Rotor speed or Rotor rpm.
NVG/NVD	Night Vision Goggles/Devices.

O

oggin	The sea or water. Devon/RN expression.
ogwash	As above.
Ozz	Australia.
Ozzie	Australian.

P

Pan Call	Emergency less severe than Mayday.
PAR	Precision Approach Radar. Allows ATC to talk an aircraft down to the runway very accurately. Used by the military but not available at civilian airfields.
PFD	Primary Flight Display. Part of a glass cockpit. A flat panel display showing the main flying instruments.
PFL	Practice Forced Landing – usually achieved by throttling the engine back to idle power – or in a helicopter lowering the collective to enter into autorotation.
Phugoid	An oscillatory flightpath where, without pilot intervention, the aircraft climbs, levels. dives, levels and climbs again. If the phugoid is divergent the various oscillations get bigger with each cycle. The motion can be likened to being on a roller coaster but can be almost unnoticeable on a large transport aircraft.

Pipe	An RN Tannoy announcement.
PPL	Private Pilot's Licence
Pronger	Or Third Pronger – Fleet Air Arm Helicopter pilots of the third prong (flying Wasp, Lynx, Wildcat). The first prong includes anti-submarine warfare ASW. Pilots flying ASW are known as Pingers (flying Wessex 3, Sea King HAS 1/2/5/7, Merlin). The second prong includes Commando/Support Helicopters. Pilots flying SH are known as Junglies (flying Wessex 1/5, Sea King Mk4, Merlin Mk4).
Prop	Propeller – mounted on an engine and, by rotating, creates thrust.
PTSC	Principle Tutor Short Courses – my final three years at Boscombe Down.
PTSD	Post-Traumatic Stress Disorder – often suffered by those exposed to mortal danger and/or combat.
Pusser	Navy expression meaning supply officer or anything issued by the Navy – a pusser's steamer being a Royal Navy warship etc.

Q

QFI	Qualified Flying Instructor.
QHI	Qualified Helicopter Instructor.
QOI	Qualified Observer Instructor.
QSP	Qualified Service Pilot.

R

RAAF	Royal Australian Air Force.
RAC	Royal Automobile Club.
Rad-Alt – Radio Altimeter	Rad-Alt uses radio waves fired from under the aircraft to bounce back from the ground/sea surface which gives a very accurate height above the said surface. Essential for aircraft operating low level over the sea, for example.
RAE	Royal Aircraft Establishment – Farnborough and Bedford. Became part of the DRA.

RAF	Royal Air Force – Formed on April Fool's Day 1918 by merging the Royal Flying Corps (RFC) and Royal Naval Air Service (RNAS). The Royal Navy recovered its independent Fleet Air Arm in 1939 and has retained its own independent aviation capability ever since.
R&D	Research and Development.
Reg	Register, as in G Reg = on the UK register.
REP	Reference Eye Position.
RHS	Right Hand Seat
Ride Shotgun	As in the days of the Wild West, when the driver of stagecoaches would take a mate with a shotgun to help protect him and the coach from robbery – effectively meaning, act as assistant or co-pilot.
RN	Royal Navy.
RNAS	Royal Naval Air Station.
Rote	Shorthand for rotary wing pilot.
Rotors	Or rotor blades. Helicopters or Gyros have two or more rotor blades, which spin to provide lift.
RPM or rpm	Revolutions per minute – relating to engine or propeller or rotor speed.
Rudder	The vertical control surface, mounted on the tail, controlled by rudder pedals, which allows the pilot to yaw (turn) the aircraft.
RV	Rendezvous – to meet up.
RW	Rotary wing – an RW aircraft would normally be thought of as a helicopter but would include autogyros.
RWTS	Rotary Wing Test Squadron at Boscombe Down.

S

SAAF	South African Air Force.
SAR	Search and Rescue (Helicopter).
Sim	Short for simulator – A training or research aid that simulates aspects of an aircraft's flying characteristics.
Slipping the surly bonds (of earth)	Means 'getting airborne' from the poem 'High Flight' by John Gillespie Magee.

Spin	An aeroplane enters a spin when it slows down sufficiently for one wing to stall. As one wing stalls, it will drop and, if the aircraft is also allowed to yaw or turn, it will enter a descending fall, where it is gyrating around a spin axis. Generally, spinning is a bad thing and often leads to aircraft fatalities if the pilot cannot recover before hitting the ground.
Spool Up	An expression derived from cotton weaving. The spool would have to be spun faster to engage with the machinery. To 'spool up' means to be spun faster – often used in respect of jet engines where the turbines are spun up.
Sqn	Squadron – the Fleet Air Arm also uses the expression NAS = Naval Air Squadron.
Stability	This is a crucial factor for the assessment of an aircraft's handling qualities. If something has positive stability it wants to return to its original state even when displaced – imagine a marble or ball bearing at the bottom of a curved soup bowl. If you move the ball up the sides of the bowl it will, when released, roll back to the bottom of the bowl where it started from. If it stayed where you had moved it to, this would represent neutral stability; instability would be to displace the ball for it to roll up and out of the bowl of its own accord.
Stall	An aircraft 'stalls' when it is no longer flying fast enough to remain airborne. The stall speed is a very important performance test point, as from it are defined a number of other speeds, including the landing speeds, which in turn dictate the length of runway required. Some requirements, such as the definition of a Microlight, require the manufacturer to demonstrate the aircraft stalls below a certain speed.
Stick	The main control used to fly an autogyro - connected to the main rotor to directly pivot the rotor disc to control pitch and roll of the aircraft, or shorthand for an aeroplane joystick.

Glossary

Stick Force per G	See Manoeuvre Stability.

T

TCL	Thrust Control Lever – V22 Osprey power lever.
Temp	Temperature. To 'over temp' means to exceed an engine temperature limit.
Trim	Trimming the aircraft to a given condition removes the control forces being held by the pilot. Aircraft can be trimmed longitudinally using an elevator trim or pitch trim.
TP	Test Pilot.

U

US/USA	United States of America.
USAAF	United States Army Air Forces (Second World War). The United States Air Force, USAF was created in 1947.
USMC	US Marine Corps.
USNTPS	US Navy Test Pilot School.

V

VFR	Visual Flight Rules. Applicable only when the weather allows the flight to be completed using external visual references – the flight needs to be flown in VMC.
VMC	Visual Meteorological Conditions. Defined visibility and cloud base that permits a pilot to fly visually. Many light aircraft are only permitted to fly within VMC.
Vne	The speed or velocity that must not be exceeded in normal operations. Usually 10 per cent slower than Vdf.
Vs	The aircraft's stall speed in a given configuration.

W

wazzing	A term much used by FAA pilots meaning to fly low and fast – mainly for entertainment.

Wingover	A manoeuvre flown by all types of aircraft whether they have wings or not! Involves a gentle climb from relatively high-speed flight. As the speed reduces the aircraft is rolled into a steep turn of 60–90 degree angle of bank – the aircraft is then dived to its original speed and height. Operationally this is used by helicopters to achieve a rapid reversal of direction but it is also used by all types in air-displays etc.
WRNS	Women's Royal Naval Service – or the Wrens. When I joined the Royal Navy, women were able to join the WRNS but not go to sea in the RN proper.

Y

Yaw	Yaw is the name we give to turning around the centre of the aircraft. A yaw to port would mean the aircraft turning anti-clockwise when viewed from above.
Yaw Pedals	These pedals are operated by a helicopter pilot's feet. Pushing the left pedal yaws the aircraft left. In a conventional helicopter the yaw pedals effectively change the thrust from the tail rotor, which allows the aircraft to yaw in each direction.
Yomping	A Royal Marines term for walking across open country – usually laden with equipment.

Index

45 (Reserve) Squadron, 13, 232
702 NAS, 3, 85, 215–16, 223
705 NAS, 45, 183, 198
736 NAS, 146
819 NAS, 101
846 NAS, 204
Aircraft
  A-129 Mangusta, 201
  AB212, 70–7
  Airship, 72
  Alouette III, 186
  Agusta A109SP/A109P, 32, 168
  Andover, 24, 117, 150
  Apache, 65, 123, 125, 195
  AS350 Squirrel, 196
  AS355F1, 204, 229, 238
  AS355N Twin Squirrel, 165
  AS365 Dauphin, 68, 196
  B204, 68
  BAC, 1–11, 64, 78, 172
  Basset, 39, 44–7, 172–6
  Beaver, 192–3
  Bell 47, 73
  Bell 206 JetRanger, 162, 191, 196, 218, 236, 249
  Bell 430, 171
  Blackhawk, 194
  Bo105, 60, 69
  Buccaneer, 3
  C130 Hercules, 70
  CAP10, 198
  Cessna 150/152/172, 14, 212
  Cheetah, 185
  Chipmunk T10, 3, 212–18
  Cobra, 11, 65, 71, 193
  DC-3 Dakota, 187, 198
  EC120, 196
  Enstrom, 14
  Gazelle, 23, 25, 27, 31–2, 35, 38, 45–6, 51, 55, 93, 178, 183
  Harrier, 5, 12, 199
  Harvard, 150
  Hawk, 5, 24, 30, 57, 117, 148
    Hawk, Astra XX341, 176, 184
  Huey B204/B205, 68, 168
  Hunter, 3, 24, 51, 66, 95, 147, 216
  Jaguar, 5, 24, 30, 117, 148, 150
  Jet Provost, 5
  Jetstream, 229, 231, 233, 236, 242, 247
  Lynx, 3, 6–8, 17, 29, 33, 42, 45, 47, 115, 122–41
    Lynx ZD285, 123, 141, 147
    Lynx ZD559, 123, 125, 130–1, 141
    Lynx ZD560, 28, 34, 123, 141
    Lynx HMA.8, 7, 133, 156
  Malibu, 15
  MD500, 60, 75

MD520N, 60
MD902, 62
Merlin, 106, 112
OH-58C, 191
Oryx, 185–6, 189
Otter, 193
PA 23 Apache, 14
PA 28 Cherokee, 15
Phantom, 3, 117, 172
Puma, 103, 182
R22, 218–21, 223
S208 Siai Marchetti, 75
Sea Harrier, 3, 16, 33
Sea King, 33, 38, 40, 99, 110–21
   Sea King XV371, 41–4, 72, 111, 113–16
   Sea King ZB506, 111, 113, 117, 119
   Sea King ZB507, 47, 111, 116, 125
   Sea King HAS.6 XZ576, 100, 120
   Sea King Mk.3A, 119
Sea Sprite, 194
Seneca, 219
Scout, 24–5, 28, 35, 38, 95
Schweizer 300, 218
Sikorsky CH53G, 189
Sikorsky S61N, 65
Sikorsky S76, 198
Skyship 600B, 72
Space Shuttle, 10
Super Puma, 66, 71, 78
SW3, 202
SW4, 202
TH-6B (OH-6B), 193
Tucano, 5
Twin Pioneer, 198
V22 Osprey, 11–13
VFW Fokker 614, 235
Wasp, 3, 17, 28, 35–6, 42, 82, 85–7, 94, 194
Wessex, 16, 35, 85–109, 120, 135, 158, 165, 190, 193–4, 220
Wessex XS509, 57, 101
Wessex XR503, 90, 109

Active Noise Reduction (ANR), 123–4
ADS33, 129, 170
Advanced Flight Simulator, Bedford, 127, 142
Air Experience Flight AEF, 216
Autorotation, 13, 31, 53, 69, 131, 182, 220
Avalon, Trial, 101, 133

Bedford (RAE/DRA), 6, 10, 16, 19, 79, 87, 91, 129, 131, 143, 160, 199
Bell Helicopters, 11
Blue Kestrel, 112
Boscombe Down, 6, 16, 117, 129, 143, 223
Bredasdorp, 185
BRNC Dartmouth, 3

CAE, 156
Cazaux DGA, 67
Central Flying School (CFS), 5, 7, 217, 233
Cranfield University, 231

Index

DLR, 60, 130, 235

ELPs, 138
Emmen, 66
EPNER, 79, 190
ETPS, 1, 6–7, 9, 11, 14, 19, 116, 130, 164–8, 171–6, 178, 181, 183, 185
    Autumn Term, Class of 1994, 60–84
    First Term, Class of 1994, 22–37
    Principal Tutor Rotary Wing, 188–210
    Summer Term, Class of 1994, 38–59
Eurocopter, 242
Experimental Flying Squadron (EFS), 72, 87, 90, 96

FADEC, 165
Farley, John, 79
Farnborough, 79, 95, 147
Fast Jet Test Squadron, 97
Field of View Trial, 124
Flag Officer Naval Aviation FONA, 159, 217
FRADU, 3

GEC, 64, 65, 147
Gliding, 49

Hague, Colin, 82
Heavy Aircraft Test Squadron, 97
Height- Velocity/Avoid Curve, 55
HMS *Arrow*, 106
HMS *Diomede*, 136

HMS *Iron Duke*, 103
HMS *Marlborough*, 101, 103, 109, 133, 136
HMS *Sultan*, 115

Institute of Aviation Medicine (IAM), 207

Landing Period Designator, 135
Lateral and Directional Stability, 46
Linkoping, Sweden, 68
Longitudinal Dynamic Stability, 45
Longitudinal Static Stability, 44
Lynx Simulator, 6, 156, 189, 223

McKenna, 78, 80, 209
Mission Task Elements (MTEs), 125, 130–1, 170

NAS Willow Grove, 194
NASA, Houston, 9,
Night Vision Goggles (NVG), 101, 116, 123, 140, 202
NRC, Ottawa, 130, 168

Paris Air Show, 161
Patuxent, 78
Perigueux, France, 3
Pilatus, 66
Practica de Mare, Rome, 70, 73–4
Predannack, 115
Prestwick, 101
PZL, 202

Qualified Flying Instructor (QFI), 5, 173, 233

Qualified Helicopter Instructor
(QHI), 5–6, 19, 25, 28, 165–6,
179, 183, 217
Qualified Observer Instructor
(QOI), 19

RAF Biggin Hill, 4
RAF Brawdy, 216
RAF Cranwell, 5, 13, 236
RAF Leeming, 144
RAF Manston, 109
RAF Shawbury, 87, 89, 91, 101,
158–9, 204
RAF St Athan, 216
RAF St Mawgan, 177
RFA Fort Victoria, 99
RNAS Culdrose, 40, 85, 101, 115,
148, 153, 198
RNAS Portland, 6, 8, 33, 132,
142, 221
RNAS Yeovilton, 3, 114, 147–8, 210
RN Flying Standards (Trappers), 8
Rotary Wing Test Squadron
(RWTS), 6, 57, 90, 93, 95,
97, 100–103, 108, 113, 119,
128, 237
Royal Navy Flying Scholarship, 1

SAAF, 185
Sikorsky, 130
Sorley, Ralph, 80
Switzerland, 66

Thames Television, 1

University of the West of
England, 246
Upavon, 49
USAFTPS, Edwards, 190
US Marine Corps, 11–12,
88, 189
USNTPS, Patuxent River, 160,
165, 190, 244

Westland Helicopters, 7–8, 78, 82,
88, 114, 120, 125, 127
Wroath, Sammy, 80
WTD-61, Manching, 190